Redesigning
Print for the Web

Dr. Mario R. Garcia

Hayden
Books

Redesigning Print for the Web

Acquisitions Editors
Robyn Holtzman
Jawhara Saidullah

Development Editor
Robyn Holtzman

Copy/Production Editors
Meshell Dinn
Kevin Laseau
Marta Partington

Technical Editor
John Bancroft

Publishing Coordinator
Karen Williams

Cover Designer
Karen Ruggles

Book Designer
Sandra Schroeder

Manufacturing Coordinator
Brook Farling

Production Team Supervisor
Laurie Casey

Production Team
Dan Caparo
Kim Cofer
Diana Groth
Linda Knose

Indexers
Chris Wilcox

Redesigning Print for the Web

by Dr. Mario R. Garcia

Library of Congress Catalog Number: 96-78599
ISBN: 1-56830-343-2

Printed in the United States of America 1 2 3 4 5 6 7 8 9 0

This book was produced digitally by Macmillan Computer Publishing and manufactured using computer-to-plate technology (a film-less process) by GAC/Shepard Poorman, Indianapolis, Indiana.

Warning and Disclaimer

This book is sold as is, without warranty of any kind, either express or implied. While every precaution has been taken in the preparation of this book, the authors and Hayden Books assume no responsibility for errors or omissions. Neither is any liability assumed for damages resulting from the use of the information or instructions contained herein. It is further stated that the publisher and authors are not responsible for any damage or loss to your data or your equipment that results directly or indirectly from your use of this book.

President	Richard Swadley
Associate Publisher	John Pierce
Publishing Manager	Laurie Petrycki
Managing Editor	Lisa Wilson

About the Author

Dr. Mario R. Garcia is president and senior designer of Mario Garcia New Media Design International, a Tampa-based firm specializing in the design of newspapers and online services. Dr. Garcia is a faculty associate at the Poynter Institute for Media Studies, where he founded the Graphics & Design program in 1982.

Dr. Garcia's career as an educator, author, researcher, designer, and consultant spans 27 years, during which he has held professorships at Syracuse University's Newhouse School of Public Communications as well as the University of South Florida. He has been a visiting professor at the University of Navarra in Spain, and has lectured extensively at universities in more than 14 countries.

The author of more than a dozen books, including his last one, *Newspaper Evolutions*, as well as *Contemporary Newspaper Design*, *Eyes in the News*, and *Color in American Newspapers*, Dr. Garcia travels over one million miles a year as a consultant, and has to date redesigned almost 400 newspapers in 40 countries.

Dr. Garcia's principal research in color and eye movement has been done through the Poynter Institute.

He is a frequent lecturer in professional seminars at the American Press Institute in Reston, Virginia, the IFRA Institute in Germany, the Interamerican Press Association (Miami), and has authored close to 100 articles about typography, color, and design for various magazines around the world.

Mario Garcia New Media Design International is located at 4350 W. Cypress St., Suite 830, Tampa, Florida 33607 USA, phone 1-813-872-0875, fax 1-813-872-0962, email 74632,267@compuserve.com

Garcia's home page is http://www.mariogarcia.com.

Trademark Acknowledgments

All terms mentioned in this book that are known to be trademarks or service marks have been appropriately capitalized. Hayden Books cannot attest to the accuracy of this information. Use of a term in this book should not be regarded as affecting the validity of any trademark or service mark.

All summaries of color contrasts taken from Johannes Itten, *The Elements of Color*, New York, Van Nostrand Reinhold Company, 1970. Originally published in Ravensburg, Germany, under the title *Kunst der Farbe* by Otto Maier Verlag, 1961 and 1970.

Acknowledgments

In October 1996, I flew to Indianapolis to present a keynote speech to members of the Society of Newspaper Design. My assignment was to present this group with my musings on the subject of the new media.

My presentation, "From Picas to Pixels," established differences and similarities between the world of print and that of web design, and received a good response. Outside that autumn day were Robyn Holtzman and Beth Millett, from Hayden Books in Indianapolis. It was our first meeting. We discussed how to take the 21-minute presentation to a book format. A handshake later, the foundation for this book was set.

It is my 14th book, and probably the most exciting one I have ever written. More than a book, it is a conversation held not in private, but publicly. I remember, as a child in my native Cuba, that the island's climate always invited people to the outdoors. So in those lazy hours before dusk, the men, particularly, sat outside, under the palm trees, smoking their cigars, and what followed was a two-hour unguided tour of the day's happenings. Nobody really knew, as he sat down, what the topics would be, or who would lead the conversation, or where it would all go. But there was conversation. And the pleasant breezes of those Cuban evenings, which prompted the participants to recline their chairs against the walls, took care of the rest. The mood was relaxed. Cigar smoke from here and there intertwined, clouding the circle formed by the positioning of the chairs, but not the minds of the participants, all of whom had something to say as in all lively conversations.

That is the spirit here. I have sat outside and carried lively conversations with dozens of my colleagues who are thinking of redesigning print for the web, or who have done so. I have pulled my chair next to theirs, and in front of the screen, to peruse web sites of various categories. Then we have pulled our chairs back, rested them against the walls, and talked about it some more. Other times, we have done the virtual equivalent of a Cuban evening of conversation: connecting through the email across the time zones to discuss an interesting site, why one works and another one doesn't.

I have always maintained that most good books are the result of many minds coming together. Of course, an author leads the conversation, gets the group together, engages them, pulling all their chairs into a circle. The rest is the result of how the dialog proceeds. This book, particularly, has benefited from this approach.

The men and women who have joined me in this conversation represent the best and most talented in our business. To them I am most grateful and hope that our conversations continue, in person or in cyberspace.

Specifically, I would like to thank:

Ron Reason, director of the Visual Journalism program at The Poynter Institute for Media Studies, who first established a contact between me and Robyn

Holtzman at Hayden Books. His "conversation" with Robyn got me going on the book, at a time when I thought I was not ready to tackle another project. Since then, Ron and I have shared daily chats on our mutual fascination with the new media and its potential. Many of his ideas are presented here.

Many of my other colleagues at The Poynter Institute for Media Studies supported me in this effort, as they always do. My greatest gratitude goes to them: David Shedden, always ready to offer his talent as a historian and librarian, who compiled the bibliography; Dr. Pegie Stark Adam, for contributing insights into color and its impact on web design; Jim Naughton, president and managing director of the Institute, for his guidance and thoughts on the new media; Nora Paul, Director of the Library, for making the superb resources of the Nelson Poynter Library available to me, as well as her vast knowledge of the new media; Dr. William Boyd, for contributing the type of academic insight that all authors can benefit from; Chip Scanlan, the writing coach, whose interest in writing styles for the web led to many interesting discussions, some of which translated into this book; and Jennette Smith, for the loving way in which she assisted me through the logistics of many of the tasks involved.

A group of talented individuals whose work is heralded as some of the best in their respective fields counseled me, put up with my constant requests for "more" information, and went beyond what was expected, in the midst of terrifically busy schedules, to provide the kind of information that propelled this book into much higher spheres than I could have done without their assistance. They are: Andrew Devigal, Knight-Ridder; George Rorick, Knight-Ridder; Roger Black, Interactive Bureau; and Jessica Helfand, Jessica Helfand & William Drenttel, New York.

The case studies profiled here involved tremendous amounts of information exchange between me and the sources at each of the web sites. I visited most of the web sites to do on site observation and interviewing. Others we did entirely through telephone and email. In each case, lots of preparations were required to make sure that readers could get a taste of how a specific newspaper made the transition to the web. Each case study is distinct in presentation because I wanted to make sure that readers perceived how different the processes have been, all leading to successful operations. Special thanks to those who assisted me with their case studies:

Luis Fernando Santos, Beiman Pinilla, and the staff of El Tiempo On Line at El Tiempo, Bogota, Colombia.

Jeff Garrard at CNN.com

Steve Stinson at Roanoke.com

Dave Pickel at NandO

Jamie Hutt at StarTribune.com

Howard Finberg at Phoenix Newspapers online

Bruce Koon at Mercury Center.com

Per Andersson and Peter Hjorne Jr. at the Goteborg Posten, Sweden

Bo Hok Cline at the Seattle Times

Helpful in establishing contacts for me were Jim Jennings, consultant; Dierck Casselman, USA Today Weekend; Lynn Staley, Newsweek; and Michael Keegan, The Washington Post.

Many thanks to John Bancroft, a former student at the University of South Florida, and now owner of his own new media business in Tampa, who was gracious to sit down with me and to guide me with the overall scope of the book, as well as with the technical details that appear in it. One could not have hoped for a better informed, more up to date and willing to share resource. His participation enhanced this work.

My usual thanks to my assistant, Martha Daughtry, for getting it all together, maintaining a calm approach, and guiding me from point A to point B as we juggled several projects during a year that was supposed to be easier than the last, but, as Martha had suspected, was not. And my assistant Christian Fortanet stepped out of his busy schedule as designer in my firm to produce work for the book, offer guidance, and to study web sites of interest.

All books, in fact, all projects, have a decisive moment in which it all seems clear and possible. For me, in this book, it was the day I decided to assign my oldest son, Mario Jr., project director at my firm, to be my chief assistant with the book. A multi-talented person who is trained as a lawyer but dreams of a script-writing career, and whose long days start with movie writing at 6 a.m., proceed with work at the firm, and theater workshops in the evening, Mario Jr. took to this project with his usual zest. In the process, he became the harshest editor every writer needs, and the only one who would be so honest with his dad as to write me notes that read: "Dad, this is not one of your magazine articles, it is a book, so give me more," or, "If I cannot get it the first time, neither can your readers, so rewrite." I often felt like emailing back something like: "I wrote my first book when you were two, kid, so lay off." But each time I was convinced that he was right, and each change was made according to the "editor's" specifications. For every one of those notes that I read, and disliked at the time, I thank Mario Jr. Watching him at work is a source of pride, a good reason to have written this book. Mario Jr. represents the audience for whom the new media has been created. His eyes on my copy, on the screen, deciphering and dissecting interesting web sites became a most valuable and essential part of the book. Heartfelt thanks from dad.

Thanks to my real editors at Hayden Books, to Robyn Holtzman, my first contact at Hayden, for her enormous contributions, for believing in this project and for editing with a smile. Special thanks to Beth Millett and to Jawahara Saidullah, who administered aspects of the project and who guided me with the insights.

Hayden Books

The staff of Hayden Books is committed to bringing you the best computer books. What our readers think of Hayden is important to our ability to serve our customers. If you have any comments, no matter how great or how small, we'd appreciate your taking the time to send us a note.

You can reach Hayden Books at the following:

Hayden Books
201 West 103rd Street
Indianapolis, IN 46290
317-581-3833

Email addresses:

America Online: Hayden Bks
Internet: hayden@hayden.com

Visit the Hayden Books Web site at http://www.hayden.com

Contents at a Glance

Table of Contents

10   A Symphony of Movement   165

Introduction

Information Design for a Global Audience

A woman in Paris, reading the classified pages online, purchases the baby grand piano of her dreams from a seller who advertised it in the classified section of a Swedish newspaper; meanwhile, on a wintry afternoon in New York, a homesick Argentinean sits in front of his computer looking at an online photograph of a little girl eating ice cream in Buenos Aires.

The online editions of two newspapers, the *Göteborg-Posten* (Sweden) and *Clarin* (Argentina), made it all possible.

for a GLOBAL AUDIENCE

Information Design

Figure 1

A prototype for the *Göteborg-Posten* online edition.

It's not surprising that the past decade has provided us with the ultimate tool for communication—through a network that links millions of people from the largest cities to the most remote villages. With this vast network, the single user can access everything from text documents to real-time movies, from sound to pictures and graphics. The capabilities are endless.

By the time this book is published, close to 60 million people will be able to describe themselves as "web surfers" in the United States alone, and the number is growing worldwide. These users of the new media are not abandoning other means of obtaining information. In fact, they continue to read newspapers, watch television news, and listen to the radio, in addition to reading books and magazines. They live and

work in a multimedia environment. Subconsciously, they can scan the vast amount of information bombarding them every minute, deciphering messages and making decisions as to what information is pertinent. They also, at some subconscious level, decide which medium to use to obtain most of that pertinent information. The medium, although important, becomes secondary to the information and how it is presented.

This book is about presenting information. More specifically, it is about information design—about making the right organizational choices to send information from the sender to the receiver in the most effective and fastest manner.

As a result, this book will touch upon a variety of topics, including content analysis, writing and editing, design, and color use. It will establish the similarities and differences between print and web publishing.

This book will make a strong case for information design as an academic subject of its own. As a result of how the new media will coexist in our lives, it is not far-fetched to see traditional journalism schools everywhere tearing down their internal walls. No longer will students "major" in broadcast, print, or public relations. Instead, the information school will provide them with a core curriculum applicable to all media, with specialized courses available in each of the specific media.

I have spent my entire professional career teaching and practicing what I would now refer to as "information design" (even if I rarely used the term to describe my work). During the past five years I began to realize how much the various media share in some of the basics of organizing and presenting information. In recent years, I find my work taking me from print to web design. My average day involves dealing with both. I do not wear two hats to do it. The hat of the information designer suffices for both tasks.

Hopefully, this book will be a springboard for the next generation of information designers who will be able to build upon their information expertise regardless of the specific characteristics of the medium.

Chapter 1

Enter the New Reader

From the beginning of communication, images and words have been the ultimate information tools. Whether as carvings on cave walls in prehistoric days, as graffiti on the sides of buildings, or as elements of a newspaper's front page, all these images and words served the function of passing along information. Not surprisingly, the World Wide Web—the latest communication medium to come into its own in the 20th century—relies heavily on these same tools to do the job.

How Users Read Online

The job of passing along information has never been more important. As communicators we have the immense responsibility of relaying information in an accurate and comprehensible manner to a wider audience than ever before. As time becomes a more scarce commodity, the designer must prioritize how information is presented. The first step in the design of a web site, or any other form of design for that matter, is to create a visual environment that organizes the material to be presented and that is suitable for the content. This precludes any other aesthetic decisions about the design.

We still do not know enough about how users of online services react to what they see. Newspapers and magazines have relied on market research to learn more about readers, their patterns of readership, eye movement, preference for type, color, and so on. Because online design is in its infancy, we can only make assumptions. We know that we are designing for an audience that is sophisticated and appreciates such visual elements as color, illustrations, and typography.

How Readers Get the Online News

Information designers must be realists. In addition to understanding how a reader's eyes move from element to element on the digital page, designers must understand (at least in broad strokes) how the bits of data that combine to produce the words and images get to the reader's computer. The current state of the technology imposes limitations, even as it offers the promise of real-time information for everyone with access to the web.

Technological bottlenecks define what a realistic information designer can and cannot do if her goal is to deliver information effectively to a broader audience.

Bottleneck 1: The Modem

Statistics show that, as of this writing, the most common modem speed in use among web surfers is 14.4 kbps. Even though 28.8 kbps modems are gaining market share, most people are a long way from ISDN or better speeds, which is where all the cool, techno-gizmos that appear almost daily will finally begin to realize their potential. For now, downloading a movie, a lengthy sound file, or even a large JPEG image is rarely worth the wait. Be a realist: keep your files lean and clean. For more information on bandwidth constraints, see the sidebar in Chapter 3, "Designing Information for Interdisciplinary Users."

Bottleneck 2: The Computer

Most desktop computers in use, especially in homes, are plodding machines with little RAM, no graphics accelerator, and primitive sound capabilities—at least when it comes to downloading and decoding graphics data. As an information designer, you may work on a state-of-the-art Pentium or Power Mac connected to the Net over a T1 line, but don't let that enviable situation delude you. Be a realist: design for the machine (and the pipeline) that most of your readers use. For more details, see the sidebar mentioned in Bottleneck 1.

Bottleneck 3: The Monitor

Monitor resolutions and color display capabilities vary enormously. As a designer, you may view the virtual world through a monitor the size of a picture window that is capable of displaying millions of colors at a variety of fine resolutions. Many home users consider themselves lucky if they are able to display 256 colors at a screen resolution of 640×480. And the most popular browsers share just 216 non-dithering colors. Be a realist: fashion your palette from the colors most web surfers can see.

ONE LAST NOTE FOR THE REALIST

Things change so quickly on the web that no one I know is capable of taking in the big picture on any given day all at once. But don't let that stop you from staying as current as you can with the advances (and the wrong turns) being made every day. That way, as soon as the web is truly ready for the next insanely great thing, you will be, too.

Words and Visuals

As information designers, we are in the words and visuals business. It's as simple as that. Although traditionalists tend to throw web pages and online systems together with television, it's important to note that the major difference between television and web pages is that television is seen and heard, while web pages are primarily read. Of course, the visual elements you add to your web pages help considerably. Ultimately, however, the users must obtain information that, most of the time, appears in the form of text.

From HTML to Onscreen Text

HyperText Mark-up Language, or HTML, is the lingua franca of the web. It is simple and accessible to even the most primitive text-only browser. Anyone capable of hitting View Source on a browser's toolbar and then learning by example (or copying and pasting) can have his own basic web page up and running in no time. (The quality of that amateur publisher's page is another matter, of course, and not our concern here.) HTML's simplicity is also its strength, which is why it is not apt to go away any time soon—loudly trumpeted predictions to the contrary notwithstanding.

This book is not about HTML, which is discussed, dissected, and deconstructed at length in a bewildering array of books, tracts, and articles online and in print. Still, for those who are new to the web and may have seen only the onscreen result of the underlying mark-up, here are two extremely basic examples (see Figures 1.1 and 1.2).

```
<HTML>
<HEAD>

<TITLE>The Florida Humanities Council: Welcome! (Text Only)</TITLE>

</HEAD>
<BODY BGCOLOR="#FFFFFF">
<BR>
<H1>The Florida Humanities Council</H1>
<BR>

<H4><A HREF="./News.html">Humanities News</A> ¦ <A
HREF="./Calendar.html">The FHC Calendar</A> ¦ <A
HREF="./Gathering.html">The Florida Gathering</A><P>

<A HREF="./Grants1.html">The FHC Grants Program</A> ¦ <A
HREF="./FCTintro.html">The Florida Center for Teachers</A><P>

<A HREF="./Member.html">Become A Member</A> ¦ <A
HREF="./Directory.html">The FHC Directory</A> ¦ <A
HREF="./Speakers.html">Speakers Bureau Catalog</A><P>

<A HREF="./Ink.html">Send Me Ink On Paper</A> ¦ <A
HREF="./Exhibits.html">Exhibits Service</A> ¦ <A
HREF="./Links.html">WWW Humanities Links</A></H4>
<BR>
<H2>Our Mission</H2>
The Florida Humanities Council
serves as the steward of Florida culture.<P>

We encourage Floridians to learn about the histories of our commu-
nities,<BR>
the cultures of our neighbors, and the values of our citizens.<P>

We believe in the effectiveness of thoughtful discussion and criti-
cal thinking.<P>

The tools of the humanities are essential to the survival of a
thriving democracy.
<P>
<BR>
<H3>Feedback</H3>
Welcome to Phase II of the FHC web. Detailed information on The
Florida Center for Teachers and The FHC Grants Program debut with
this phase. And there's more to come. Your views and opinions will
be of great value to us as we continue to develop this site to bet-
ter serve the citizens of our state. Won't you
take a moment to <A HREF="mailto:Feedback@flahum.org">let us hear
from you</A>?<P>

<HR><P>

<I>The Florida Humanities Council World Wide Web site is sponsored
in part by the State of Florida, Department of State, Division of
Cultural Affairs, and by the National Endowment for the
Humanities.</I><P>
<HR>

<H6>This page was last updated 13 January 1997.<BR>
Its URL is http://www.flahum.org/indexa.html<BR>
Questions or problems? Contact <A
HREF="mailto:webmaster@flahum.org">webmaster@flahum.org</A>.<BR>
Site design & consulting by <A
HREF="http://www.pictograph.com/BancServices.html">Bancroft &
Associates</A>.<P></H6>
<BR>
</BODY>
</HTML>
```

Figure 1.1

A page of simple and fairly strict HTML.

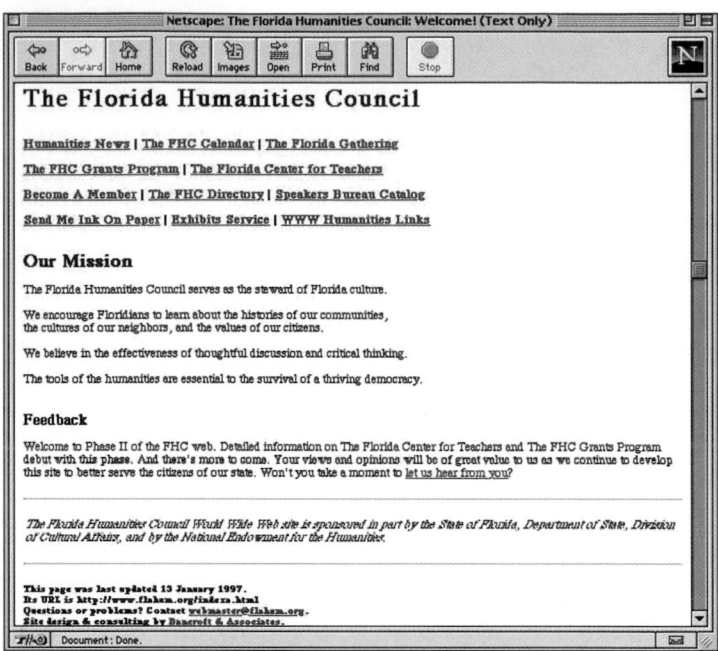

Figure 1.2

The screen image it produces in Netscape Navigator 3.0. The text blocks between angle brackets (<...>) in the markup are tags; they carry the instructions your browser interprets in order to display the information, more or less, as formatted.

This sample page is designed as a text-only, low-tech alternative index page for a site that otherwise employs graphics, tables, HTML extensions, and interactive forms to display largely text-based content in more visually engaging pages.

Text is perhaps the most important element in an online edition. The average newspaper includes more text than anything else. In fact, about 85 percent of what appears in a newspaper edition is body text, while the rest consists of headlines, photos, and illustrations. Perhaps this percentage is the same with web sites. I often hear complaints at seminars from people who criticize the design of newspapers for making too much of a visual thing of the section fronts, as in Food, Travel, and Sports sections, only to fill the rest of the section with mostly text. Ironically, the practice is even more common on web sites. Sometimes one moves from an attractive home page—a great first impression—and dives into a sea of text.

Opinions are mixed and controversial on the subject of how users react to text onscreen. Recently, a graduate student told me he had listened to two speakers during the same media conference, one promoting the value of text and the other one suggesting that users did not have the patience to read text onscreen. As mentioned earlier, we still do not have the answer to such an important question, although my experience with web sites in different parts of the world is that it is, first and foremost, a reading medium.

In fact, because the current flock of online service users tends to be highly educated, they are already predisposed to receiving information. They normally read newspapers, magazines, and lots of books, so they come to their web sites prepared to read. And read they do. There is nothing new in the formula for success: if the content is appealing, timely, and of interest to the user, then there is no limit to how much time he will spend assimilating it.

In addition, readers also are scanning the screen, looking at pictures, listening to sounds, watching animated images and, most important, writing to online publishers with their feedback.

◄ **HTML RESOURCE** ►

For HTML tips, try the Web Design Group's HTML Help Site at
http://www.htmlhelp.com.

The New and the Old Blend

Perhaps one of the greatest ironies of this new medium is how easily it is misunderstood, specifically by traditional print journalists and writers generally, who tend to see web pages as "the enemy." Quite the contrary, journalists and writers should rejoice that web pages are here to stay. I am always surprised by the number of journalists, especially those in their late 40s and 50s, who have decided they will not have anything to do with the web. I also encounter print designers, among the best in their fields, who have failed to see how they could have an impact on the new medium. Perhaps I, too, felt that way until I decided to start surfing the Net.

I am surprised because these are the same journalists who started using computer terminals to edit in the 1970s, and have spent most of their professional careers sitting in front of a computer screen. Suddenly, the new medium of web sites is here and so many of them confess they have not been curious to see what it is all about, even though it *is* new, it's news, and they are media people. The potential they are missing is to suddenly have the largest archives in the world, what all journalists dream of, available and ready at the click of a button.

It did not take me too long to realize that here was a medium that enabled immediate satisfaction in three of the most important areas of information:

▶ **Access:** The information desired is as accessible as the touch of a "link" (see Figure 1.3).

▶ **Depth:** There is no limit as to how much information one may obtain if he is willing to spend the time (see Figure 1.4).

▶ **Interactivity:** The capability to communicate with others and to obtain feedback almost instantly (see Figure 1.5).

Figure 1.3

On the *USA Today* web site, the user has access to a number of sections and stories, as well as advertisements—all by clicking one of many links. Along the top of this page, the user can go directly to a specific section or to a lead story. The left of the page enables the user direct access to particular subjects. The middle of the page leads the users to stories of the day.

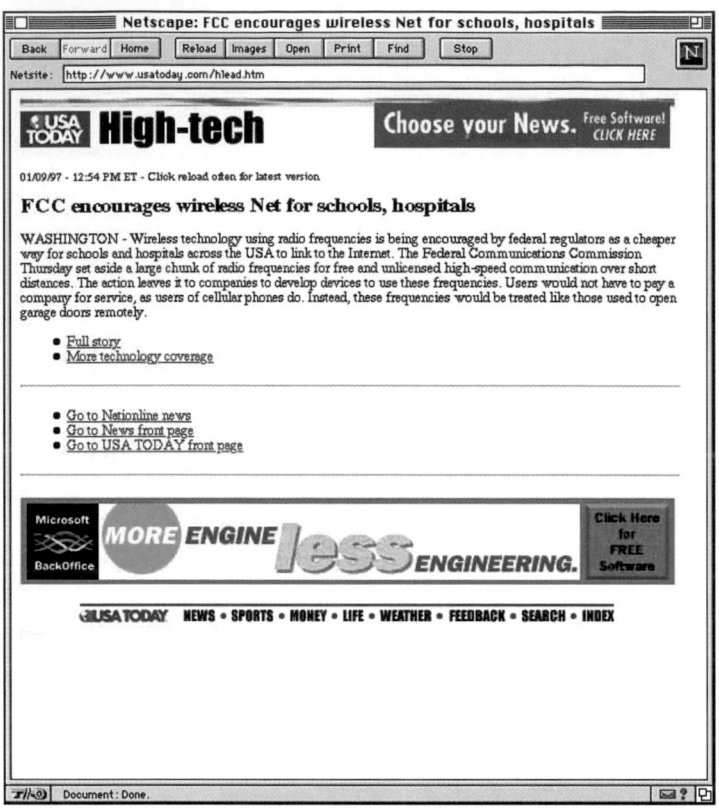

Figure 1.4

After the user has decided where to go, the following page gives the user the brief story. He also has the option of reading the full story, of reading other stories regarding similar subject matter, or returning to the *USA Today* front page.

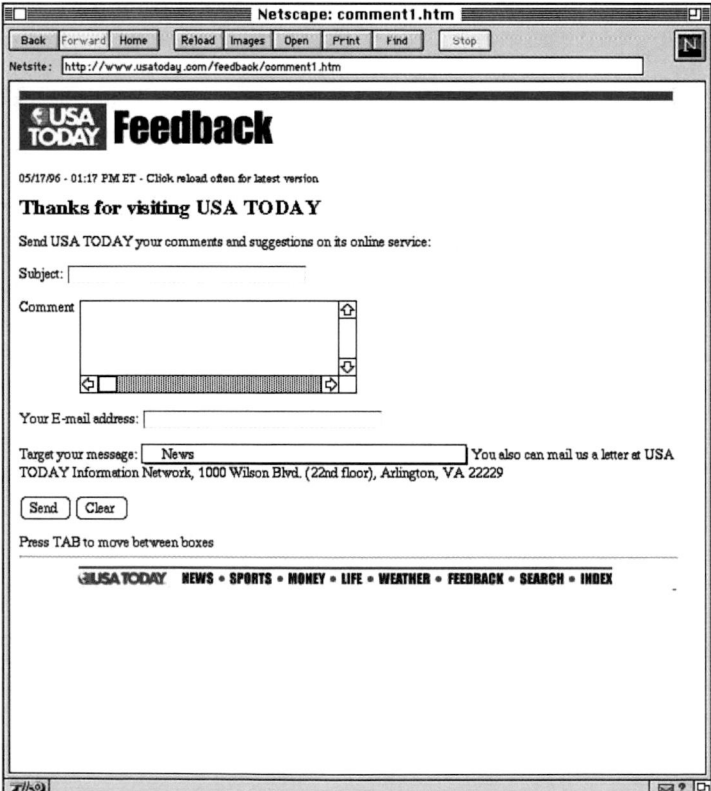

Figure 1.5

The user is welcome to send suggestions or comments back to *USA Today* via the Internet on any particular subject.

And so here we are, a few years from the new century, in one of the most exciting media to come along in a long time, and reading prevails. Literature is being read on the web, the same way that we read stock listings, gallery postings, the news of the day and letters to the editor. A new generation of writers are writing exclusively for online systems.

The task of the information designer is to make all the words that do fit more accessible, and to make sure that once the user "hits" that link word, he stays on that site beyond the first few paragraphs. Nothing new here for anyone who ever edited a publication, although the challenge is greater, and the time spent capturing that busy reader/user gets shorter all the time.

The Challenge

It is the challenge of getting that reader that we discuss in the next chapter, detailing strategies for the information designer at work. Just like the reader of web sites presents his own characteristics: moves fast, scans often, but stops for serious interpretation, navigates with the speed of TV channel surfers and has an insatiable appetite for information, the designers creating materials for these readers must also think fast, design with movement in mind, and provide, in the relatively small canvas of the screen, a sense of organization, hierarchy, and visual attractiveness.

Chapter 2

The Information Designer at Work

Information design is not a new discipline. Whoever created the first Sears catalog was an information designer with a lot of information to present in a limited amount of space and in a restricted format. Anyone who first constructed a university catalog probably had an even more difficult task to face, as did the person designing the menu or wine list of a large restaurant. Annual reports, stock listings, sports results, gallery samplings, and auction offerings, not to mention the more established examples of information design in newspapers, magazines, and television programming are all compiled by information designers.

What all of these examples have in common is that they require a variety of processes to be successful, from gathering and discussing the data to executing the actual presentation. The steps in between may vary according to the scope of the medium, the size of the organization handling it, and the audience for which the information is intended, but many of the processes required to guarantee that the information is designed properly are the same.

The Basic Formula

Information designers, regardless of the medium in which they work, carry out a basic formula as they conceptualize the means to present the information. This is a time-tested way of going through a checklist that ensures that various strategies are in place before a final concept is created. As this is done, the information designer reviews a multi-task process that includes bringing together message, audience, size of the canvas on which information will be presented,

Figure 2.1

The Sears web site (http://www.sears.com) is similar to a catalog, showing products and prices as well as discussing credit details, essentially functioning as a sales tool.

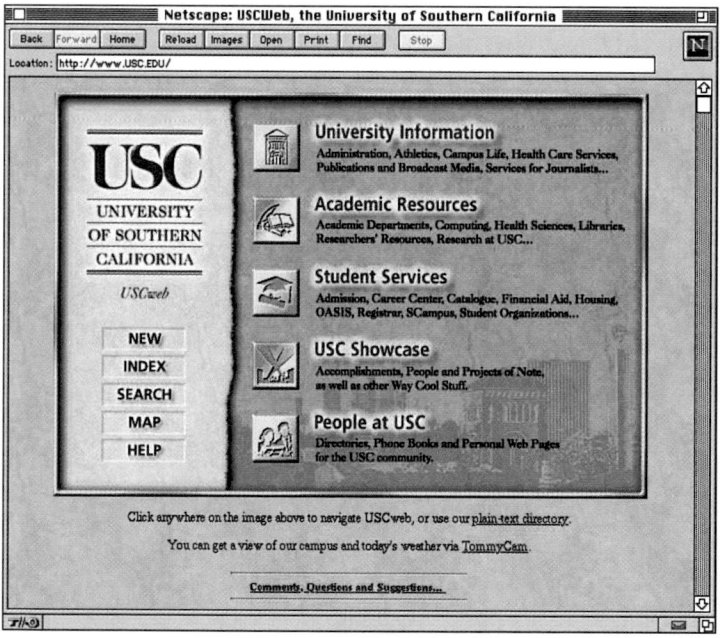

Figure 2.2

The web site for the University of Southern California (http://www.usc.edu) is tailored specifically for students and prospective students looking for information about the university. Also, this site is for alumni, faculty, and others generally connected to the school. Although other users are welcomed, the site is primarily tailored for the informational needs of the specific users mentioned.

potential for visual development, and legibility. The formula, then, consists of a strong relationship between content and visual environment, the two areas that create many of the dilemmas and lead to various decisions facing the information designer.

A good model for effective information design consists of the following:

▶ Understanding the nature of the information to be presented

▶ Focusing strongly on a specific audience

▶ Simplifying the message

▶ Integrating words and visuals

▶ Recognizing the differences between print and electronic media

Understanding the Nature of the Information to be Presented

There is a difference between presenting assorted items in the Sears catalog to prospective shoppers and providing university information to students or sparking interest in an upcoming movie. Some information must sell, other information must inform a specific audience, and some must entice (see Figures 2.1 through 2.3).

Focusing on a Specific Audience

The creators of a film's web site know before they start designing the first item on the screen who the film is expected to attract. All the words, visuals, and interactive elements on the site are strategically aimed at that audience. The most difficult information designs to create, and sometimes the less successful ones, are those that are aimed at too general an audience, thus failing to capture any one segment of the population. More and more, we are beginning to see the importance of marketing analysis as a primary tool of the information designer.

Communication Arts and *The Red Herring* are two very different magazines with one core strength in common: both know who their readers are and both tightly target their content to those audiences, in print and online.

Communication Arts, long the bible of graphic designers, illustrators, and art directors in the print world, has thrown itself into new media (see Figure 2.4). That doesn't mean it has abandoned its stance in defense of restrained, technically superb design. Instead, it has carried that message to the web and has embodied its philosophy in the clean, understated design of its own site.

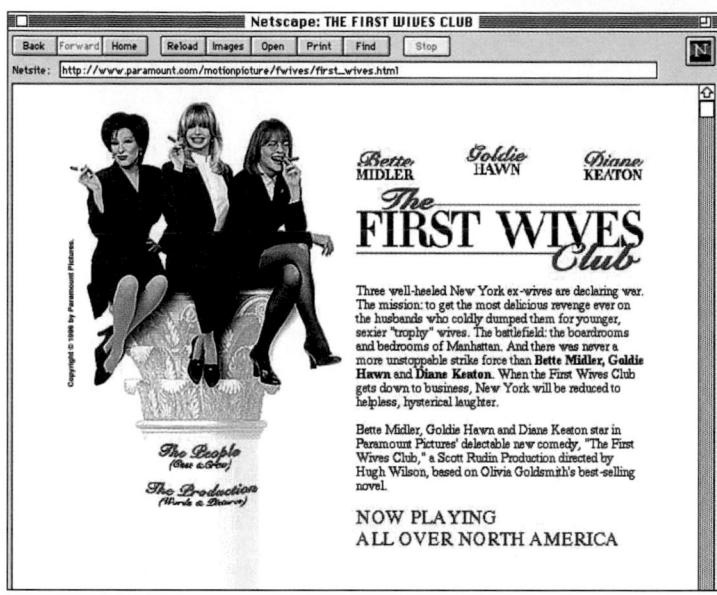

Figure 2.3

Paramount Pictures (http://www.paramount.com) has created this site to plug their movie, "The First Wives Club." The site talks about the film and gives the user a behind-the-scenes look at the production in the hopes of sparking interest in the movie.

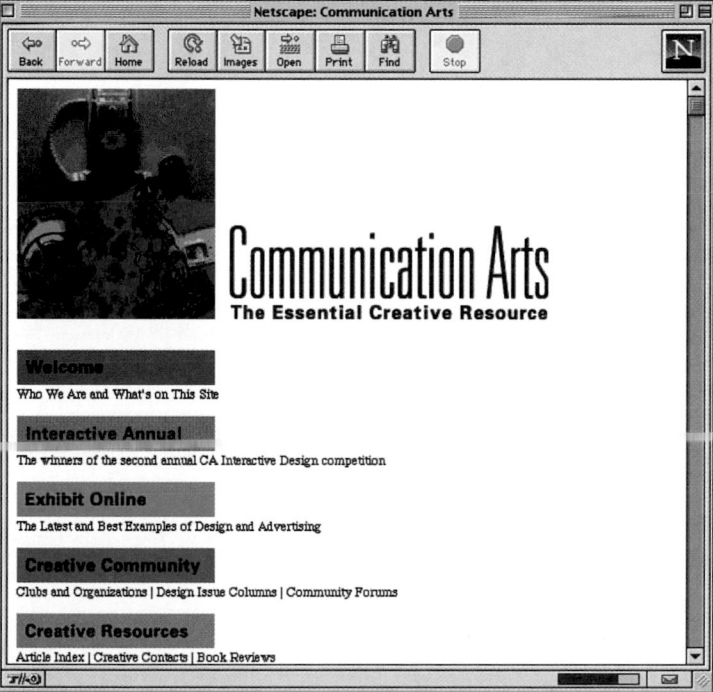

Figure 2.4

The Communication Arts web site (http://www.comarts.com).

The Red Herring is a creature of its time (see Figure 2.5). Its target audience is found in the flashier milieu of technology and entertainment, and its front door (right) reflects its focus. Like CA, *The Red Herring* combines traditional content from its print editions with departments created exclusively for the web. In this way, both magazines extend their reach online, rather than simply attempting to change the purpose of editorial content for a new medium.

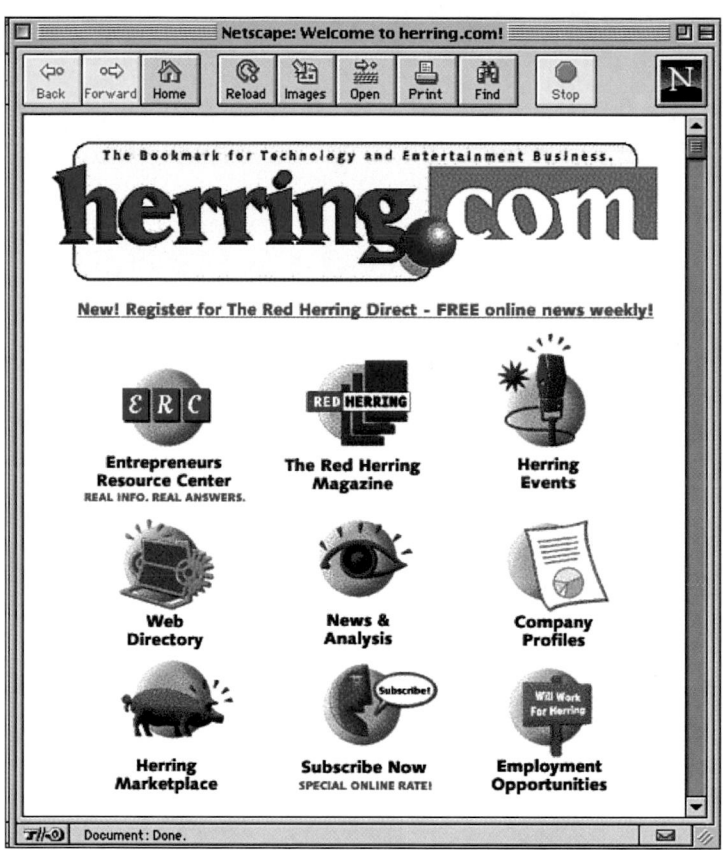

Figure 2.5

The *Red Herring* web site (`http://www.herring.com`).

Simplifying the Message

Complicated messages fail to attract users. Simple, straightforward messages grab attention and keep you reading, listening, or watching. A newspaper front page is rejected if it is cluttered, lacks hierarchy, and does not offer a good visual point of entry. A front page with a definitive lead headline and photo, however, grabs the reader (see Figure 2.6). A home page is the same way; one that resembles the window of a hardware store becomes a five-second stopover on the way to the next web site.

If the client is unable to provide a simplified message, then it is up to the designer to work toward that goal. Cooperation and team effort, even in a playful way, can get to clarification of messages. I often ask the simple question: What do we wish to achieve here? What do we want the user to do? Move? Stop and read? Seek a link? Interact? By the time one reviews these basic questions, suddenly the ideas have been focused and the message simplified. It is not as simple as it sounds, but it can be done through dialog.

Two things help to instantly organize the *San Francisco Examiner's* web site (`http://www.examiner.com`) for the user: the photograph and the simple words. The photograph becomes the main point of entry and the simple words, Top Stories, in large, visible, elongated type, lead the user to a menu of headlines. The navigational column, left, is practical and simple to approach, dividing the content into four baskets of information.

Integrating Words and Visuals

An information designer has a bag of tools that includes words and images working together. Sometimes the words create the images. Often the images substitute for the words. Most of the time the two coexist like flowers in the same garden, breathing the same air, basking in the same light, yet retaining their individual characteristics. The information designer succeeds when she is a master of both the words and the images; the messages she produces reflect that mastery.

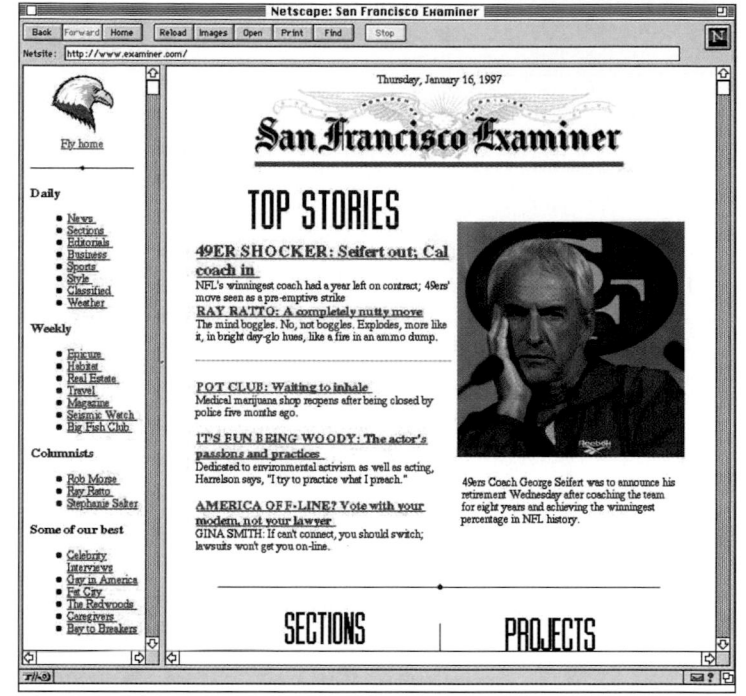

Figure 2.6

This front page from the *San Francisco Examiner* web site gets the reader's attention with a definitive headline and photo.

EXAMINER

Five rules for integrating words and visuals:

1. Read the words carefully. Good writing is descriptive. Descriptions lead to visuals. Seek those opportunities.

2. Establish the importance of visuals with writers. If writers begin to think graphically, not only will their writing be more visual, but they will come up with ideas to illustrate their stories.

3. Ask the question: what is the graphic potential of the story?

4. Think beyond one visual medium: not all contents lend themselves to photos. Sometimes a graphic, a simple icon, provides tons of information. And many times an illustration sets the mood long before one reads a word.

5. Adapt to occasions when the words should be left alone. There is such a thing as a wonderful narrative that does not need visuals.

Figure 2.7

The *Los Angeles Times* web site is a perfect example of words and visuals coexisting. This is a very clean page where the words are more prominent than the visuals, but not so much that they dominate the entire page.

Good examples of sites where words and visuals coexist well are the *Los Angeles Times* (`http://www.latimes.com`) and *The Seattle Times* (`http://www.seattletimes.com`) (see Figures 2.7 and 2.8). In both cases, it is obvious that planning has taken place for the content of stories and the images used to illustrate them have been coordinated well. In addition, headlines are written to match the point of view of text and the visual point of view of illustration elements.

Figure 2.8

The *Seattle Times* web site is different from the *L.A. Times* site in that there are more visuals. Still, the visuals coexist with the words and neither dominates the page.

Discovering an information designer

In early 1997 at a Poynter Institute for Media Studies seminar devoted to web design, the first so-called Web Track seminar, the Florida-based Institute attracted young designers from a variety of online services. At one point, designer Bo Hok Cline, from the Seattle Times On-Line, described a highlight from her site: a High School Guide that describes itself as the most comprehensive report ever published on the public and private high schools of the greater Seattle area, complete with updated information about everything a prospective student, or his parents, might want to know about specific school districts and/or schools. Ron Reason, director of Visual Journalism at Poynter, turned to me and said, "Here is one very good information designer, and her product shows the careful consideration she has given the information."

Bo seemed a bit confused when we called her an information designer, as she had never heard the expression before, or at least not until we told her she was, indeed, a very excellent one. Her background? Print designer for Seattle Times *for 8 years, doing everything from feature pages to special sections. As she tells it, it was not a glamorous transition into online design. She simply was eager to go into the new media, the opportunity came and she designed the personal technology section of the then new online edition. She remarked that what impresses the most as a distinct difference between print and web design is the sense of immediacy in the latter. Online design "feels like nailing down Jell-O art, design in motion, that is the challenge."*

The high school project began with a manager who created the database, contacted each of the schools, and prepared student questionnaires and faculty surveys. By the time Bo got involved, she had all the information available. "To me, " she explains, "This was a great example of a newspaper and its online edition working well together, maximizing their resources and providing service.

We received lots of emails from users, including prospective citizens of Seattle, who were able to access valuable information prior to moving to the area. We planned the project from the beginning with a designer and the material appeared on paper as well, as a special supplement." So successful was the High School Guide, says Bo, that next the staff planned to compile the elementary and junior high listings as well.

For this project, the initial questionnaire sent to students and faculty led to the baskets of information that eventually appeared on the guide's home page.

Reporters as well as editors were involved. Bill Ristow, education editor; a team of reporters and researchers; and Betsy Aoki, online content development specialist, took all the information that rates schools in academics, vocational programs and school climate, charting school performance, profiling everything from curriculum to student activities, to helping students and parents choose a school.

The design of the site is attractive in its simplicity, capitalizing on a color coding system, inspired by a pastel color palette, to list each of the items in the navigational column (see Figure 2.10).

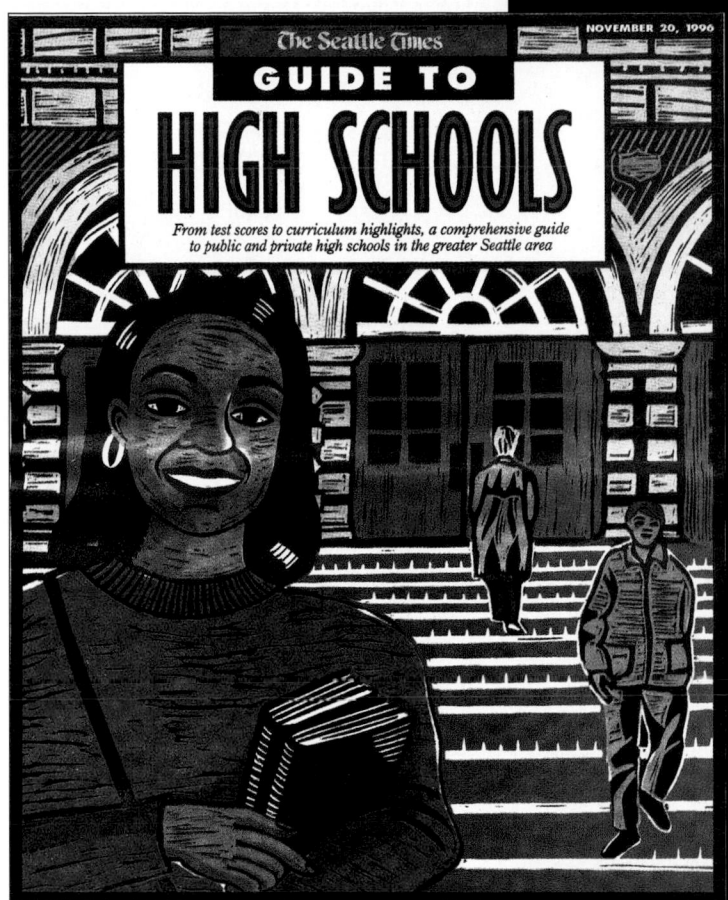

Figure 2.9

This is how the printed edition of the High School guide appeared in the *Seattle Times*, as designed by art director Marian Wachter.

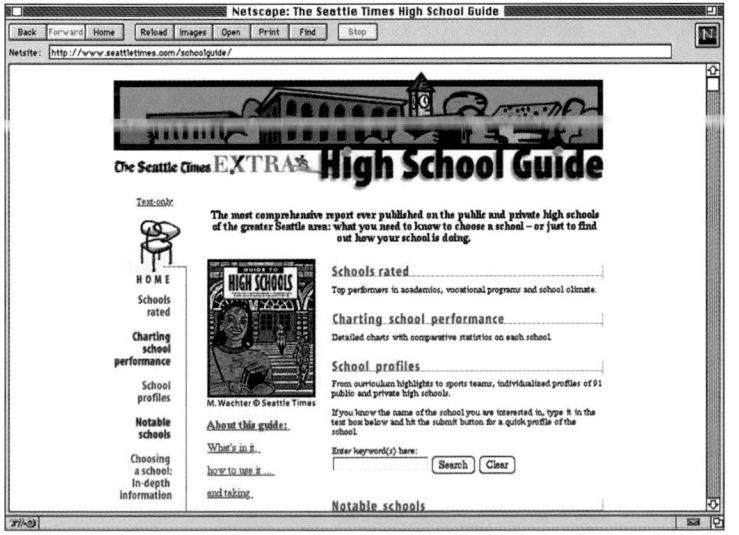

Figure 2.10

This is the home page of the High School Guide, complete with a soft color palette for the navigational elements on the left, which are then reflected for each of the sections inside.

Recognizing the Differences Between Print and Electronic Media

After the information designer has gathered the data to be "designed," the next step is to accommodate such information in a way appropriate to screen (web) versions as opposed to printed versions (see Chapter 8, "The Basic Recipe").

Ideally, it is not unusual for the same information designer to be responsible for the design of a message in various media, creating it simultaneously for both print and the web. It should all be part of a day's work, executed by the same team, with one message and even one basic design concept, but applicable to various media.

Because information design comes together in a systematic way, information designers must be extremely observant and analytical, and they must develop expertise in at least five disciplines:

▶ Management

▶ Visual arts

▶ Language

▶ Technology

▶ Journalism

Management

The initial creation of an information design begins with a series of meetings to deal with important details such as the following:

▶ Message

▶ Personnel

▶ Medium

▶ Scope of presentation

▶ Follow-up

Before there is any information to be designed, there are meetings to plan the project. As experienced information designers know, management plays a key role here. Who decides what information to use and how to proceed with its design? Who attends meetings? Who follows up on the various processes leading to execution? The answers to these questions are the result of management strategies that are basic ingredients of an information design strategy. The information designer may not label himself a manager, but in some way all information designers are managers, and they must learn the idiosyncrasies of management. Good information designs are managed well.

The Mentality of Editors

This a conversation I have heard various times at the newsrooms of many newspapers in different countries. The languages, the people, and the cultures may be radically different. The question seems to be the same: why are some journalists in the newsroom of newspapers so reluctant to get involved with the online editions ?

Like much of what is related to new media, nobody has conducted the definitive study on this matter. As a matter of observation, I have put down some constants that happen regardless of where I am working:

▶ *The online operation of many newspapers has started without much input from the journalists in the print medium.*

▶ *The online operation has relied heavily on "technical people" to get the edition off the ground, giving this new medium an aura of technicality that traditional journalists seldom want to get involved with. Let us remember that journalists have always refused to know more than what is necessary concerning production aspects of the newspaper. Many journalists today cannot explain how color photographs appear in the newspaper, they just know what a good color photograph is, and leave the technical details to someone else. That someone else, in the mind of the journalist, may be a person in another room, another world, perhaps with dirt under their fingernails! Suddenly, there are additional technical people in the midst of these traditional journalists, talking about pixels, bytes, frequencies and transmission codes. It is no wonder that the reception these online staffers get is somewhat cold. They might as well be guests from Mars touring the newsroom for the day.*

▶ *There exists a sense that the new medium of online electronic editions is a passing fad. Some traditional newspaper and even magazine journalists believe that the printed editions they produce will never be replaced, and these young guys working on online editions better realize that. Of course, printed editions are not likely to disappear, but they must coexist with their online counterparts.*

▶ *One of the first tasks of good on line staffs is to tear down geographical barriers. Make sure that the online operation is physically close to where journalists work. In some newsrooms, even after this is accomplished, only geographical distance exists, with psychological distance prevailing.*

THE MENTALITY OF EDITORS

▶ *Effective online staffs make it a part of their job to recruit journalists in their ranks, to create awareness of what the Internet is, how it works, how to benefit from its offerings. Once journalists realize what a marvelous research and information tool the Internet is, things begin to happen.*

▶ *Start by getting everyone in the organization to surf your own online edition. I am always surprised by the number of journalists who confess that they have never visited the site of their own newspaper.*

▶ *Hold periodic short sessions to introduce people in the newsrooms to interesting sites, specifically newspaper ones, to show innovation, creativity and how other "respectable journalists" take to the new media, and use it to showcase their journalistic talents.*

▶ *When all else fails, remind the diehards in the newsroom that with online comes abundant opportunities for writers to present their material to a new audience. Yes, remind them that journalism, as they know it, is very much alive, and, indeed, enjoying a renaissance online.*

Figure 2.11

This basic home page model relies entirely on type, Poynter Roman Text, to lead the user into the menu.

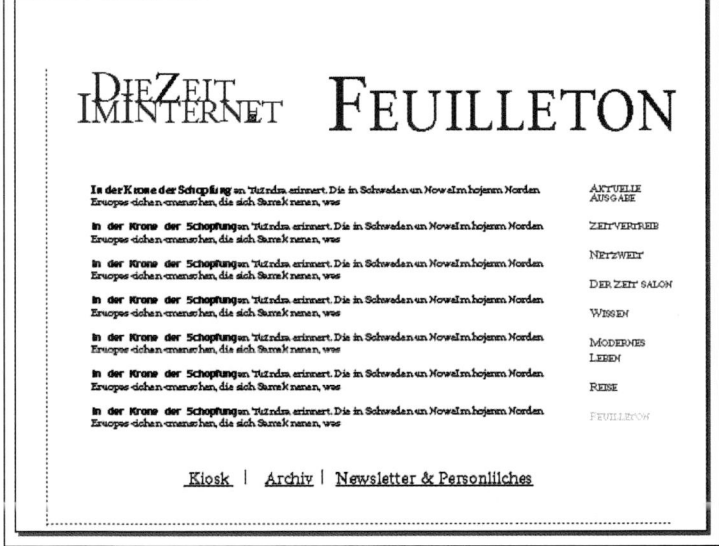

Figure 2.12

From the home page, users find a listing of all the important content for a given section, clicking to access their desired destination.

Visual Arts

It is no longer sufficient to throw text on a page or a screen without considering the information's graphic potential. Icons, photos, illustrations, informational graphics, color, typography, and space architecture all combine in various forms to shape the way information is presented and the way users perceive it. It is up to the information designer to create the appropriate visual environment, or framing, for the information.

The creation of a visual environment depends on several factors, such as preoccupations with the use of photos or graphics that may slow down the process of transmission. More than that, when creating a proper visual environment, one must be concerned with the appropriateness of how visuals integrate with the rest of what appears in a site.

A good example is my project with the German newspaper *Die Zeit*, one of the country's leading publications that has an elite readership including intellectuals, university professors, students, high-ranking businessmen, and politicians (see Figures 2.11 through 2.13). In 1997, as I redesigned the print edition, I was invited also to take a look at their Die Zeit Im Internet, an electronic edition with a good following of users who came to it to read long pieces written by philosophers and literary authors. From the beginning I felt that I had to create a pleasant visual environment in which these massive amounts of text could stand out, while making the reading process easy and interesting. Several versions came through my head as I conceptualized, as seen here:

Soon after the initial concept was created, I decided to break away from the concept, and returned later to more colorful and visually appealing versions of this site (with black as a background color and with more use of bright and pastel hues for type, and so on). The result was an interesting mix, that although visually appealing, seemed less appropriate for this serious publication (see Figures 2.14 through 2.16).

Figure 2.13

This is how an actual reportage opens, perhaps with the use of a photograph to create some visual interest.

Figure 2.14

Home page test shows a black background, along with red type.

Language

Words sometimes can be the most visual of elements. Although we all know a photograph is worth a thousand words, we must remind ourselves that one word can trigger a thousand reactions. In the case of web sites, words take less time to publish or transmit on the screen and, in that sense, can save us a thousand seconds of waiting. Words have existed from nearly the beginning of communication, a medium as casual as graffiti on a wall. Words will continue to work their magic and information designers must capitalize on their use, mastering the selection of appropriate words, linking several words together, and putting writing in a special place in the emerging form of journalism.

Figure 2.15

Another home page emphasizes the sharp contrast of black and lavender.

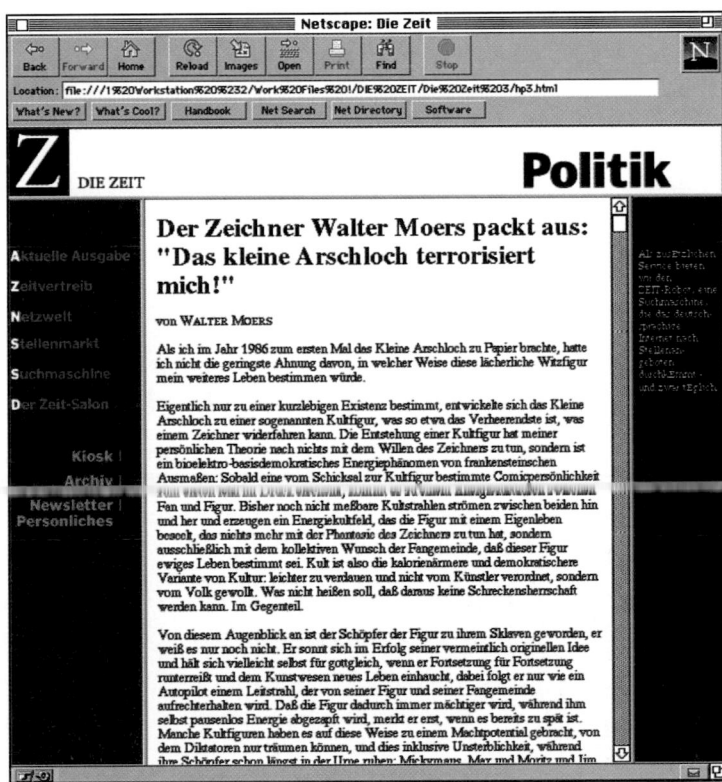

Figure 2.16

An inside page shows a staircasing effect from left to right, which would enable the user to move more efficiently into the text.

Regardless of how graphic a site is, one begins with a discussion of words, content, and how these will affect the graphics. So words, in a sense, are there at the moment of creation. Good web sites are an outgrowth of words.

Technology

It is no longer possible to separate technology from information design, not that it ever was. With the invention of the printing process an era of information developed. The evolution of information systems has walked hand in hand with developments in technology. Information designers are forever linked to technology that affects everything they do.

Information designers may have grand ideas, but it is my experience that ultimately some of those must fit into the technical plan, the system used, the availability of technical resources, from memory available to what the software can realize, many ideas end up on a sketch pad, never traveling the next step onto the screen. Adapting to what can be done is a trait most good information designers must possess.

With electronic publishing, technology has reached such a plateau that it is difficult to separate the more content-oriented aspects of information from the technological functions that make it possible. Information designers understand the technology that serves as the basis of their craft.

There is hardly any discussion, at any level or stage of a web design project, where technology is not involved. First, considerations regarding users and how they may receive the information, or how a certain technique may slow down the process too much; then, discussions of how to translate an idea (something as simple as the creation of a logo or illustration) into a high resolution image on the screen. The technical side is always important and usually takes center stage.

Almost every chapter in the book deals with some aspect of technology. The early chapters, however, plus typography, color, and animation do have special technical components.

Journalism

All information design is based on many of the basic principles that traditionally have been associated with journalism, such as the following:

- ▶ Hierarchy (setting priorities for bits of information according to their importance)

- ▶ Brevity (knowing how to convey information without redundancy)

- ▶ Accuracy (checking every detail twice)

- ▶ Relativity (using comparison and contrast to remind users of where this content has been presented before and where they can access more if they wish)

- ▶ Consistency (creating styles of clarity that provide continuity for the information presented)

Many information designers are products of a traditional journalistic education. Those who come from other disciplines must train themselves to think journalistically. Until a better word appears, the word journalism will be used in this book to convey the ideas of style, hierarchy, and accuracy that all information designers must master.

Elements of Information Design

No matter what information you have to present, chances are that four essential elements will be discussed before and during execution of a design:

- ▶ **Story structures.** How various types of content are presented, detailing how many points of entry (from titles to subtitles) are included.

▶▶ **DEVELOPING ROUGH DRAFTS**

▶▶ **DEVELOPING ROUGH DRAFTS**

My experience with both print and web designers is that pencil sketching seems to be more practical than "sketching" onscreen, but a new generation of young designers may abandon paper altogether to doodle on their screens.

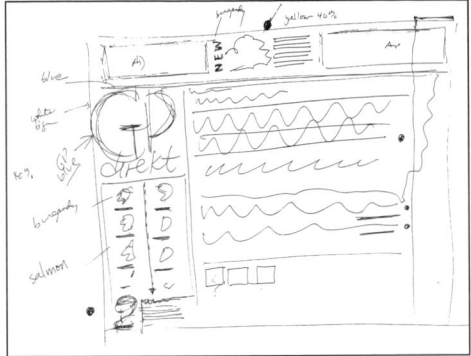

Figure 2.17

These sketches represent the work I did with GP Direkt, the web site for the *Göteborgs-Posten* in Sweden, in its primitive stage.

▶ **Typography.** The element that creates a sense of familiarity for a certain web site, as it always has done for a page.

▶ **Architecture.** The physical structure of the web site; how columns of text and navigational elements are presented.

▶ **Color palette.** How colorization has been approached, from classic or subtle shades, to brighter or brightest ones.

The order of these elements, and how they come into view during the information design process, does not matter. First, of course, there is a message (or messages) to be conveyed. Then there is a medium through which that message will be presented. After these have been established, the information designer is free to engage in the process of thinking about how to utilize the four elements that will give life to his creation.

Many information designers confess that it takes as little as 20 seconds to "visualize" a concept. In that visualization, they "see" the story structures, in a given type font, architecturally displayed as columns or lines, and in a certain color palette. Of course, this first burst of creativity, the birth of an idea, rarely ends up as 100% of what the first sketch reveals. It is important, however, to get this down on paper or on the screen (see Figure 2.17).

With the sketches at hand and the idea already set to run, the real work begins. As an information designer you have cleared the first hurdle, which is organizing the content in some logical framework—but not necessarily in the same way the information was presented in print. The chapters that follow discuss story structures, site architecture, typography, and color palettes, bringing some sequential order to the disciplines that constitute information design.

Chapter 3

Designing Information for Interdisciplinary Users

It's 9:15 a.m. in the office of the university professor. She turns on her computer and accesses the Internet. Suddenly, she must decide which of thousands of possible sources of information to tap into. Should she read one or more newspaper web sites to catch up on the news, or should she turn to CNN online for the latest news and weather, or, faced with an important 11 a.m. meeting, perhaps it would be more advisable to access sites that deal with the subject to be discussed in the meeting. Along the way, there are possible detours, to a magazine site, an entertainment site, and so on.

By the time this scenario takes place, the user already has glanced at the headlines in the morning newspaper at home, scanning more than reading, but nonetheless, getting an overall picture of the day's happenings. On the way to work, she has listened to the radio for additional information, perhaps of a more local nature. Last night before going to bed, she watched television and even read two news magazine articles before the end of a busy day.

Enter the interdisciplinary user, a person compulsive about seeking information, obsessed about getting more of information whenever possible, and surrounded by a variety of information tools that help nurture the obsession. The emergence of the web not only satisfies the voracious appetite of this interdisciplinary user, but it does so in a way that is practical, fun, and intuitive, especially to anyone familiar with computers.

Designing Information for Interdisciplinary Users

What these compulsive information-seekers enjoy most about the new medium is how it enables them to access virtually unlimited information, while providing interactivity that is instantaneous and puts them in the driver's seat.

So on the one hand you have the information seeker, hungry for more information, delivered faster. On the other, the information designer, who can hardly keep up with the challenges of providing what these information seekers expect.

Each day at a newspaper, we begin to prepare all the information that goes into the paper's many sections and editions. Those same rules of creating hierarchy and selecting content apply to all web sites. You could just as easily be in charge of turning the traditional print version of an annual report into a web version.

Rethinking the Model

With electronic publishing, several things happen. Suddenly, you must imagine that you have a new book or section of the newspaper, or that the traditional annual report or newsletter has an added section. You must not, however, go into the project thinking that the web site is an identical duplication of the printed material, because it is not.

The downfalls of thinking that way involve two important considerations.

Audience

The audience for the web site may be totally new (and different) from that of the printed version, with a different set of interests and priorities. Web sites users, for example, are highly interested in anything related to computer technology, and thus, a story about faster modems speed, for example, which may be secondary to the printed edition of a publication, could be the lead item, the first to appear on the home page of the web site.

Constraints of the Medium

As a new medium that is not read on a printed page, the dimensions of the screen, the way users handle the keyboard, look at the screen, maneuver with a mouse all influence how the information is obtained—which is quite different from holding printed pages in one's hands.

Unfortunately, and because this new medium is so highly technical, we all tend to lose sight of its merits as an information tool. There is no question that technology, not reporting or editing, is what most web site projects emphasize in their early development. Ideally, the two disciplines must be approached with equal zest for a web site to be successfully launched.

The work involved deserves the journalistic attention to detail, to freshness, and to content that we have traditionally given to printed work. Transmitting information, which is what you learned if you attended journalism school, continues to be at the heart of what one does.

What a dream it is for journalists to be able to update information constantly, to be able to provide entire databases of research and resources to readers who want it, and to do so without having to deal with so many of the traditional obstacles of paper, ink, printing, and delivery trucks. True, other challenges abound here, including being at the mercy of telephone lines and a technology that is in its infancy, but one cannot afford not to enter the promising field of electronic publishing.

How Publishers Deliver Online News

Earth is imperfectly wired. The situation is changing hour by hour, but it still will take time to connect the entire planet to that big data pipe we've all heard so much about—the World Wide Web.

This maddening gap between potential and (temporary) fact usually is addressed under the catch-all techno-label "bandwidth," as in: "Will insufficient bandwidth strangle the web in its cradle?"

The answer to that question is no. But there is a problem. It is one of unevenly developed telecommunications infrastructures, which translates into an overabundance of puny telephone wires, antique switching mechanisms, and fragmented (rather than interlocking) land line networks. This is true to some extent even in the rich post-industrial nations; the problem is compounded in the developing nations.

For publishers, the simplest form of the truth at the moment is this: You can deliver the digital news much faster than your average reader can receive it. Does this mean publishers should serve their sites to readers via 14.4 modems over least-common–denominator copper wires? Of course not. It does mean the information designer should check his site regularly over such a connection, just to stay in touch with the real world—and real readers.

Modern Information Consumers

When one embarks on a project in electronic publishing, it helps to have a good understanding of the sociology of modern information consumers. The printed newspaper is, for the most part, a medium for the general audience of people who want to be informed and who consider it important to do so. The web product is, by my definition, a more tailor-made information system for a more "obsessed" type of user. As anyone with an obsession will do, the user will pursue the desired information at length. The topics could be as varied as the history of the Olympics, to a day-by-day account of events in Bosnia, to every detail about a sports team, movie studio, or national industry. It is all information, and it is information that every newspaper has an abundance of stored away in its library archives (see Figure 3.1).

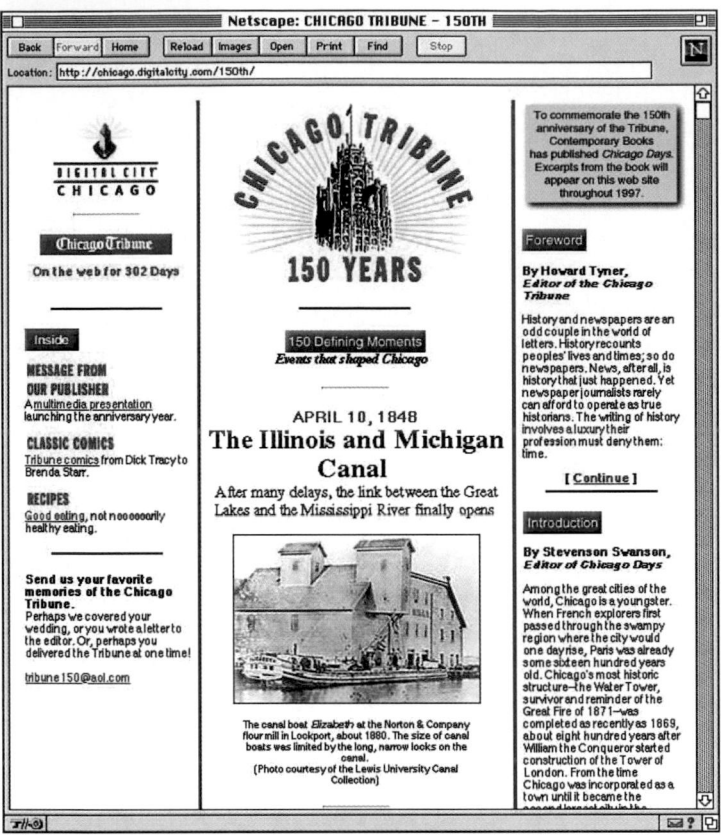

Figure 3.1

The *Chicago Tribune's* web site, aside from the day's news and events, offers visitors a link to read about the newspaper's 150 year history. This is a large amount of information that would take up too much space in print, but the web site offers it in its entirety to those users who desire to pursue it at length.

Living Environments

Good information designers always imagine the environment in which their product is consumed. Users of web sites represent a variety of people, of all ages, who feel they are better informed than the average person and who thrive on becoming more informed all the time.

These users normally dwell in environments that include cluttered desks, where the presence of computers has not totally eradicated that of paper. Not only are they surfing through "baskets" of information on their computer screens, but they also have overflowing baskets on their desks. There is the "In" basket, the "Out" basket, and the "Must Do Now" basket.

Consumption of Information

Unlike readers of newspapers, who normally do their reading at a set time (a majority in the early morning or in the evening), users of the web see the their medium in a more casual and serendipitous manner. There are no set patterns established for surfing the Net. Some users do it between telephone calls or while waiting for an appointment or while waiting for their spouses to get ready for an outing. Because their consumption habits are hard to track, it represents a challenge for the information designer to focus on the most effective strategies to attract and to maintain these users.

During the 1980s, newspaper, magazine editors, and designers spent considerable time discovering the world of so-called "scanners"—readers who browse the pages, stopping primarily at headlines, photos, and photo captions. As a result, these elements in the overall design of printed pages took up a certain importance that led to better written headlines, more prominently displayed photos, and more intelligent captions.

Likewise, information designers for web sites must take the habits of web users into account to attract them to a site and to make sure they stay.

To grab attention, an opening home page must have the following:

▶ Colors that attract the user.

▶ Type that immediately identifies the site and creates a point of view for it (serious, fun, informative, and so on), and that is clear and easy to read.

▶ An easy to see navigational area (primarily menus) that offers the user an instant glance at what there is to sample on the site.

▶ An informative headline that tells the user content is a key part of the site. Don't forget that content is what first attracts us into a site for exploration, and then holds on to us for further discovery.

How that web page title is written is a key to whether users stay with the site. This applies to any areas of promotion that may appear anywhere on a site page. Linking is undoubtedly dependent on words that arouse interest.

Ultimately, as it is in print, content is the key to hold the user's attention. Content that is relevant, timely and that implies DISCOVERY ("I did not know this before") as opposed to repetition or reaffirmation of stories already in other media is what good web sites are all about. A few good sites for leading the user deep into the information are *The Wall Street Journal's* web site (http://www.wsj.com), *The Christian Science Monitor* (http://www.christian-science.com) and *The New York Times* (http://www.nyt.com) (see Figures 3.2 through 3.4).

Figure 3.2

The Wall Street Journal's web site (http://www.wsj.com) offers one of the best examples of a site specifically designed to make sure that the words entice users to link beyond the home page.

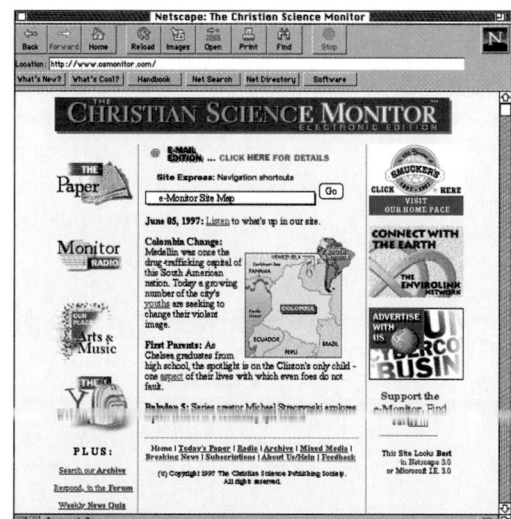

Figure 3.3

The Christian Science Monitor's web site (http://www.christianscience.com).

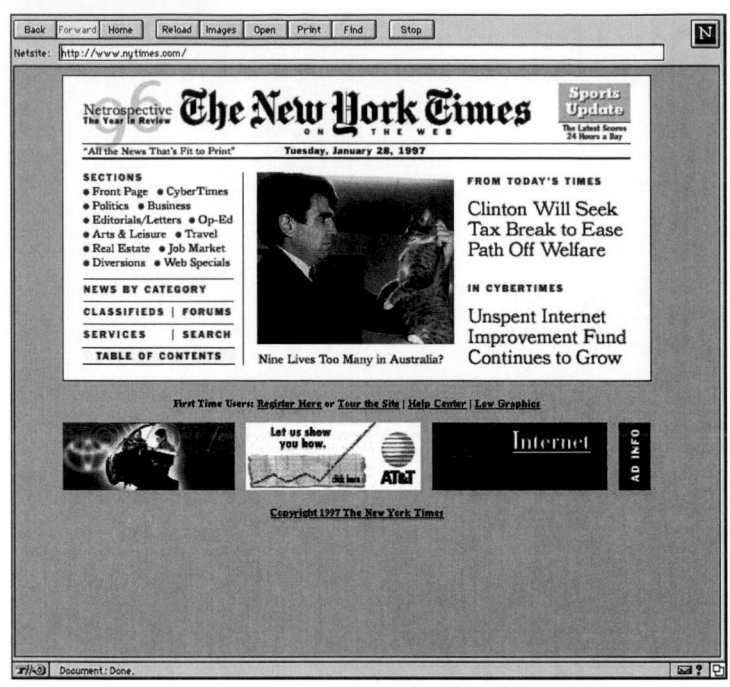

Figure 3.4

The New York Times' web site (`http://www.nyt.com`).

enhance their products' visibility and increase a shopper's desire to buy them through the presence of movement and interactivity that only this new medium can offer.

Interactivity is Essential

Knowing that interactivity is such an essential element of the web, information designers must seek opportunities to provide it in their products. This affects the thought process of designers as they go about the creation of their web sites. Ask yourself the following questions:

▶ Beyond the regular "email" component that most web sites include, how can my site offer opportunities for interactivity? Will I offer forms, bulletin boards, or other devices to stimulate interaction?

▶ Do I have my own interactive mode created to accompany the text on my web site? Does the content make room for such interaction?

▶ Do I take every possible opportunity to offer "links" to related subjects or to interactive sections of sites that enable discussion of specific topics? (A columnist on a web site who is discussing the ethics of cloning, for example, may have links to other sites and writers who have explored the subject, and who are seeking opinions.)

Newspaper web sites can accomplish the same effect by taking advantage of what the new media offers. Incorporating video or sound can make the still photograph of that fire or rescue

A Web Site Is Not a Newspaper

If you think of creating a web site as a matter of duplicating your "paper" product, it is best not to enter this field. If, however, you see an online edition as a good extension of, but not a duplication of the newspaper, then possibilities develop.

Using the Medium to its Fullest

For one, you can create items for your own electronic edition that do not appear in the printed edition. You can market it so that users of one will want to be readers of the other, and vice versa. One cannot compare a printed version of Walt Disney's annual report, for example, with the prospect of an "animated" version of it as it may appear on their web site. Retail catalogs effort that appears on the printed edition seem passive by comparison. In addition, informational graphics become more educational and more useful when they are animated (see Figure 3.2).

We begin to get the picture of why everything that is printable is not transferable to the web, and vice versa. On any good day, only 60% of what appears in print should go into the online edition. The rest is information for the "obsessed" and a good team of online journalists can dig into that and find lots to be obsessed about. Begin with sports, business, and entertainment.

Add history and trivia for good measure. In other words, to make it good, the team of developers need imagination and the ability to grow with the medium. In terms of newspapers and even magazines, a good online edition can help to revitalize the printed edition if a professional effort is put into it. It can do so by not duplicating content. Just like a printed edition of a newspaper could, for example, inform users that the entire text of the President's Inaugural Address appears on its web site, it can also attract attention to columnists and features generally that are not on the web, but that appear (along with photographic content) on its printed edition. Making users travel between the two media is not a strange phenomenon and, in fact, is one that smart editors—both for print and web sites—will make part of their everyday planning and logistics.

Figure 3.5

The progression of this animated infographic from *The Chicago Tribune's* web site shows the course of a fire through the city. The animation gives the user a better visualization of how the fire spread, as opposed to a static graphic with just the numbering.

Rethinking Content

The areas where interactivity works best are those that involve controversial subjects, such as interviews with celebrities or experts that enable live chats—user exchanges (especially among students) and most importantly in the specific area of computer and new media information. This is an important point to remember. Although traditional print publications have always emphasized "beats" (areas of coverage) to reporters, and normally considered the local news as the main beat, web sites are produced for consumption in a computer and consumption by people who are into computers. The result is that anything about computers, new media, and technology become the best beat to include.

At the CNN web site (http://www.cnn.com), Science & Technology is one of the most important sections, although it may not necessarily be the most important one in their broadcast edition (see Figure 3.6). Why? Although not everyone who watches television may have an interest in computers and new media, it is almost certain that users of web sites bring with them an incredible amount of interest in the subject.

The nature of the new media is to be an encyclopedic medium, one that offers substance and depth for those seeking it. If one can add to that interactivity the ability of the user to "connect" with the encyclopedia and its expertise, then nothing can compete with this offering. Information designers should take every possible opportunity to link the user with the experts. It is here, indeed, that some of the magic of this medium resides.

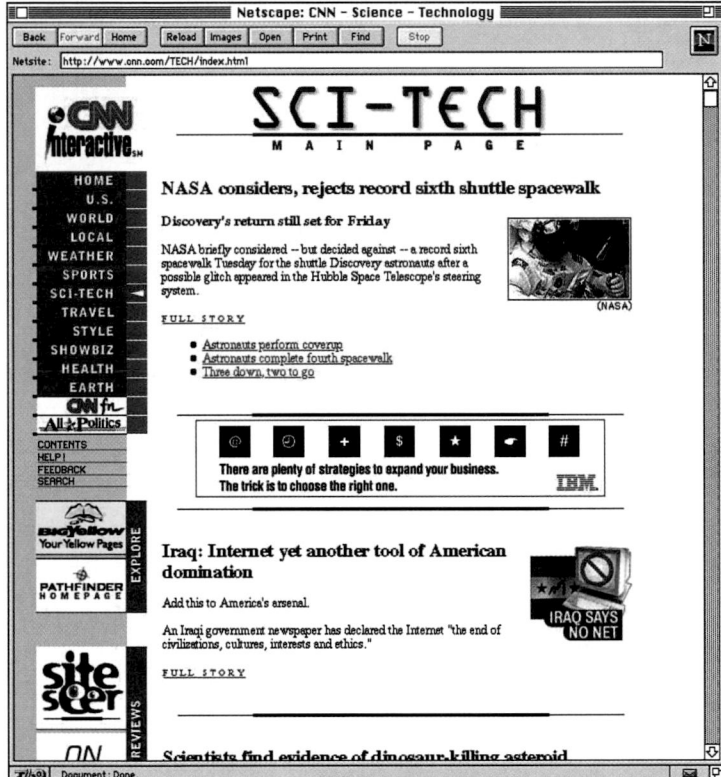

Figure 3.6

The CNN web site's popular Sci-Tech page.

Bandwidth Conservation: Lean Graphics = Fast Downloads

Few things are more frustrating for the web surfer than waiting endlessly for bloated graphic files to download. And because it is so easy for the surfer to ride her desktop bus away to a more promising site, frustration means missed opportunity for the online publisher. To avoid driving readers away, be sure that your graphic is needed (would HTML text be just as use-ful?) and that the graphics files you choose to display, whether still or animated, are as lean as possible.

There are always exceptions, of course, but here is a good three-part rule of thumb for fast downloads over a broad range of standard modem speeds: For navigation buttons, do not exceed 3 K; for ad banners, do not exceed 10 K; for all other graphic images, do not exceed 20 K.

It's not the whole solution by any means, but three more good places to start are:

▶ *Use as few colors as you can and still convey the information your photo, infographic, or animated sequence was intended to contribute to the story*

▶ *Whenever feasible, use the 216 non-dithering (on 256-color machines and better) colors shared by Netscape Navigator and Internet Explorer*

▶ *Choose the right format (usually GIFs for graphics with large areas of flat color and JPEGs for photographs with many subtle shifts of tone)*

There's much more to the equation that adds up to crisp images and fast downloads, of course. For a thorough exploration of a complex subject, an excellent source is The Bandwidth Conservation Society's eminently useful GIF Images page at (http://www.infohiway.com/faster/tuts/gif.html). *After reading through the intro-ductory material there, scroll back to the top and select the "Palette" link at the end of the first bulleted entry. The most useful link from that page is "Victor Engel's No Dither Netscape Color Palette," where information in still greater depth is available. To download versions of the indispensable 216-color palette (arranged by hue or value), which you then can load directly into the equally indispensable Adobe Photoshop image editing package, go to Lynda Weinman's Non-Dithering Colors In Browsers page* (http://www.lynda.com/hex.html).

Two excellent books are Lynda Weinman's Designing Web Graphics: How To Prepare Images and Media for the Web *(1996, New Riders Publishing) and David Siegel's* Creating Killer Web Sites: The Art of Third-Generation Site Design *(1996, Hayden Books). Both books are written by web designers, rather than techies; they approach complex technical issues in a way that makes sense to information designers.*

The World is Getting Smaller

For newspaper web sites, the new media offers an opportunity to explore information baskets of items that are unique to a specific circulation area and its readers, for instance, to a state, province, or country.

Baskets are groupings of information. Combining all consumer related items into one button (as part of the navigation and titling that consumer news), for example, constitutes one basket of information.

These baskets are placed on the web page for users to sample. We are no longer limited by geographic boundaries. There is the possibility that users may be visiting your site from anywhere in the world. No one should cover your area as well as your online edition does.

The world is indeed getting smaller as this new media continues to grow. Chat rooms make it possible for a person in Seattle to have a conversation with someone in Florida. Newspapers also can develop online chats with experts who may be especially suitable to write for the new medium. These chat rooms should include humor, analysis, a brief diversion along the way, or a chat in the corner cafe.

Advertising Online

Finally, commercial possibilities must be considered. I believe that advertising can and should be a pivotal part of online publishing. True, it is not going to be easy to attract these advertisers at first. If, however, you market the edition properly, establish a base clientele of upwardly mobile readers—executives, professors, lawyers, and intellectuals—then you can measure the number of hits and use that information to attract advertising groups from there.

The placement of advertising on web sites should be removed from the traditional print version metaphor. We have no evidence to indicate that advertising should always appear relegated to the bottom of a screen, or to the side. Instead, advertising messages may appear almost anywhere on the screen (see Figures 3.7 and 3.8).

In this new medium, the texture of advertising and that of non-advertising material can, and should, coexist in a happier, more harmonious environment that it has traditionally done in print. Some suggestions:

▶ Place ads on the top right of the screen, perhaps next to some often-used menus.

▶ Position ads toward the center of the screen, keeping them boxed, and separated slightly from other content, but visible.

▶ Set ads at the bottom left of the screen, directly under (or in the middle of) a menu bar.

▶ Place ads at the top of the sites and next to logos of a section, or on the right side or left side of the content, and not just at the bottom of the screen.

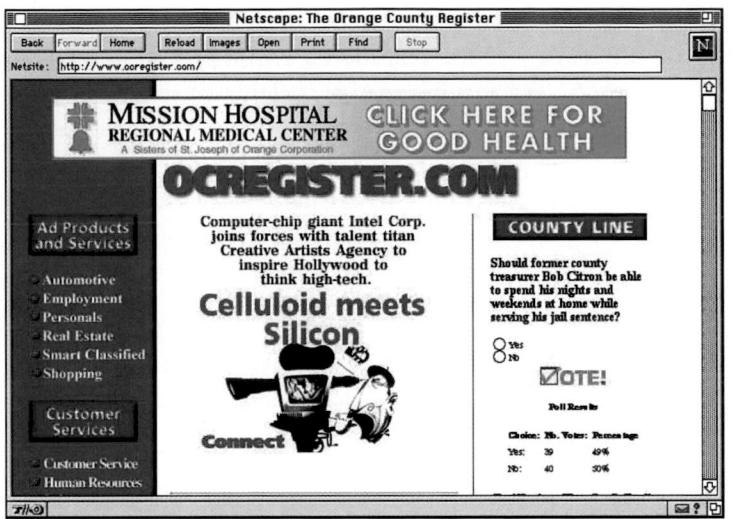

Figure 3.7

The *Orange County Register's* web site prominently displays advertising along the top of the screen.

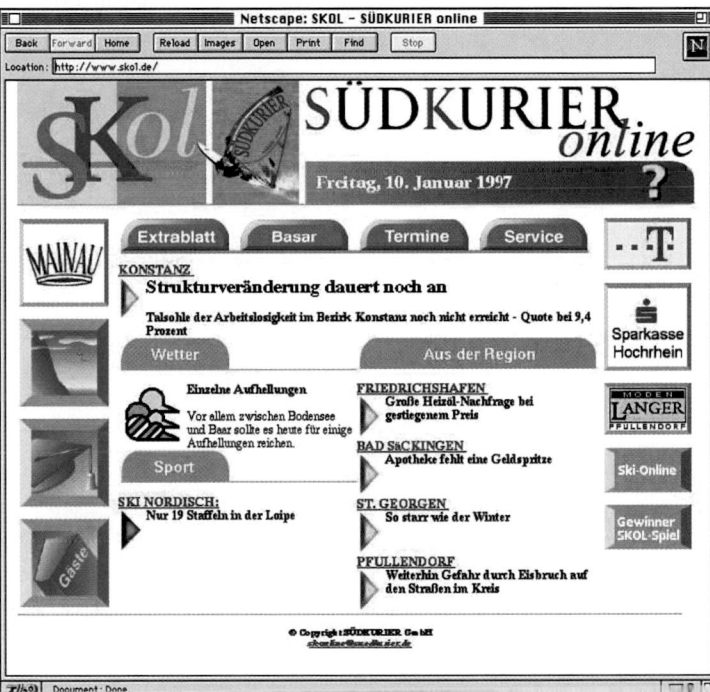

Figure 3.8

Germany's Südkurier Online scatters its advertising among the icons.

As advertising becomes more important in web sites, its design should try to incorporate less congestion, more white space around the central elements, and a color palette that harmonizes with other elements on the screen.

As more advertising appears on web sites, here are some tips to remember:

► Users like advertising.

► This is a new medium and information designers should create the type of visual canvas in which advertising and editorial content do more than coexist (as they now do in print). Beyond coexisting, I think we will begin to see greater connection between advertising and editorial materials.

► Divide the screen so that half is advertising and half is editorial, but without dividing lines.

► Advertorials, the mixing of advertising and information so popular on television, will find its way into the more reduced environment of a computer screen. A perfect medium for it exists on the web.

This is a perfect medium for advertising because the majority of its users are attracted to and view advertising positively, using it to guide their purchases, and seeking from it relevant, timely information. The interactivity that many web sites provide also makes "impulse" buying here as quick as if one was walking down the aisle of a store. There is nothing to keep us from acting on impulse. A print ad may entice us, but we must wait before we act on our impulse. Reaching for a credit card number while surfing the Net is as easy as pulling it out of one's wallet at the toy store!

The new medium should finally echo the feelings of media users in many focus groups: advertising is information, too, and users are not adverse to it.

Quite the contrary, advertising messages are considered a vital part of information today. It is only some traditional editors who still refuse to accept this as reality. Web sites offer a great opportunity to revitalize the presence of advertising, to let it join with editorial matter on the screen.

Information Design as a Discipline

Information design as a discipline is as interdisciplinary as are the users of information today. We are beginning to evolve into a world where many people specialize in one field academically, only to work in situations where their specialization is only secondary to their main task. As it becomes more difficult to focus on single subjects in the workplace or in academic settings, the work of information designers becomes more visual and the role of information design more important.

Although it is true that traditional journalism always attracted people with a variety of backgrounds (from politics to literature to economics, and not necessarily journalism majors), the need for variety is greater among information designers.

What will be new, I believe, will be the integration of new disciplines, from architecture to engineering and the sciences, people for whom the challenge of a laboratory environment was always a top priority in seeking employment. The new media offer such a laboratory. The traditional communication major is likely to expand beyond speech and logic, the subject of expression, to embrace other disciplines such as architecture and engineering, where expression mixes with the logistics of constructing, programming, and experimenting.

Experimenting was never more important. We must remind ourselves that for those of us who started in print and followed a career path in that area, when we arrived at our first newspaper or magazine job, we inherited structures and processes that were, in a sense, part of a legacy. The average publication had clearly distinctive patterns such as sports, national news, business, entertainment, and so on. We came into our jobs and trained, but did little creative experimenting.

Today, the new medium continues to use print as a metaphor, but this is passing fast. Most of us involved in new media dwell in an environment of daily discoveries—the result of experimentation. Little research exists, so we as information designers are creating the structures and processes that another generation may inherit as their legacy. Legacies are not going to grow old in this medium, however, and rightly so.

Each generation of information designers will bring in new processes. And although one can predict what newspapers and magazines may look like 20 years from now, it would be difficult to predict what web sites will be like in 10 years. The good news is that all of these media will coexist.

Chapter 4

Story Structures

For years, I have begun many of my projects by creating an environment, a sort of "house" in which type elements dwell. I call them story structures, and they are the combinations of words, sentences, and paragraphs that lead to the comprehension of story units.

A story structure may be as basic as a headline (or title) followed by text. Although the most basic combination, it is highly effective (see Figure 4.1). In an environment where users are the ultimate quick scanners—in a hurry, fighting against time and an avalanche of information—sometimes other "hooks" must be used. These "hooks" may be as simple as adding an overline above the headline or title (see Figure 4.2), a paragraph that summarizes the highlights of a story (see Figure 4.3), or even a full second line, or deck, under the headline (see Figure 4.4).

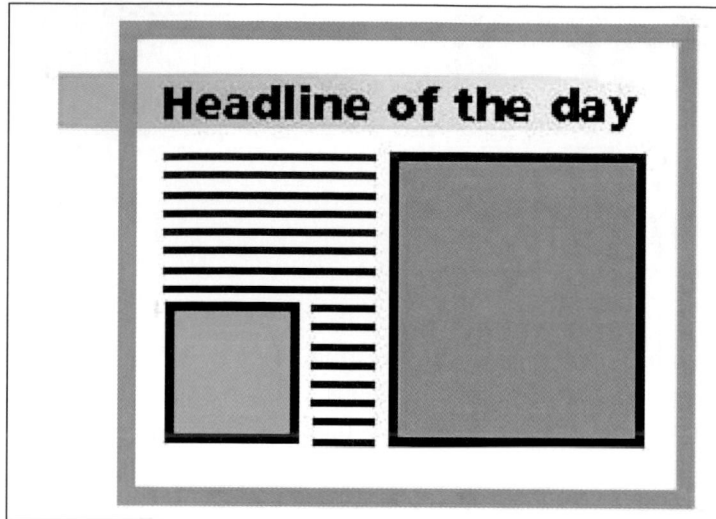

Figure 4.1

This simple story structure is very effective in getting the reader right to the text. It relies heavily on the headline to guide the reader.

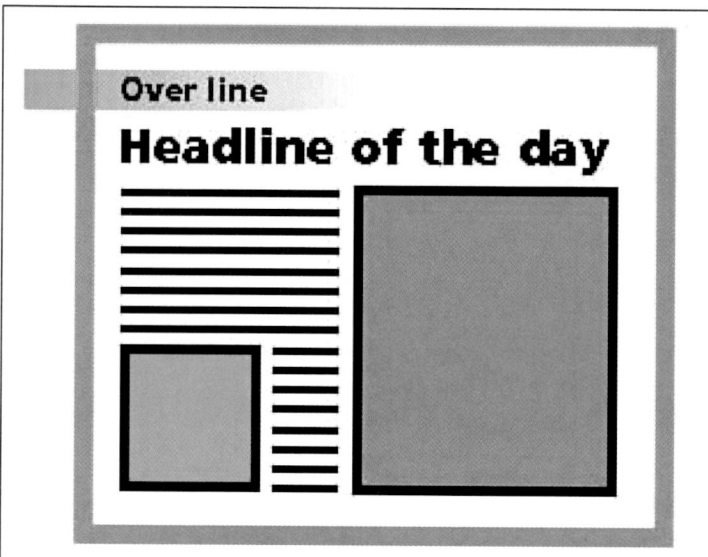

Figure 4.2

The overline head is commonly used to generalize or briefly describe the story and add more information than the headline. It may guide the reader to the headline or even right into the text.

This chapter emphasizes the importance of story structures, and how their creation can facilitate the job of the information designer by offering a foundation on which to build everything, from creation of typographic schemes, to architectural formats, and, in the case of some of the most dynamic web sites, the colorization of certain titles or elements in a story structure.

Story Structures in Action

Story structures are all around us, in everything we read. Literature, to take an obvious example, provides us with story structures: how an author divides the various chapters and how those are presented constitutes an element of story structuring. When an author decides to include type breakers, or subheads, to move the reader along, he is helping structure the information to be presented.

Story structures relate directly to content. Readers, and users, seek information with one of two intentions in mind: to discover new information, or to reaffirm the information they may have heard somewhere already. As such, if we heard on the radio about a bomb exploding somewhere, or the Dow Jones average reaching its highest level ever, we may go to a publication or to a web site for a "glimpse" of the news item, but go somewhere else desiring to hear more.

This is how story structures become important. Reaffirmation news normally appears in briefer structures than, let's say, discovery items. The more discovery there is in a news item, the longer it is,

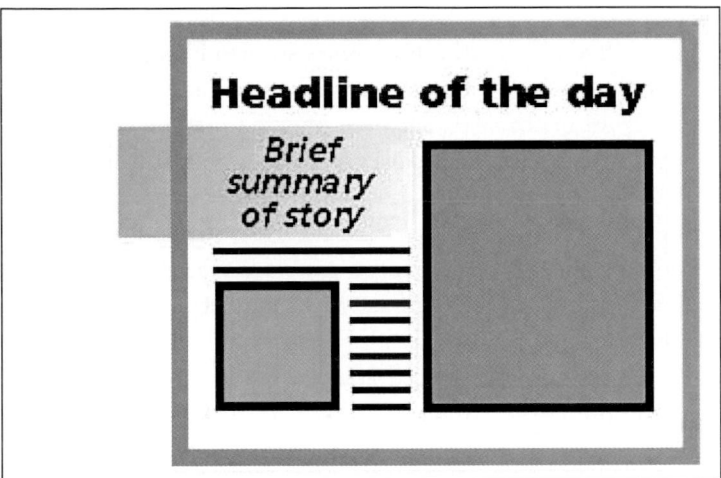

Figure 4.3

A summary paragraph is extremely effective for the "quick reader" or "scanner." It provides the "television" briefing of what is to follow, and it is not to be confused with the "lead" or main paragraph of the story.

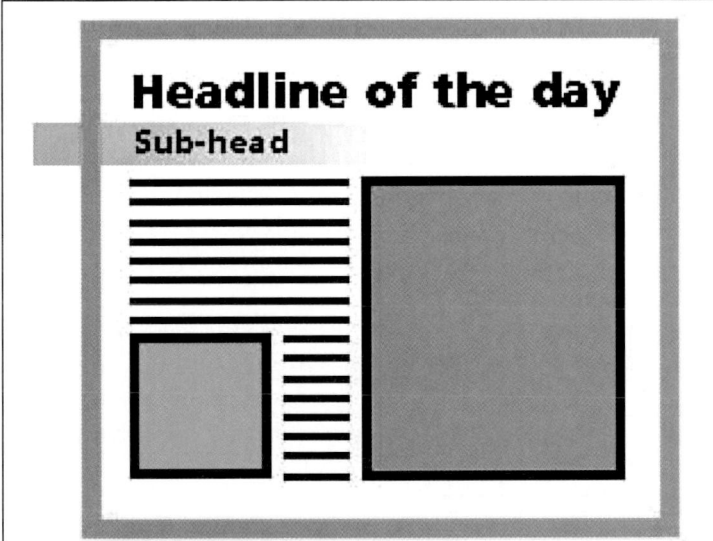

Figure 4.4

A second line under the headline or a "sub-head" works very much like the overline, but it often gives the reader a bit of additional information that the main headline may not provide. This is also effective in helping the reader decide whether or not to read the story.

the larger the headline, and perhaps the more comprehensive the summary. A story structure for a new, substantial presentation of news shows, through its graphic presentation, greater flair than a repetition of the bomb explosion that we know about, may appear in what is commonly referred to as a "brief" (a three-paragraph structure with a small two-line headline).

There is much editorial intention in how story structures are used, of course. An editor decides how to play a news item, selects the appropriate story structure, and the user (reader) gets a message of its importance by the way the structure is displayed. To the story, story structuring is a process; to the user (reader), it is a rather subconscious one.

Story structures also reflect the medium in which they are used. In television, for example, a "brief" item may be "read" on the air in 10 seconds, whereas a full report may include video and last longer. Newspaper story structures emphasize briefness to expedite readers and scanners who are moving rapidly through the pages. Magazine story structures, on the other hand, tend to be more leisurely paced, with several headlines and subheads, longer texts, and more images.

Print Publications

How one starts a magazine article—whether with a summary paragraph, a simple one line heading under the main headline, or with quotes and interruptions in the middle of the text—is story structuring at work.

Newspapers have experimented with story structures for as long as they've been in existence, but especially in the last 15 years, as readership has decreased and editors have been forced to adopt more efficient techniques to make text and reading more palatable and accessible. Magazines, with easier deadlines, better paper to print on, and a more focused readership, have always made story structures a part of their design and a part of the publications' overall visual continuity.

Eye Movement

The specifics of eye movement onscreen need to be understood first, along with a comparison with the printed page. Granted, not much research has been conducted on how users approach and move about while accessing information on a typical computer screen. In fact, it was only in recent years that more conclusive research, including the Poynter Institute for Media Studies' Eye-Track research (which I conducted with my Poynter colleague, Dr. Pegie Stark Adam), provided us with some specific clues as to how newspaper readers' eyes move on a printed page.

We know that the typical movement on a printed page goes something like this: reader enters the page through a visual element, primarily photographs or illustrations that are the largest visual mass on the canvas of the page. From there, specific movement is rather difficult to track, but larger headlines generally capture attention first, then smaller ones. Other factors, such as placement of elements and the presence of color also can alter the trajectory of the eyes on a printed page.

In the Poynter study, we also found that the placement of elements on a page determines, to a large degree, how the reader penetrates and travels through a page. Normally, it is a photo or illustration that draws us in, but the presence of color, or the lack of it, can also determine patterns of readership. Specifically, an element in a bright, forward color such as red immediately created attention, whereas the same element in a gray, or more muted color, such as a pale blue, did not have the same immediate effect. A hierarchy is created systematically through the size of an element (large elements dominating), the placement (whatever is above the fold of a page gains immediate attention), and, of course, color (the bright primaries dominate, soft pastels play back in the choir).

Most importantly, we discovered that if one can point out a specific pattern of movement on a printed page, it tends to be mostly in a diagonal sweeping motion from top to bottom and back up.

Focus groups and very early studies conducted with small groups when web sites are designed, however, lead us to believe that the eye movement onscreen tends to be more horizontal—with quick sweeping motions from left to right—as opposed to diagonally.

Observing the Eyes

The Poynter Eye-Track Research was conducted in 1990. Using a prototype of a daily newspaper, consisting of four sections, we set out to print the same paper in color, as well as totally in black and white.

The purpose of the study was to use two different sets of readers, in four

American cities, who would look at different versions of the newspapers. Some readers saw the newspaper entirely in color, others in black and white. The contents of both prototypes were identical.

Drawing Conclusions

We concluded that the presence of black and white or color was secondary to the following: placement of an element, size of an element, and content. A large photograph, if it was good and interesting, commanded the same amount of interest and became the point of entry on the page despite its color. Elements placed above the fold were looked at faster and had greater impact than those below the fold. Ultimately, and not too surprising to us, it was the subject matter of elements that determined how readers looked at them and how long they stayed on a given page.

We did find out that color played a more vital role in advertising. Ads in color had greater visibility, more reader traffic, and were remembered longer than the same ads in black and white. Readers also preferred color images in such feature sections as food and travel, but the issue of color versus black and white was secondary in news and sports sections.

My own research using Eye-Track equipment to record eye movement across a written page (published in a report called "Eyes on the News" in 1991) revealed that story structures are, indeed, extremely important in guaranteeing that readers proceed beyond the headline. Many readers routinely fail to read past a headline, but the use of summary paragraphs in 12 points or larger

tends to retain readers a bit longer and, in many cases, to lure them into the text. I do not know of any research to test the same principles on a web site, but the results are likely to be similar.

This makes the job of the editor extremely important. Good story structures are clear, direct, and sequential. Words are not repeated in any of the different points of entry to the structure. Each element provides new information. Good story structures contain interchangeable elements that work well for both print and web editions (see Figure 4.5).

Figure 4.5

This page from *People* magazine is reflective of the effectiveness of good story structure. The brief headline is supplemented by a brief "sub-head" telling what the story is about and inviting the reader to read on or continue to another story.

Good story structures can result from the following strategies:

▶ Provide the necessary elements for approaching and following a story.

▶ Use consistent typography, so that a brief item always uses the same typographic elements, regardless of what section of the site is in. The same would be true for a personal column, or a long reportage.

▶ Imply a sense of hierarchy by the size of type, and the number of points of entry leading into the text of the story.

▶ Classify stories according to their importance, establishing whether the news they contain is of a reaffirmation or discovery nature.

Advertising

Advertising information designers take their cue from newspapers and magazines, combining headlines and text in limited spaces to convey messages that accompany photographs or illustrations (see Figure 4.6).

For advertising information designers, the space is more limited than for anyone else. In addition, they must deal with "catch phrases" or tag lines that will be remembered and a product that must be presented prominently, while not allowing the message to seem too terribly like pure advertising. Thus, the answer is to take the newspaper/magazine article metaphor and try to lure readers into their message thinking that it is "another page" from the editorial

Figure 4.6

This advertising for Seiko combines a curious headline followed by a few lines of text explaining it and a large photograph. Like newspapers and magazines, this ad also relies on story structure to effectively distribute information.

section of the publication. This, I am convinced, can be done even more successfully online that it has ever been accomplished in print. The reason? The more limited canvas of the screen enables less compartmentalizing of editorial and advertising. The mixing of messages, if done properly, can even be attractive. A new way of presenting advertising is upon us.

Just How Big Is the Screen?

Story Structures and the Web

Story structures figure prominently on the web as well; in fact, they are one of the top considerations when designing a web site. Specifically with newspapers and magazines, one important question to ask is whether story structures transfer to the web exactly as they appear in print.

A newspaper whose story structures normally dictate an overline, a headline, and text (including a summary paragraph), for example, probably finds it relatively easy to transfer that entire structure directly to the web. For others, the transition may involve creating a totally new story structure for the screen. (See Chapter 8, "The Basic Recipe").

For web sites, story structures need to emphasize good "hooks" (headlines, summaries, and secondary lines) at the beginning, but they should avoid loading the text with too many interruptions—graphics and photos that delay the process of scrolling and reading.

Although I notice that one can transfer 90 percent of a story structure from print to web, it is clear that some of the interruptive elements that break text so well on a printed page can become obtrusive when scrolling up and down through text onscreen.

A lengthy article that might take up an entire page of a newspaper, for example, or a double spread in a magazine or newsletter, benefits from the thoughtful placement of quotes, boxes, and other elements to make the reader's journey through the text easier.

Onscreen, however, getting to the text requires some navigation before the initial story structure appears, and it is here that the real reading process begins. Now we are "hooked" with the story content and proceed to "dive" into the text. Because the screen is smaller than a newspaper or magazine page, we do not perceive the length of the text in the same way we do when faced with a printed page. As a result, there is no need to interrupt the flow of text on the screen with unnecessary elements.

Just How Big Is the Screen?

There is no default screen size—just as, from the user's point of view, there are no defaults for image resolution, browser software, modem speed, or raw computing power. Indeed, some users choose not to load images at all, preferring the download speed of straight text. But, as web designers, we have to begin somewhere. I find 640×480 pixels to be a reasonable working estimate of screen size (meaning content that comes into view as a web site loads), as opposed to page size (which includes content that comes into view only as a reader scrolls downward). This assumption enables me to construct balanced tables, to arrange images and display type, or to calculate the amount of screen real estate to be displayed within each of several frames. The result won't look the same to all users, but the proportions should hold up.

It is clear that much research is needed in this area. It took years of newspaper and magazine publishing before any valuable research on readership patterns became available. With luck, it will take less time before we can begin to gauge how web page readers move their eyes, what makes them "click," the effect of typographic elements in easing legibility, and so on. In time, it may be possible to create story structures exclusively for web sites.

Is it necessary, for example, to have a traditional headline over the text, in the form of an umbrella, inspired by the newspaper/magazine metaphor, or could we simply use a one word entry into the text, and proceed from there (see Figure 4.7)?

One word should be enough, especially if there are visuals to aid our understanding of the story. In addition, we must keep in mind that the canvas of

the screen we are looking at is much less than the size of a newspaper or a magazine page, thus key points of entry (such as one word, or even a word and an icon) can be enough to get us into the content. The one weakness of using "one word" hooks is that sometimes a story includes a variety of topics that are difficult to summarize in one word, thus a full title with a subject and verb is more recommended.

Another good technique for a web story structure may be to box the topic and heading, using colors and reverse type, before plunging the user into a mass of text (see Figure 4.8).

This type of arrangement makes the user see the heading as an illustration, because of the boxing and the colorization. Information designers should never go too far with these techniques, as we must keep in mind that the purpose of a story structure is to lure users to read, not to simply create visual impact onscreen.

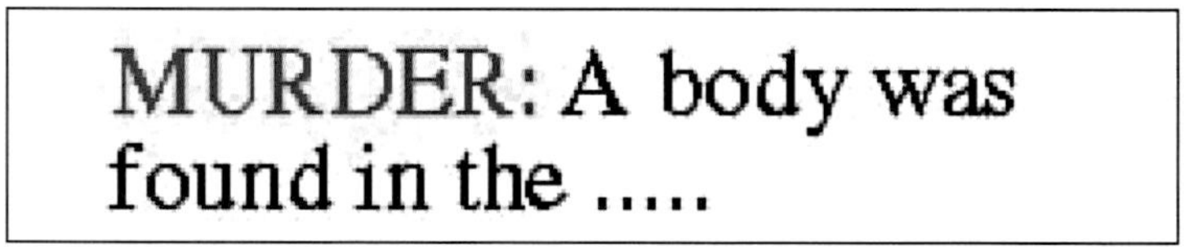

MURDER: A body was found in the .....

Figure 4.7

A one word entry may be enough to "hook" the reader when we consider that the screen is much smaller that a newspaper page and there is much less to compete with. On a smaller screen, the reader will look at everything and the entry word may be all it takes.

MURDER
A body was found in the .....

Figure 4.8

A reverse box can be even more effective than a one word entry when we are talking about a screen as opposed to a newspaper page. The reversed text in a colored box is also a "hook"; it can give the user the right amount of information he needs before deciding to read the story.

The Purpose of Story Structure

Part of the challenge of new media is to continuously experiment with all aspects of its creation. As for story structures, they have been there from the beginning. Samuel Clemens' idea of a good story structure is one that follows a *circular format*: if a scene opens in a kitchen, it should end there as well.

Creating story structures serves the primary purpose of establishing a format, or a forum for presenting information. A second useful purpose, both in print and online, is that it presents the designer with a skeleton to support typographic elements. The minute the story structures are established the designer can begin to assign typographic components.

If two or three different type fonts are being utilized on a project, for example—and we shall see this in more detail in the typography chapter of this book—then the story structures must accommodate them to establish visual continuity.

Fashioning a Unique Structure

Using the examples of story structures presented earlier in this chapter, assume that a web site incorporates Times Bold, Times Italic, and Helvetica Light. As such, the overline on top of the headline could be set in Helvetica Light, while the main headline is set in Times Bold, with the underline, or summary, in Times Italic. Various combinations are possible, giving the story structure a special characteristic while contributing to the overall typographic unity of the site or the publication (see Figure 4.9).

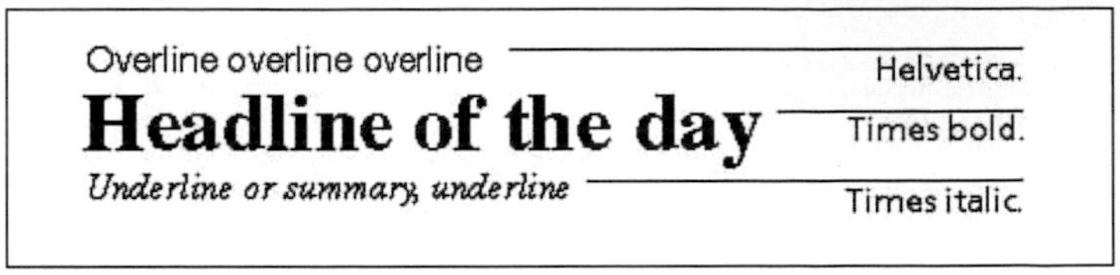

If, as we mentioned at the beginning of this chapter, story structures are "houses" or dwellings for information, then populating them with interesting content, and dressing them up with legible and attractive type fonts are an important part of the task of the editor and designer.

Print designers have always had a set of guidelines, measurements, and tips that they keep handy, insisting that it is not worth memorizing so much of what can be looked at on a piece of paper. For the web information designer, the list is short, but because most of us still

Overline overline overline ——————— Helvetica.

Headline of the day
Times bold.

Underline or summary, underline ——— Times italic.

Figure 4.9

A story structure gives the information designer more liberty to make the information being transferred more "readable." In the case of typography, for example, this particular story structure allows for the use of three typographic units in various combinations.

◀ CONVERTING PICAS TO PIXELS ▶

The following equation is quick and dirty, rather than exact, but it gives the web designer a feel for how the analog measure translates to the digital. Park it behind your ear to keep it handy, like a stub of copy pencil in the old days:

1 pica = about 10 pixels

think in terms of picas, the units of measurements used in print (six picas equals one inch), then it is convenient to deal with the following guidelines for the pica equivalent on the screen: pixels.

Story structures reflect the very essence of the information presented. Next in importance is how the structures themselves fit into easy to follow patterns of organization inside the screen, which is where screen architecture comes into play.

We have learned about the importance of story structures as the foundation of all design, the elements that turn words and stories into clearly defined models of how the information is presented. Information designers will find that taking care of story structures early in the conceptualizing of a web site saves them time later. More importantly, as we shall see in the next chapter, story structures facilitate everything from how the architecture of the web site is designed to the typographic elements designed for each structure.

DRESSING up

INFORMATION

Figure 4.10

A home page on the special report presented an index of each of the seven baskets of information included in the package. With a headline and a three-line description, the user could get a glimpse of what each installment related to. A photo accompanies each description.

Dressing up Information

The presentation of special reports finds a particular receptive medium on the web. Unlike its appearance on a printed newspaper page, where the length of the piece becomes immediately obvious, and may even overwhelm the reader, special reports written in narrative style tend to allow for what appears to be more leisured reading on the screen.

The Los Angeles Times *published such a piece on its web site, titled "Homicide... and justice for some," (*http://www.latimes.com/homicide/*) and did so in a manner that was visually attractive, and journalistically well organized. (See Figures 4.10 and 4.11).*

Perhaps one of the most notable design elements in this presentation is the use of text set in a 30-pica wide column, as opposed to filling up the entire width of the screen. As such, the reader tends to move easily from line to line. It is well known in print design that column widths beyond 22 picas are not as easy to read. The same concept applies to screen text setting. In addition, the "neutral" space left on the side of the screen makes the presentation more attractive.

Notice the use of graphics to interrupt the masses of text, as well as to provide additional information. The use of color here, black and brown, set the appropriate mood for the topic of the special report.

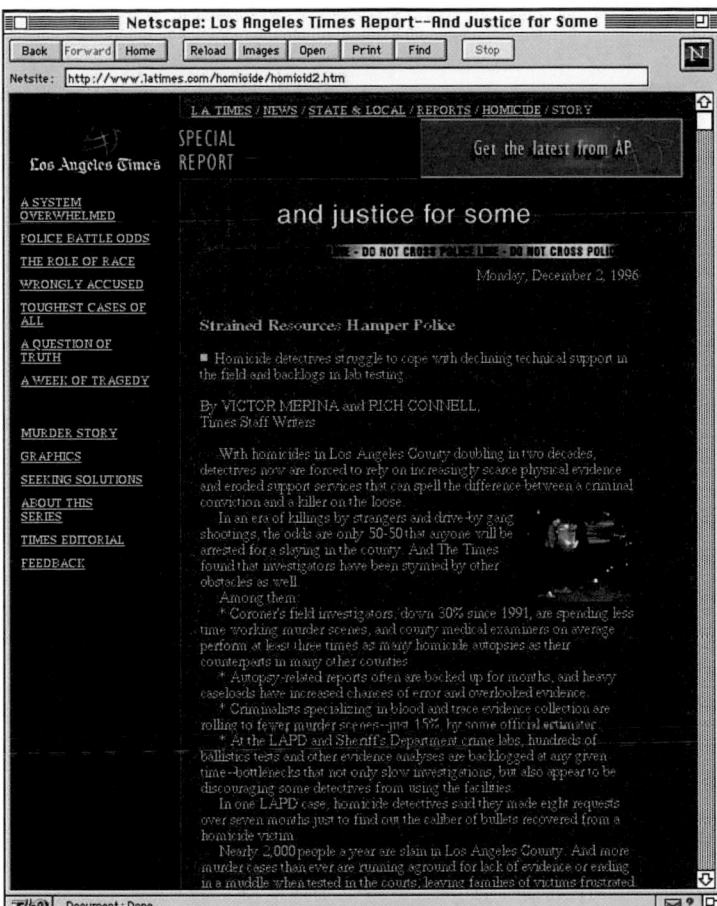

Figure 4.11

Click the headline and go inside the narrative. On the left side of the screen you still have the menu choices to move to another narrative or back to the home page.

Chapter 5

The Information Designer as Architect

Grids, columns, white space, movement, and overall effect…the architect's jargon is also that of the information designer when it comes to putting images on a surface to communicate a message more effectively. Web sites are miniature architectural landscapes. Like precious boxes in a collector's display, the space in which to create is limited—but the possibilities are not.

But these possibilities are better explored through a strong knowledge of how users access and digest information, how their eyes move on the screen, how visual hierarchy creates organization, as well as how to effectively use white space. This chapter discusses and illustrates the most effective ways to orchestrate the display of visual elements on the screen.

Architecture for the Screen

With the computer screen, architectural applications must take into account that dramatically smaller canvas on which the designer paints and the user canvases the information (see "Just How Big Is the Screen?" in Chapter 4, "Story Structures"). Still, it is important to have a center of visual impact that creates the hierarchy for movement on the screen. Early returns from focus groups conducted for various online projects in which I have been involved indicate that a more horizontal sweeping of the screen, from left to right, seems to be in order (see Figure 5.1).

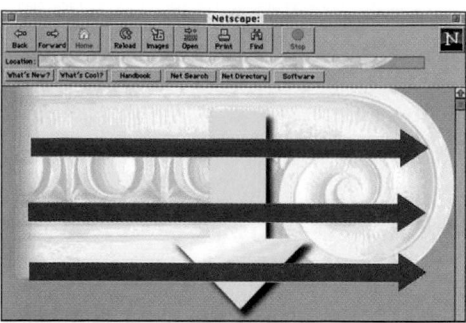

Figure 5.1

Unlike a newspaper or magazine page, in which the eye moves normally from top to bottom, following diagonal lines of motion from the top left hand corner of the page to the bottom right, on the screen, the motion of the eyes seems to be first to the center, top to bottom, then it is a steady left to right movement.

This, no doubt, will determine how "layers" of various elements will be placed on screens, and how the hierarchy of weights on the screen will appear.

Generally, design is a combination of elements, some of which may be layered, almost on top of each other. We may have a title that touches an illustration, for example, but we have done it in such a way that hierarchically, the illustration is secondary to the title, or vice versa. This is layering at work.

Weight has more to do with dominance. A photo may carry more weight than a title, or a color may carry the weight of the screen (dominating visually). Perhaps the best definition of weights takes place with typographic elements, how we can go from bold to medium to light, thus defining hierarchy.

Color Across Media

Because most web sites are designed in color, there is no need to dwell on the power of color as opposed to black and white on the screen, a subject much discussed and researched in terms of newspapers. There is still a set mentality among certain print editors, for example, that a "serious" newspaper should always be in black and white. I encounter plenty of publishers, primarily in Europe these days, who cling to the idea that color on a printed page translates into a sort of "boulevard, sensational" product. We know through focus groups that to a generation of readers who grew up with color television and color magazines, this is no longer so.

But in terms of web design, there is no black and white antecedent. Web sites are designed in color. The same newspapers that look at color with a great deal of caution, such as *The New York Times* (which uses it in its feature sections, but not yet on page one), or the German weekly, *Die Zeit*, have web sites in color.

Nobody in these newspapers even considered going with a black and white web site. This provides web designers with an excellent opportunity to experiment with and display color with greater freedom than print designers in many publications (see Figures 5.2 through 5.4).

Figure 5.2

This is a front page of the prestigious German weekly, *Die Zeit*, published in Hamburg, and read by an elite group, representing the intellectual readership of the country.

Begin with an Element of Visual Impact

One thing that print pages and screens have in common is that they both require one dominant element to capture the reader's attention. Call it a center of visual impact, or a dominant lead visual, this is the initial point of entry for the user. This element could be a photograph or illustration, or perhaps a large headline, logo, or even a color block.

The size of this element should be two times bigger than any other element on the screen. The user unconsciously penetrates through this one element, and then decides how to move on the screen from there.

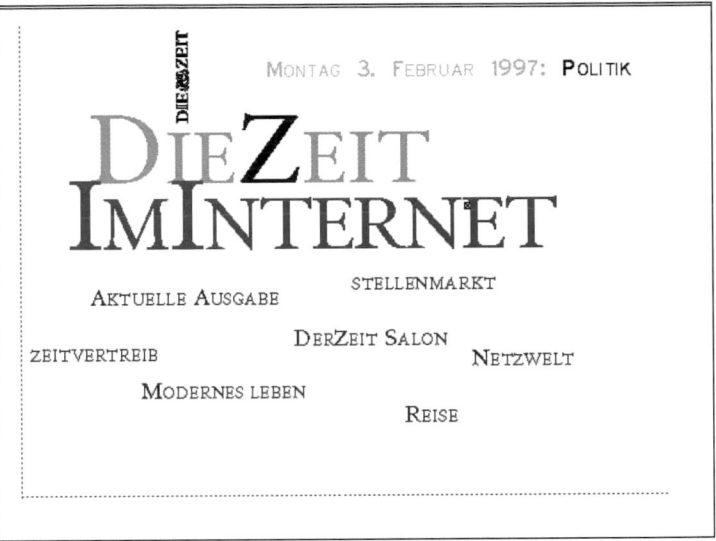

Figure 5.3

This is a prototype concept for Die Zeit Im Internet, the electronic edition, trying to convey the same conservative feel and typography of the printed edition.

Figure 5.4

Another model presented as a prototype for Die Zeit goes one step beyond, emphasizing greater use of color, and more dynamic visuals.

The Grid

Unlike print grids, where sizes may vary to accommodate a broad sheet newspaper, a tabloid (of which there are at least four different "standard" sizes around the world), or a variety of magazine sizes, the screen "grid" is more standard in its format. The screen proportions enable a variety of grids. The imagination of the information designer can lead to a one-column grid, or many columns, or no visible grid at all. The following are examples of different grid structures that may prove helpful to the designer.

Inverted 7 Grid

The inverted 7 grid enables the left hand side of the screen to be open, with the column of navigational tools to the right, and sometimes a bar of additional navigational tools, or even advertising, at the bottom of the screen.

This is an ideal grid for sites where the designer knows, from the start, that there will be heavy use of images (photos and illustrations), and therefore it is important not to block entrance to the site with a frame on the left (see Figure 5.5).

Figure 5.5

Horizontal panel dominates the top, vertical navigation on left of screen.

L-shaped Grid

The L-shaped grid is one of the most commonly used for web sites world-wide. The left hand side of the screen provides a vertical element normally utilized for navigation. The bottom is used for advertising or for additional navigational tools.

This is an ideal grid for more text-heavy sites. Users can always move to the left to abandon the page on the screen and move on to further reading inside the site. (see Figure 5.6).

Figure 5.6

Vertical column for navigation on the left, bottom of screen horizontal unit.

Double-track Grid

The double-track grid uses vertical columns both on the left and right of the screen, with the changeable (text) elements dominating in the center of the screen.

This is the least recommended of all the grids, as it tends to crowd whatever moveable elements, such as text and images, we put in the center. But it might be an economical way to get more onto the screen, especially when the menu is extensive, and advertising is also an integral part of the site (see Figure 5.7).

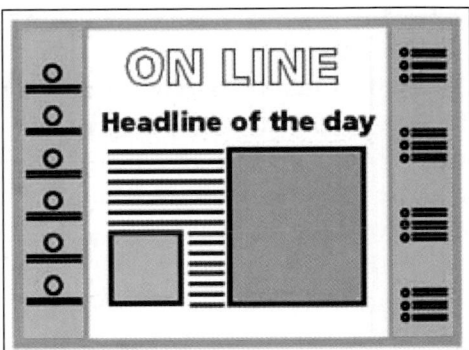

Figure 5.7

Vertical columns dominate on the left and right of the screen.

Open Grid

This is one of the cleanest and perhaps easiest to use of the grids (see Figure 5.8). The navigational elements appear only at the top of the screen. The rest of the page is open and changes from day to day.

This grid is ideal for sites where the number of navigational "buttons" is reduced, therefore enabling easy distribution at the top.

Figure 5.8

No set structures appear but the designer must maintain balance and contrast, while incorporating white space.

Invisible Grid

This is the single-image screen, in which the grid is not visible; users see one visual splash upon connecting, then nothing else until they link to a second page (see Figure 5.9).

This is definitely the ideal grid for more artistic sites, the ones where large images may be presented, as when a creative portfolio appears, or a photographic treatment of a story that opens with large images. It is, in a sense, the open canvas landscape that designers dream of, but rarely can get in real life situations—most likely to be used for special purposes inside an already existing site.

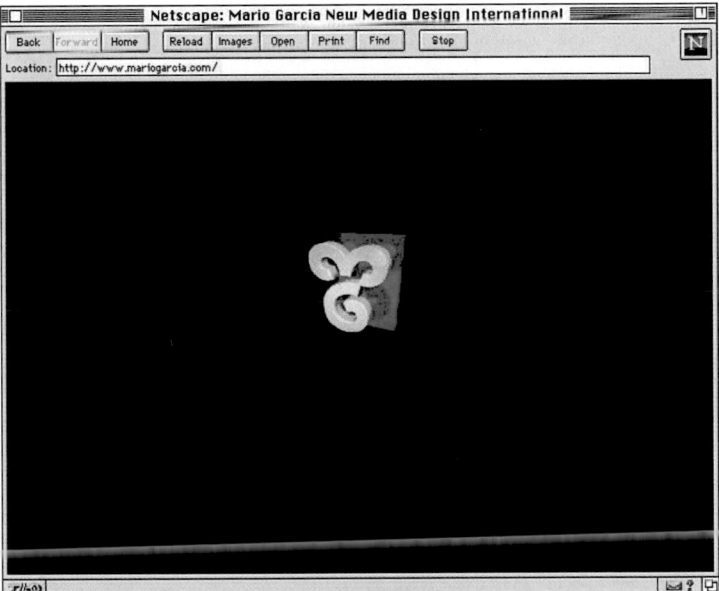

Figure 5.9

The home page for Mario Garcia New Media Design International offers an invisible grid, with the major navigational tools centered under the logo. After the user moves to the inside screens the grid becomes more visible, with the navigational tools on the left.

Visible Grid

Another style is to have a highly visible, very specific grid, where the frames or columns are part of how the designer paints on the screen. Here a certain organization prevails, one that is highly recommended, especially if it leads the user to navigational tools (see Figure 5.10).

This more visible grid is recommended for sites where advertising is going to be a presence on each screen, for example. The visible grid can be designed so that advertising content is part of a grid (wider, narrower, more colorful), whereas the non-advertising content remains in a less structured grid.

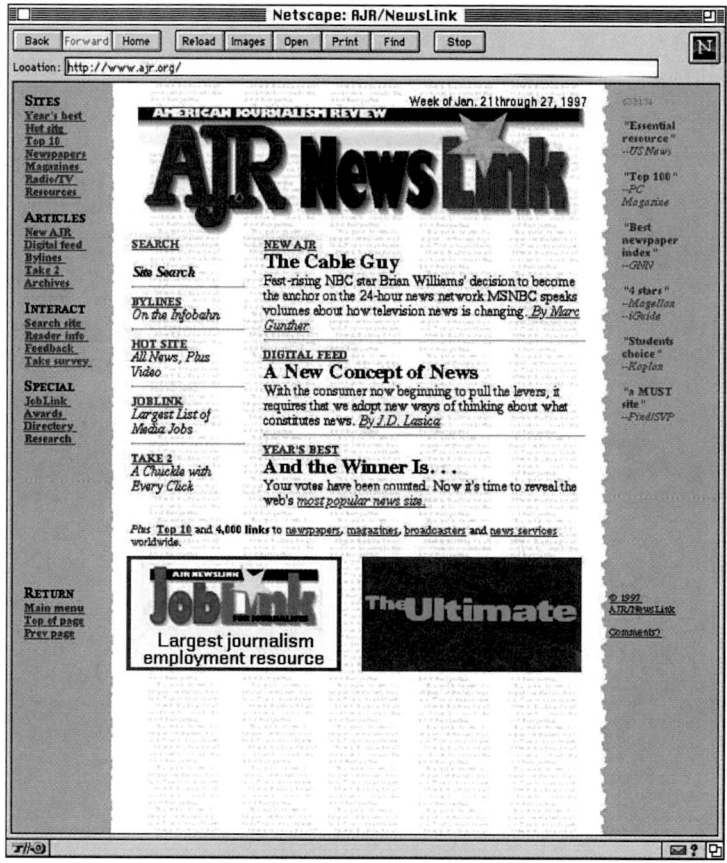

Figure 5.10

The *American Journalism Review* magazine home page is clearly structured with one vertical unit of navigation on the left, then a wider column in the middle to include the main headlines accessible on that edition. A clear distinction is made, architecturally, between the narrow column on the left and the wider one in the middle. This grid is preserved through every page of the site.

Tables and FRANES

Both tables and frames have become de facto standards for web designers. They enable the designer to construct a screen layout grid without going outside the bounds set by the HTML extensions implemented by Netscape Navigator and MS Internet Explorer (as of this writing).

Tables can be displayed with or without visible borders, the latter being generally preferred for our purposes. In this form, tables enable the designer to construct an invisible grid and then to arrange images and type within the rows and cells (see the following code and Figure 5.11).

```
<HTML>
<HEAD>
<TITLE> The Florida Humanities Council: Welcome!</TITLE>
</HEAD>

<BODY BACKGROUND="./GIFs/parchmnt.gif" TEXT="#000099" LINK="#990000" ALINK="#3366FF"
VLINK="#6699FF">

<A NAME="home"><A HREF="./indexa.html"><FONT SIZE="-1">A text-only version<BR>
of this page is available.</FONT></A><BR><IMG SRC="./GIFs/dot_clear.gif" WIDTH="1" HEIGHT="1"
VSPACE="2"><BR>
<IMG SRC="./GIFs/dot_clear.gif" WIDTH="1" HEIGHT="1" HSPACE="3"><IMG SRC="./GIFs/FHClogoT.gif"
ALIGN=MIDDLE WIDTH="379" HEIGHT="127" VSPACE="5">

<TABLE CELLPADDING="3" WIDTH="480" BORDER="0">
<TR>

        <TD ALIGN=CENTER VALIGN=TOP WIDTH="98">
<A HREF="./News.html"><IMG SRC="./GIFs/9_man.gif" ALIGN=MIDDLE WIDTH="65" HEIGHT="55" BOR-
DER="0"></A><BR>
<A HREF="./News.html"><FONT SIZE="-1">Humanities News</FONT></A><BR><IMG
SRC="./GIFs/dot_clear.gif" WIDTH="1" HEIGHT="1" VSPACE="10"><BR>

<A HREF="./Calendar.html"><IMG SRC="./GIFs/8_woman.gif" ALIGN=MIDDLE WIDTH="65" HEIGHT="55"
BORDER="0"></A><BR>
<A HREF="./Calendar.html"><FONT SIZE="-1">The FHC Calendar</FONT></A><BR><IMG
SRC="./GIFs/dot_clear.gif" WIDTH="1" HEIGHT="1" VSPACE="10"><BR>

<A HREF="./Gathering.html"><IMG SRC="./GIFs/1_man.gif" ALIGN=MIDDLE WIDTH="65" HEIGHT="55"
BORDER="0"></A><BR>
<A HREF="./Gathering.html"><FONT SIZE="-1">The Florida Gathering</FONT></A><BR><IMG
SRC="./GIFs/dot_clear.gif" WIDTH="1" HEIGHT="1" VSPACE="10"><BR>
```

TABLES and FRAMES

```
<!--MORE NAVIGATION ICONS & LINKS GO HERE-->
      </TD>

      <TD ALIGN=LEFT VALIGN=TOP>
<BR><IMG SRC="./GIFs/dot_clear.gif" WIDTH="1" HEIGHT="1" VSPACE="15"><BR>

<IMG SRC="./GIFs/dot_clear.gif" WIDTH="1" HEIGHT="1" HSPACE="9"><FONT SIZE="+2"><FONT
SIZE="+3" COLOR="#FF9900"><B>O</B></FONT> u r<IMG SRC="./GIFs/dot_clear.gif" WIDTH="1"
HEIGHT="1" HSPACE="3"><FONT SIZE="+3" COLOR="#FF9900"><B>M</B></FONT> i s s i o n
</FONT><BR><IMG SRC="./GIFs/dot_clear.gif" WIDTH="1" HEIGHT="1" VSPACE="5"><BR>
<FONT SIZE="+1"><FONT SIZE="+3" COLOR="#990000">T</FONT>he Florida Humanities Council<BR>
<IMG SRC="./GIFs/dot_clear.gif" WIDTH="1" HEIGHT="1" HSPACE="10">serves as the steward of
Florida culture.<BR><IMG SRC="./GIFs/dot_clear.gif" WIDTH="1" HEIGHT="1" VSPACE="1"><BR>

<FONT SIZE="+2" COLOR="#FF9900">W</FONT>e encourage Floridians to learn about<BR><IMG
SRC="./GIFs/dot_clear.gif" WIDTH="1" HEIGHT="1" VSPACE="2"><BR>
<IMG SRC="./GIFs/dot_clear.gif" WIDTH="1" HEIGHT="1" HSPACE="10">the histories of our communi-
ties,<BR><IMG SRC="./GIFs/dot_clear.gif" WIDTH="1" HEIGHT="1" VSPACE="2"><BR>
<IMG SRC="./GIFs/dot_clear.gif" WIDTH="1" HEIGHT="1" HSPACE="10">the cultures of our neigh-
bors,<BR><IMG SRC="./GIFs/dot_clear.gif" WIDTH="1" HEIGHT="1" VSPACE="2"><BR>
<IMG SRC="./GIFs/dot_clear.gif" WIDTH="1" HEIGHT="1" HSPACE="10">and the values of our citi-
zens.<BR><IMG SRC="./GIFs/dot_clear.gif" WIDTH="1" HEIGHT="1" VSPACE="2"><BR>

<FONT SIZE="+2" COLOR="#FF9900">W</FONT>e believe in the effectiveness of<BR><IMG
SRC="./GIFs/dot_clear.gif" WIDTH="1" HEIGHT="1" VSPACE="1"><BR>
<IMG SRC="./GIFs/dot_clear.gif" WIDTH="1" HEIGHT="1" HSPACE="10">thoughtful discussion and
critical thinking.<BR><IMG SRC="./GIFs/dot_clear.gif" WIDTH="1" HEIGHT="1" VSPACE="2"><BR>

<FONT SIZE="+2" COLOR="#FF9900">T</FONT>he tools of the humanities are essential<BR><IMG
SRC="./GIFs/dot_clear.gif" WIDTH="1" HEIGHT="1" VSPACE="2"><BR>
<IMG SRC="./GIFs/dot_clear.gif" WIDTH="1" HEIGHT="1" HSPACE="10">to the survival of a thriving
democracy.</FONT><BR><IMG SRC="./GIFs/dot_clear.gif" WIDTH="1" HEIGHT="1" VSPACE="7"><BR>

<IMG SRC="./GIFs/fleurTsmall.GIF" ALIGN=MIDDLE WIDTH="35" HEIGHT="19"><BR><IMG
SRC="./GIFs/dot_clear.gif" WIDTH="1" HEIGHT="1" VSPACE="7"><BR>

<!--REMAINDER OF CONTENT GOES HERE-->
      </TD>
</TR>
</TABLE>
</BODY>
</HTML>
```

Frames require a bit more work than tables, as well as a number of separate, but linked pages of HTML. Framesets (the package of related pages to be displayed on screen within frames) are particularly useful for navigation. But be warned: they can take longer to load than tables and some users have developed a virulent dislike for them. I use them, but sparingly, and in the simplest configuration suitable to the information displayed (see the following code and Figure 5.12).

Tables and FRAMES

```
<HTML>
<HEAD>
<TITLE> The Virtual Ink Bookstall</TITLE>
<META name="resource-type" content="docu-
ment">
<META name="description" content="At The
Virtual Ink Bookstall you can always find a
selection of hand-picked good books at a dis-
count. Frequent updates.">
<META name="keywords" content="books, book-
stores, book reviews">
<META name="distribution" content="global">
</HEAD>
<FRAMESET rows="30,70">
<FRAME SRC="VirtBkStallHed.html" NORESIZE
scrolling=auto>
<FRAME SRC="VirtBkStallCat.html" name="con-
tent" NORESIZE scrolling=auto>
</FRAMESET>

<NO FRAMES>
<BODY>
<!--COMPLETE TEXT & GRAPHICS FOR NON-FRAMES
BROWSERS GOES HERE-->
</BODY>
</NO FRAMES>
</HTML>
```

This is a basic mark-up for a two-frame (split-window) frameset. It is not the mark-up for individual pages of content, nor does it include the actual text and images to be displayed if a reader's browser does not support frames, although including that content is essential. This mark-up does include META tags within the HEAD element to facilitate indexing by certain search engines. The numbers within the initial FRAMESET tag are percentages; they mean that 30 percent of any frames-capable browser window will be occupied by the first FRAME SRC and 70 percent by the second FRAME SRC.

The result is a frameset intended to keep visitors anchored at the parent site even

Figure 5.11

This is the result in Netscape Navigator 3.01 on a Macintosh set to display 256 colors. (This is the graphical version of the text-only home page pictured in "From HTML To Onscreen Text" in Chapter 1.)

TABLES and FRAMES

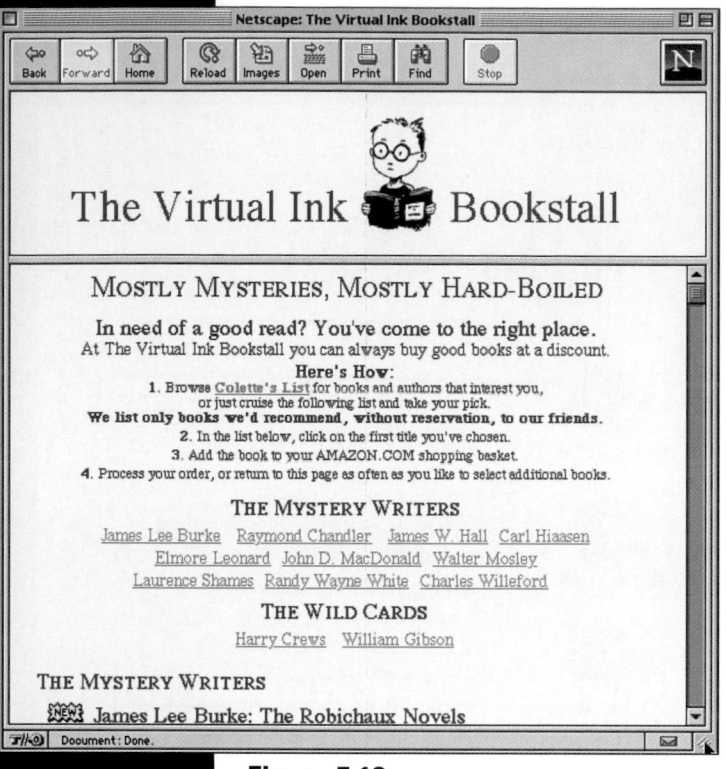

Figure 5.12

This is the page the frames code creates.

when they click off to other destinations; remote sites open within the bottom frame, leaving the bookshop's nameplate in place. Note that the dividers between frames are visible in this example, but that they can be turned off, just as the borders in tables can be turned off.

Confused? To make sense of all this, check out Netscape's authoritative tables and frames primers at:
`http://home.netscape.com/`
`assist/net_sites/frames.html` *and*
`http://home.netscape.`
`com/assist/net_sites/tables.html.`
Then find some sites that you think use these constructs well and hit your browser's "View...Source" button to see how the designer did it.

Horizontal Grid

With this grid, most of the elements standard to the screen design appear in horizontal frames, with ample white space separating them and giving the user a sense of openness from one side to the other (see Figure 5.13). It has a breezy style that many web sites capitalize on. A main criticism is that it may be too static and not enable large images to be used.

Vertical Grid

This grid, popular with three-dimensional sites, enables clear distinctions in the grid. (See Figure 5.14.) Normally, a left-hand frame includes buttons or labels to enable navigation; another column on the right may carry advertising. A top horizontal frame may include logos and other permanent elements, in addition to navigational elements.

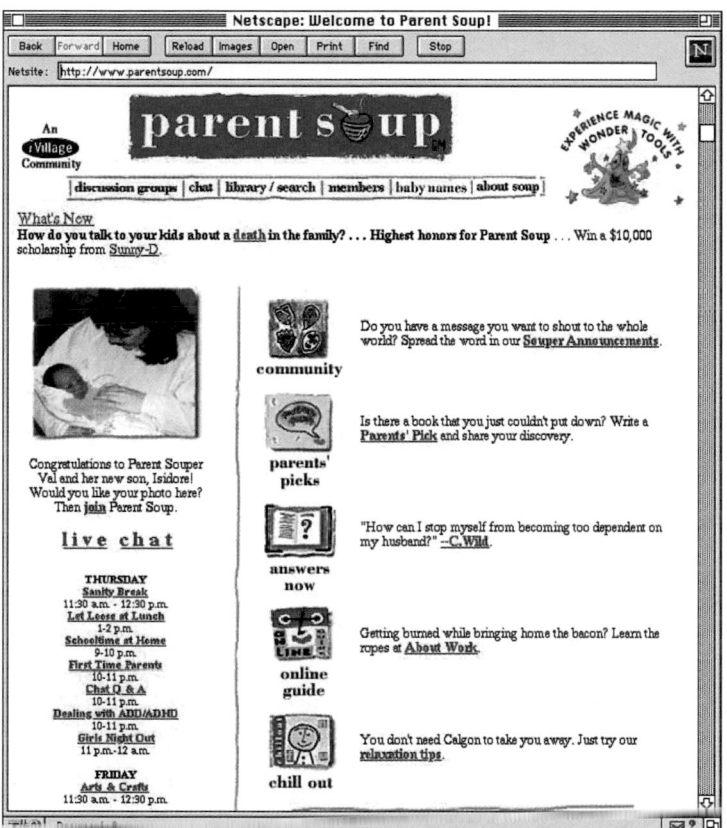

Figure 5.13

An almost entirely horizontal grid is displayed in the home page of Parent Soup, beginning with the logo, which extends, centered, at the top, and followed by the various blocks of text. The color red is used for headlines here, enabling the user to move from one unit to the next through color. Used as a staircase, color is a smart way to add to the effective architecture of this site.

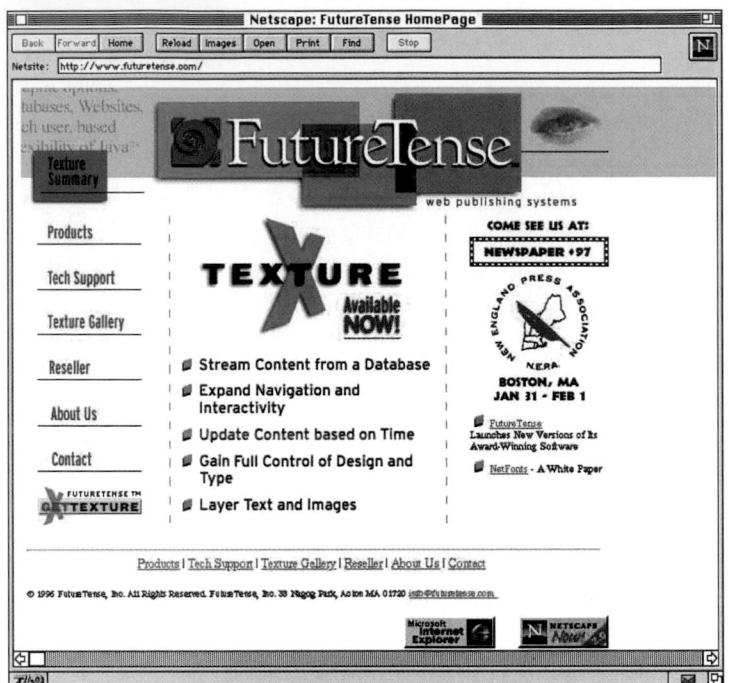

Figure 5.14

It is unusual to find an almost all-vertical grid, but the FutureTense web site divides the screen into three full units, of different widths, the one on the left used for navigation, the center, wider column for main headlines of that edition, and the right for calendar and extra baskets of information. A smaller, horizontal unit of navigation appears at the bottom of the page.

This is an ideal grid for sites that are not text-heavy, but that include a variety of navigational tools, and where graphics and illustrations are a key part of the overall design. Because scrolling is primarily a vertical function, this grid tends to be less conducive to such movement, and is, indeed, more generally preferred for the highly illustrated or art-oriented site.

Hierarchy

The average screen is going to consist of three layers that the eye captures as it enters it (see Figure 5.15). Ideally, and knowing this information, the information designer may decide how to allot different weights, or hierarchy, to each of the three layers on the screen, remembering that this can be established through an interplay of such basic design elements as typography, photography, illustration or color (see Figure 5.16).

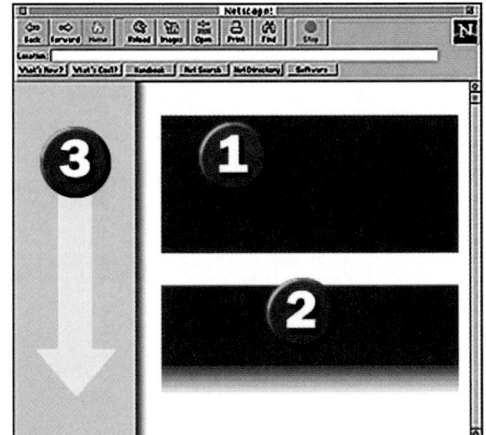

Figure 5.15

The user looks for the one center of visual impact (the lead visual element), enters the screen through that point, then seeks the second heaviest element on the screen, and then the third.

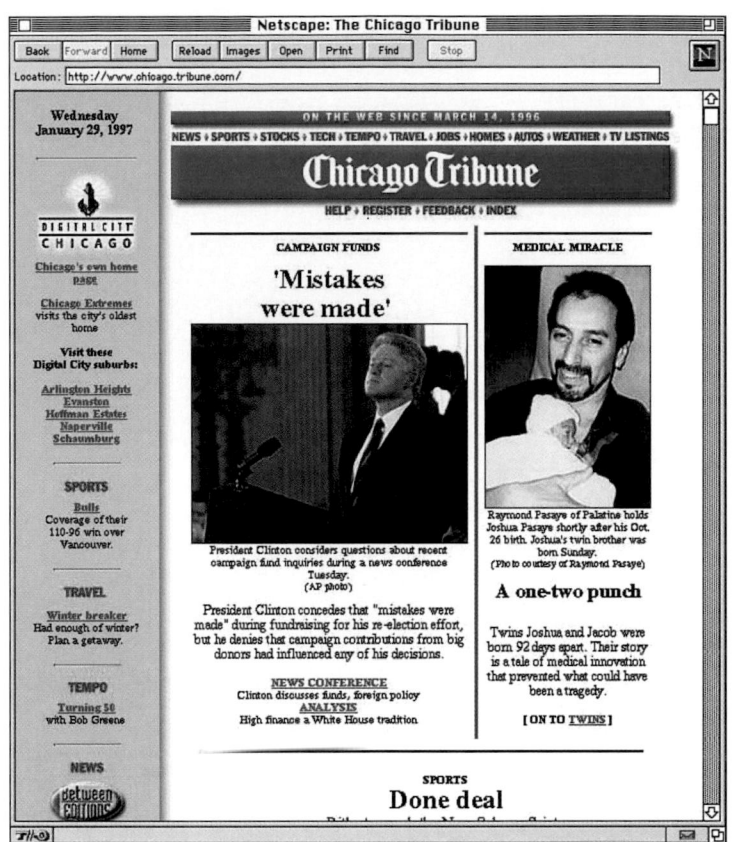

Figure 5.16

The *Chicago Tribune's* web site demonstrates the three layers on the screen and how much weight is allotted to them. The one center of visual impact is the main photo in the center. The second heaviest element may be the story under the photograph, and the third element is the bar along the left of the screen.

Many print designers are aware that each page must "attack" the reader visually. Good pages, however, and good screens, do not incorporate "attacks" that fight each other. When typography is going to be the lead layer, the first point of entry is a large word. Then the other elements become secondary. In a "type attack," photos lay low in the background, in smaller sizes (see Figure 5.17); if, however, a "photo attack" is the lead visual element on the screen or page, then type is not the protagonist (see Figure 5.18).

Figure 5.17

Nothing but typography appears on this Champion Paper site. Contrast is achieved through variation in type sizes.

Sometimes a screen leads with color, as in such sites as the home page of Ferrari cars (http://www.ferrari.it). In the event that all of these elements attack the user simultaneously, the result can be effective, but the eye is going to feel the competition as it enters the page. Sometimes, as in the case of the German tabloid daily Bild (http://www.bild.de), these multiple attacks are achieved by design. The user gets a feeling of a lot happening, but the publication designers and editors want them to think that way (see Figures 5.19 and 5.20).

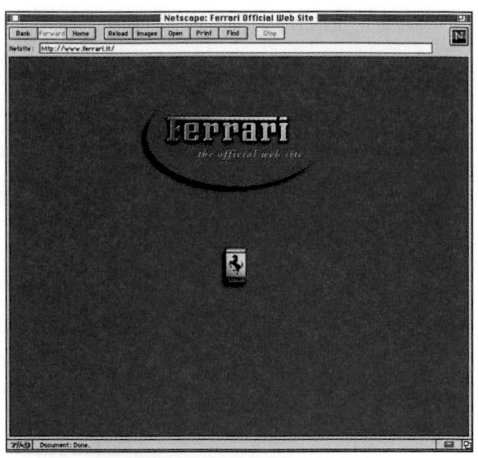

Figure 5.19

Red is prominent the instant you enter the Ferrari web site. This is an effective result as there is little to compete with it.

Figure 5.20

Although the Bild web site combines multiple attacks through color, photo, and type, it achieves an effective result through the design and placement of these elements.

Figure 5.18

The web site for *El Pais* of Uruguay displays an example of "photo attack" hierarchy, where the lead visual element is the photograph and the typography becomes secondary.

When the American supermarket tabloids do go online, it will not be surprising if the multi-attack approach is used. Users of the site would be reminded of the product they have grown accustomed to reading on the run while at the supermarket checkout counter. For more serious sites, the layering system of creating hierarchy and sticking to it, might prove more beneficial and elegant.

White Space

If there is one characteristic that appears to be universal to all information design, it is white space. Printed pages benefit from it, classic advertisements build it into their designs, magazines use it to achieve the optical illusion of less copy, and web designs must have it as punctuation.

Punctuation here means that white space takes the place of a comma in a sentence (it indicates a pause), or a period (a transition on to another topic. One punctuates the design with white space, to indicate pauses, separations, and transitions, just as in writing.

White space should be present on every screen. Good use of white space makes it an almost invisible element as part of the design, but its presence works to support and to enhance other visual parts of the screen, such as an image, display type, or text (see Figure 5.21). White space that works well will push, tuck, align, and highlight the elements around it. In the case of color, white space can create the necessary equilibrium to enhance it.

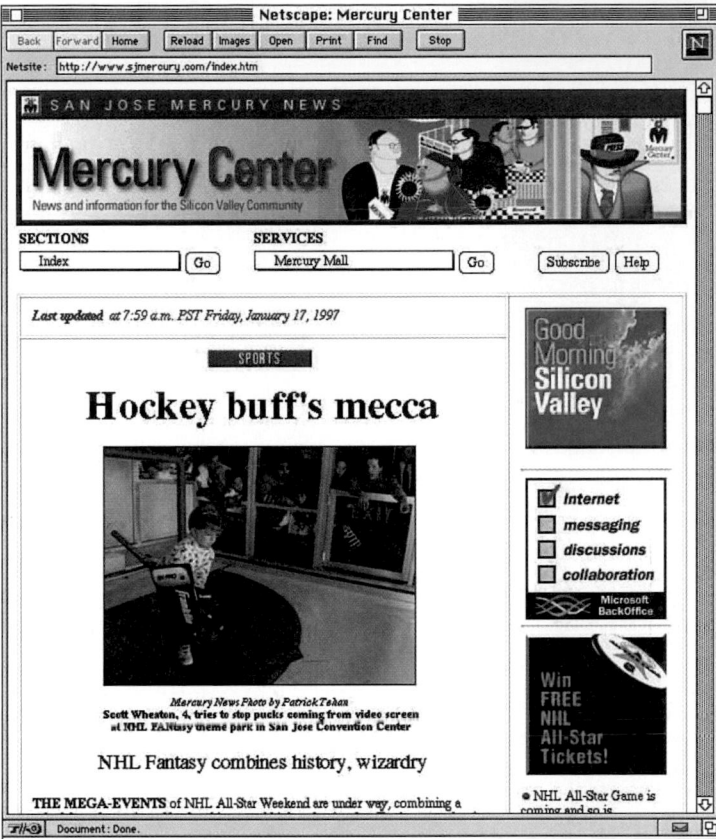

Figure 5.21

With a halo or white space around the main center of visual impact, the photograph creates immediate interest on the *San Jose Mercury News* web site, the Mercury Center. The dramatically vertical column for navigation on the left attracts our attention, as well as the more designed boxes, which promote distinctive features inside the site. Space is well used here, and the white space is, more than luxury, a necessity to get us around the page easier.

CONTROLLING White Space with SINGLE-pixel GIFs

David Siegel, author of the best-selling Creating Killer Web Sites *(Hayden Books), is the web designer's web designer. Not only does he produce exemplary sites, he shares what he has learned with the rest of us—who, until very recently, were flying by the seat of our pants in this brave new medium.*

One of Siegel's first gifts to information designers was this "trick," a simple way to outsmart older, design-challenged web browsers. It consists, in its simplest form, of adding a tiny (1 pixel ×1 pixel) clear (no visible image) GIF to a site's images directory and then manipulating that little transparent box in a seemingly limitless number of ways: to indent paragraphs, to control space between lines of display type and text, to introduce vertical or horizontal white space into a screen layout, to tweak alignments of image and text, and so on.

GIF is shorthand for Graphics Interchange File. GIF employs something called the LZW (Lempel-Ziv-Welch) compression algorithm, which is a "lossless" method of reducing file size for faster transfer over the web.

Lossless means, in essence, that the decompressed image eventually reconstiututed on your computer monitor will look just as good as the original image. By any name (or acronym), GIF is the default web file format for simple graphics that incorporate large areas of flat color; it conforms easily to a designer's use of the cross-platform (or "web-safe") 216-color palette (GIFs are 8-bit graphics and can handle a maximum of 256 colors) and produces nice lean files when properly executed. To further complicate the issue, GIFs come in two flavors: 87a (often referred to as CompuServe GIFs) and 89a (often referred to as Transparent GIFs because transparency is an attribute that can be specified in the 89a format); both flavors can be made to load by a method called interlacing, which means that the graphic appears piece by piece, giving the illusion of a faster download.

For photographs and continuous tone images with subtle shifts of color and/or shading, the default file format (at the moment) is JPEG, a "lossy" 24-bit format; the Joint Photographic Experts Group gave its initials to this one. In mark-up, JPEG sometimes is shortened to JPG.

PNG, a competing 24-bit file format, has appeared and is much loved by some web designers for its potential to encode much more information than GIF or JPEG, while still offering good compression. The problem is that PNG is not, as of this writing, widely supported by web browsers.

CONTROLLING White Space with SINGLE-pixel GIFs

Even with the greater control over these elements being built into HTML itself, as well as all the adjunct scripting languages and add-ons introduced daily, I still use this low-tech trick in nearly every page I build, both because it gives me the fine control I need and because it is neither a bandwidth hog nor tech for tech's sake.

You can learn the details—and even download the essential "dot_clear.gif"—at Maestro Siegel's web site:
`http://www.dsiegel.com/tips/wonk5/single.html`

White space's main function (on the screen or page) is that of alignment. There are both vertical and horizontal varieties of white space.

Vertical White Space

In terms of punctuation, vertical white space represents a comma. It enables the eyes to "breathe" a little as they move from one unit of thought to the next. As with all white space, vertical white space should be a systematic part of the design, not an improvisation. As such, the information designer must allocate it in terms of specific units (see Figure 5.22).

Vertical white space, if used properly as visual punctuation of the page, eliminates the need for rules. The white space provides the separation; no need to express it directly by inserting a rule into the layout.

Figure 5.22

Hot CoCo, the *Contra Costa Times'* web site, utilizes an internal grid of white space to separate the left-hand unit of navigational tools from the rest of the page. The white space is a separator, but also enables space for photos to appear, thus avoiding excessive waste of space.

Horizontal White Space

Horizontal white space is most evident and useful between lines of text, in what is normally referred to as "leading," a term that evolves from the days of hot typesetting when printers inserted metal slivers of various thickness to separate lines of metal type (see Figure 5.23).

What horizontal white space does, whether in print or on the web, is to provide a sense of visual relief for the reader. Lines of type that touch create a crowded sensation that translates into slower reading.

In addition to its aesthetic benefits (nobody likes to see descenders of letters such as g and p hugging the ascenders of letters such as the d and the b), the presence of good interline spacing brings about a sense of regulated white space running through an entire page or screen. If those pioneer typographers who first inserted pieces of metal between lines of type to give us some visual relief were creating web sites today, they would carry metal pieces in their pockets to insert between the lines presented on the screen! Because the eye moves more horizontally than diagonally on a screen, it is safe to assert that horizontal white space is even more beneficial here in speeding legibility than it may be in print. Horizontal white space is like milk: white, pure, and good for you, and few question its benefits.

Most recently, a generation of information designers who never touched lead refer to leading as interline spacing. Leading is a musical term; interline spacing is not.

Figure 5.23

The Champion Paper company, in a highly typographic display for its opening screen, introduces excellent horizontal white space, which enables greater legibility and creates a breezy sense of movement through the entire design. Notice that words are used to link users to the inside of this site.

Alignment

Whether the elements appear on a printed page or on the screen, alignment is a prerequisite to good visual presentation. A screen, like a page, consists of four corners, and it is important that elements appearing on the canvas of this rectangular space align properly.

Top Alignment

Top alignment is where frames, headlines, text, and images all come to rest along a horizon at the top of the screen. This positioning is preferred to bottom of the screen alignment.

Top alignment is preferred because of our general tendency to start reading at the top of pages (or screens), with movement from left to right, top to bottom. Elements that are properly aligned at the top tend to give the rest of the screen a greater sense of unity—this is where the user begins to read, and then follows from there.

Perhaps top alignment is the most basic of all alignments, but also the one that makes the most visual sense, and a technique that seems to be effective in most cases. Let the excitement of the design take place elsewhere, but get most of the elements lined up at the top if possible, although as we have seen, this is *not* the only way to align.

Left Alignment

Left alignment is where frames, headlines, text, and images all come to rest at the left of the screen, enabling more of a ragged, or unfinished, look on the right. Left alignment is preferred to right alignment, as screens where elements align to the right rarely look as organized (although there may be exceptions).

Bottom Alignment

Although bottom alignment can play very well on a printed page, creating what is commonly referred to as "skyline effect," it is hard to imagine doing much of this on a screen, due, of course, to scrolling. The skyline would very soon disintegrate when the user begins to scroll down into the "basement" of his computer screen.

The skyline effect, as the name implies, does not create a perfect alignment at the top of the screen (or page). Instead, the elements at the very top appear at different heights. This is easier to achieve on a printed page than on a screen, but for especially designed web sites that emphasize photos and illustrations, it can be an effective and attractive tool.

Right Alignment

Right alignment is possible, but it creates a ragged environment in that very important entry point on the screen, which is the left hand side.

Scrolling versus Linking

What information designer has not had to deal with the topic of legibility on the screen? How much does the user scroll before he stops? Is it true that if the topic is of interest to the user, and if the writing is excellent, then, to use the old newspaper metaphor, the reader takes it all in, regardless of the pain we may inflict on him or her?

Print designers have heard this all along from sometimes overconfident writers and editors. Of course, there is an element of truth here. The ultimate test of legibility is the content. If we are primarily interested in the results of the stock market today, then we will struggle with the usually small type used for listings. And when that narrative is so absolutely enticing that we cannot put it away, we, of course, go along with the text flow, jumping twice if necessary.

On the screen, however, there is no jumping; it is more like skipping from one title to the next. We must keep our balance, maintain our interest, and not get distracted. Just as with print, we are always discussing the merits or demerits of jumping text from one page to another; the equivalent on the screen is whether it is better, and more functional, to link or to scroll.

Scrolling is a totally linear activity. Linking is less so. Users are more likely to enjoy the motion of linking than that of scrolling, especially after three or more screens.

As technology and new design solutions come about, the challenge a designer faces regarding linking and scrolling becomes more critical. With the advent of frames, and the soon-to-be available style sheets and layer capability, the issue of linking and scrolling

Scrolling versus Linking

becomes less based on a user's habit but more of a designer's decision and physical layout of the page. The latter, of course, is more pertinent on the designer's decision on when to use scrolling text or hyperlinks (see Figure 5.24).

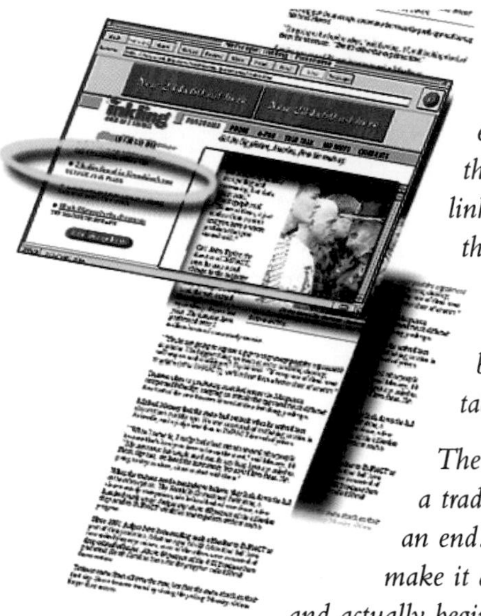

The decision, when given the right content, is easy. Basically, we choose to scroll the text when the part of the story is linear. We choose to hyperlink the part of the story when we come to a fork in the storytelling process. A fork here can range from enabling the user to choose which part of the story she wants to read next or from the very beginning in enabling the reader to choose from a table of content.

The challenge here comes when the designer is handed a traditional linear story, where there's a beginning and an end. Here the designer will either breakdown and make it a really long linear story or take it a step further and actually begin to layer the story in pertinent parts.

In inventing this new way of storytelling, it is critical to involve both the writer and the designer.

Figure 5.24

Story elements should be selected carefully for use on a web site.

This chapter has outlined the most systematic aspects of screen design architecture, which are only a part of the process. Information designers are in charge of using the system and combining it with the creative aspects of the craft. Surprises land on the screen when the serendipitous meet the systematic. Perhaps one of the areas most ideally suited to mix serendipity and system is that of typography, the subject of the next chapter.

Chapter 6

Typography for the Screen

Let us assume that Johann Gensfleisch Gutenberg is creating type for a home page, perhaps his own, instead of for the newly created medium of print. What would this man—who in 1440 was experimenting in the "new" method of book production, including letter design, punch cutting, matrix fitting, typecasting, composing, and preparation of inks and paper—create for screen use?

Chances are, nothing too radically different, if we realize that a majority (if not 99 percent) of the typefaces used on web sites are the same fonts we have grown accustomed to in print design. Undoubtedly, the design of web sites, circa 2000, will be inspired by the metaphor of print media, just as Gutenberg's style for his famous 42-line Bible was an imitation of black letter book hands of that era. Many print designers today have crossed over to the new media, inevitably bringing with them their knowledge and intuition about type utilization.

Although a majority of the typefaces that work in print work onscreen, remember that the screen is best suited for low-resolution fonts that adapt much better to a pixel-based format and enable clearer shapes of letters, a more distinctive serif (those endings of certain letter forms), and where the roundness of letters such as o and c, stand out more sharply, for example. A good test for designers is to see how certain letters look, beginning with the letter x, which gives us a sense of how the widest letters might appear; the letters l and d, to verify how thin ascenders move; and, of course the roundness of b, c, o, and d. Later in this chapter we cover the specifics of letter forms, as well as alphabets totally designed for the web.

A Typography Lover Puts Her Spin on the Web

A Typography Lover Puts Her Spin on the Web: Jessica Helfand

When I met Jessica Helfand during my redesign of The Philadelphia Inquirer, *she was art director of the* Inquirer Magazine. *Each Sunday, the pages of the magazine showcased interesting use of typography as the reader moved from page to page. Our conversations of design were mostly of typographic design, alphabets, type contrast, and typography as the heart of all good design. So I always envisioned that Jessica would move on to the world of book publishing, to continue her love affair with typography in a medium that best accommodates it.*

Instead, Jessica reappears as one of the nation's premiere online designers. But, alas, her typographic background is omnipresent in what she does. She sculptures typographic images on the screen and is likely to inspire every designer who doubts that there are typographic possibilities in the new medium. She has been an inspiration to me as she helped me with the chapter on typography for this book. That is why I asked her to recommend her favorite type sites, included in Appendix B "Site Catalog."

What Gutenberg and his successors created has continued to be used by various other media. The new media of online design is no exception; today, however, some type fonts are designed specifically for online use. Those type fonts are explored in this chapter, but first let's concentrate on the specific characteristics of online typography and their use in effective design.

The Basics

So you are about to select a typeface to use on your web site. Many different alphabets stare at you, and you are confused by all the different fonts that you seem to like.

Step 1: The Anatomy of Letter Forms

It is helpful to know the terminology of type, or the name for each part of a letter. Art directors often find themselves referring to these in front of clients, especially journalists, who sometimes have no clue as to the difference, for example, between a counter and a baseline (see Figure 6.1).

The important terms are the following:

- ▶ **Ascender:** The part of a lowercase letter that extends beyond the x-height of the letter, as in b, d, or l.

- ▶ **Descender:** The parts of letters such as p, q, and g that extend below the baseline.

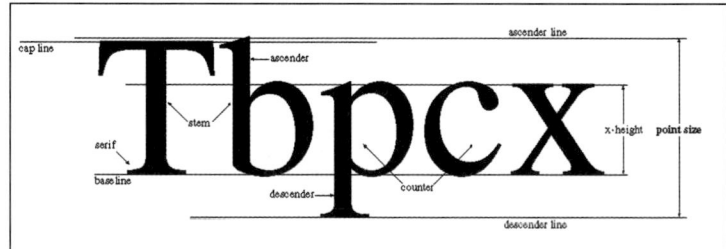

Figure 6.1

A diagram of letterform features.

► **Counter:** The enclosed or partially enclosed parts of a letter such as p, g, and c.

► **Serif:** The strokes that appear as endings on the letters and guide the eye from one character to the next. A style of letter that does not include serifs is referred to as sans serif.

► **X-Height:** The height of the lowercase letters, not including the ascenders or descenders.

Step 2: Think Appropriateness

What is the content of your web site? What are you trying to communicate and to whom? The aesthetics of the typeface, the size of the type, the use of color or black and white for the letters—all of these are decisions that depend on content and your audience (see Figures 6.2 and 6.3).

The classic Roman typefaces with their elegant serifs, for example, are ideal for conveying a feeling of seriousness and stability on a web site or in printed material. Selecting Bodoni, Caslon, Baskerville, or Times (or their variations) immediately gives the reader a feeling of tradition on certain projects, but a site aimed at very young readers

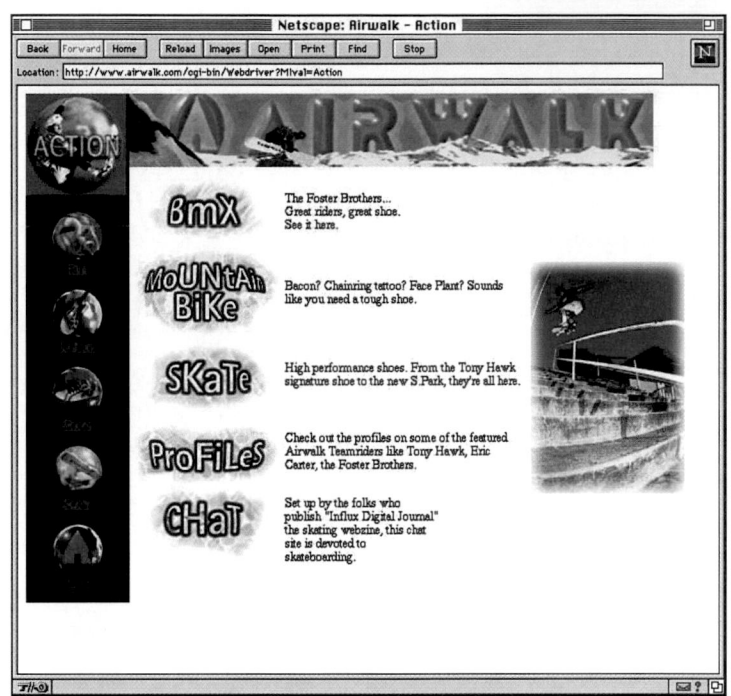

Figure 6.2

Visitors to the Airwalk web site encounter an "appropriate" environment of expanded and distorted typefaces, taken to an extreme, which is where the usual reader of this site takes everything.

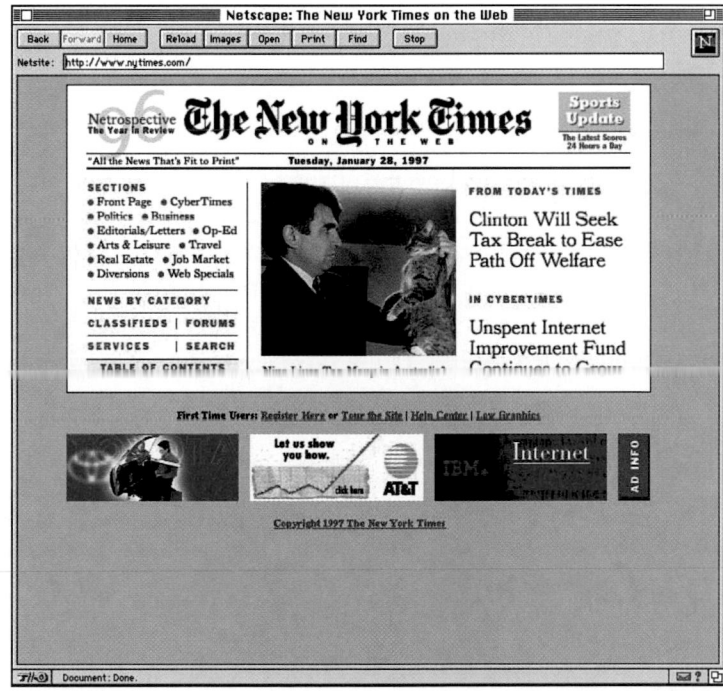

Figure 6.3

A traditional reader of *The New York Times* encounters the same "appropriate" environment of tradition, seriousness, and order in the newspaper's online edition as he experiences in the printed version. This is a good mixture of appropriateness in design and content.

might do better utilizing a sans serif such as Interstate, Franklin, Helvetica, Futura, or Gill Sans. An interesting logo can be dressed up with a typeface that may be ideal to convey a feeling of informality through one word or two but not in large quantities. With more than 8,000 typefaces available to choose from today, designers must be both careful and adventurous.

Step 3: PostScript and TrueType Fonts

Although many font formats have appeared, the two standards are PostScript Type 1 and TrueType. They are not likely to disappear, either, although they may change periodically to accommodate new systems. Both formats are quite acceptable and are based on a relative measurement system called an em-square. The em is a unit of distance equal to the point size so that, for example, in 12-point type an em is 12 points wide and in 64-point type it is 64 points wide.

Step 4: Classifications of Typefaces

It is not necessary for a type designer to become an expert in the details and idiosyncrasies that constitute these classifications of type; however, a working knowledge of the terminology helps when discussing type and also when making certain selections. The following classifications of type are some of the most important ones.

The Old Styles

Elegant and classic, and even romantic, according to some typographers, the old styles of fonts are still very much used today. A Frenchman, Claude Garamond, is credited with the design of the Old Style letter, in which the height of the lowercase letters, or x-height, is small in relation to the uppercase letters. Interesting typefaces included in this style include Garamond, Caslon, and Bembo.

AaBbCc

An example of Caslon regular (Old Style).

AaBbCc

Caslon italic (Old Style).

AaBbCc

Caslon bold (Old Style).

AaBbCc

Garamond regular (Old Style).

AaBbCc

Garamond italic (Old Style).

AaBbCc

Garamond bold (Old Style).

The Transitionals

These letterforms represent the in-between period, evolving from Old Style to Modern. An Englishman, John Baskerville, designed a representative transitional typeface at the end of the 18th century during the Neoclassical period, showing greater contrast between thicks and thins than Old Style and more vertical stress. The serifs tend to be symmetrical, more mathematically based than aesthetically inspired perhaps, and the relationship of the height of the lowercase characters to the uppercase is less pronounced. Almost everyone who designs anything comes into contact with Transitional fonts, such as Times, Baskerville, Bookman, and Perpetua.

The Moderns

It was Giambattista Bodoni, a Parmesan printer, who gave us one of the most widely used typefaces and ushered in the so-called Modern style of type. His typeface is characterized by flat, unbracketed serifs, with the highest contrast seen to that time between thick and thin strokes, and with perfect vertical stress. Bodoni is synonymous with newspaper type. The Moderns imitate the classic styles but appear more geometric and often easier to read. Take, for example, Walbaum, an ideal typeface for headlines, titles, and even text. Walbaum looks good in its condensed versions, as well, and can mix harmoniously with sans serif styles, such as Futura, Gill Sans, and Frutiger.

AaBbCc

Baskerville regular (Transitional).

AaBbCc

Bodoni regular (Modern).

AaBbCc

Baskerville italic (Transitional).

AaBbCc

Bodoni italic (Modern).

AaBbCc

Baskerville bold (Transitional).

AaBbCc

Bodoni bold (Modern).

Walbaum regular (Modern).

AaBbCc

Walbaum italic (Modern).

AaBbCc

Walbaum bold (Modern).

The Slab Serifs

Perhaps one of the most ideal styles for a solid and dramatic presence on the screen, the slab serifs were designed in the 19th century and have always been popular for advertising, magazine, and poster design. During my work with newspapers, I normally stayed away from slab serifs, especially for text, as they tend to be overwhelming in the way they fill the space. Their presence onscreen, however, makes them an ideal choice—the ultimate protagonist to tell stories in a way that impacts the reader visually, while enhancing legibility. Among the most popular and useful slab serifs is Clarendon.

The Sans Serifs

A result of rebellion against the overly decorated letterforms of the Victorian or Gay Nineties, sans serif appeared as a skeletal, minimalist representation of the letters. The serifs disappear. Writes Edmund Arnold, the legendary newspaper designer, "…after World War I, creative people rebelled against all reminders of that gaudy era, they began stripping gingerbread off furniture and architecture. Functional became the watchword." (From *Ink on Paper,* New York, Harper & Row, 1972.)

A group of artists at the Bauhaus in Germany began to experiment with the alphabet, getting rid of some of the elegant serifs in the process, but emerging with a style that became a standard choice of many newspapers and magazines.

Eventually, television news graphic artists chose sans serif fonts as their preferred style, claiming that, indeed, the simple designs of the letters made them more visible and easier to read onscreen. Ben Blank, a pioneer of television news graphics and a long-time art director of ABC News, explains that there was no substitute for a good, solid sans serif letter under a graphic over the shoulder of a news commentator. Serifs, he said, tended to disappear onscreen, and lacked the strong presence of the Helvetica, Franklin Gothic, and Universe fonts. If the sans serifs did so well on television screens, perhaps they may find favor with online designers, too.

AaBbCc

Franklin Gothic Roman (Sans Serif).

AaBbCc

Franklin Gothic condensed (Sans Serif).

AaBbCc

Franklin Gothic extra condensed (Sans Serif).

AaBbCc

Helvetica medium (Sans Serif).

AaBbCc

Helvetica regular (Sans Serif).

AaBbCc

Helvetica condensed light (Sans Serif).

Helvetica extra condensed (Sans Serif).

AaBbCc

Futura light (Sans Serif).

AaBbCc

Futura regular (Sans Serif).

AaBbCc

Futura extra bold (Sans Serif).

AaBbCc

Frutiger light (Sans Serif).

AaBbCc

Frutiger regular (Sans Serif).

AaBbCc

Frutiger bold (Sans Serif).

AaBbCc

Gill sans light (Sans Serif).

AaBbCc

Gill sans regular (Sans Serif).

AaBbCc

Gill sans ultra bold (Sans Serif).

The Gallery Fonts

So many artistically designed fonts exist today that it is simply difficult to put them into the usual baskets of script faces or contemporary fonts, and so on. It is more like a gallery, a display of many interesting, sometimes even beautiful, typefaces that do not fit into any of the categories described here. Some are so ornate that they deserve a one-time use consideration for a special logo or as the heading of a newsletter. Some belong on the menu of an exclusive restaurant or a funky café. Others were designed to be forgotten but perhaps can lure the less conservative user to connect with a section of a web site. Their names sometimes are as unusual as the faces themselves, including Mistral and Unical.

The New Online Fonts

Type designers are working to create type fonts that are especially designed and engineered for online use. At the Font Bureau (http://www.fontbureau.com) in Boston, typographer David Berlow and his colleagues have designed system, multimedia, and online fonts. Many of the usual concerns of print, such as proper font selection and arrangement, are transferable to the online medium. But to best utilize type online, the networking and resolution aspects of the online medium, and their effect on specifics of type composition and type design itself should be briefly examined.

The issues of playback fidelity across wide area networks and resolution online operate under a very different set of rules when compared to any other medium, including print.

Fidelity, Berlow says, is something you take for granted in print: you calibrate the screen color to the output, for example, set the fonts, and perhaps go to the press and make sure it is all right, but you can nail it, both images and text, with fidelity if you want to. Online, in the foreseeable future, users are going to have control over the colors, sizes, and styles of the text face they see online. So online designers must consider fidelity in light of the difference between their own and the users' computers. With this in mind, designers are pretty much forced to compose the text in a standard typeface, such as Times Roman, and concentrate on the headlines, buttons, and other large type elements to create their designs.

This may be fine for some kinds of documents, or sites, but for a whole medium to be limited in such a way is impossible for the long term. And as fidelity from the largest graphics to the smallest text is an accomplishable option, look for it to spread.

Examples of fidelity critical systems are corporate intranets, online ventures such as @Home (see Chapter 11, "Designing Magazines and Features Online"), and operating systems such as Macintosh and Windows, all of which have included specific fonts for text to unify the appearance of their online look. Getting mass audience standardization of software and fonts for the mass of online typography—that is, for hundreds of thousands of sites—is another thing.

Resolution would still be a challenge to online typography even if fidelity were no longer an issue on the farthest flung servers and sites of the web. For that to happen, there would have to be some technological breakthrough so that all the type you composed was instantly packed in an automatically downloaded, installed, and rendered font that worked on any user's computer in any user's browser, exactly as you used it in your design.

Resolution, Berlow says, is the measure of how fine an image can be rendered. Oil paint is really high resolution, around a million paint molecules per inch. In print a good resolution is 2,400 lines per inch, but resolution online is 72–96 lines per inch! This means a couple of things, Berlow adds. One measurable thing is that a 12-point font at 2,400 dpi is 400 pixels tall and as many wide as you need to define each letter, which enables plenty of detail in each letter. But at 12-point, a 96 dpi font is

14 pixels tall and 14 or so wide. The subtle and cunning letter forms we read in print as curves become straight, little, one-pixel-wide lines online. Every single pixel becomes an essential element in the making of a legible font. A single stray pixel can destroy the readability of a font. So, unless resolution rises miraculously, or grayscale fonts succeed, forget about distinguishing your publications with great text type for some time. The best thing to do for small type is to rely on the finely designed and hinted fonts provided by operating systems vendors. The second thing to remember about resolution and online type is its production requirements and effect on file size. "Resolution," Berlow says, "is also the measure of how long an image takes to be rendered."

Online, with text as an uncontrollable element, the designer tends to work with display type as image files, complete with graphics, type effects, and small movies, to distinguish the publication from the rest. This slows down transmission.

The following are some samples of the typefaces created exclusively for online use by the FontBureau:

▶ Agenda Condensed

▶ Agenda Medium

▶ Agenda Bold

▶ FBI Online Serif

▶ Interstate-Bold

▶ Proforma Medium

▶ Proforma Bold Condensed

▶ Proforma Bold

TYPOGRAPHY and the WEB

Typography and the Web

For the moment, however, realists want to bear in mind that typographic control in HTML is still quite primitive. Both Netscape Navigator and Microsoft's Internet Explorer have added some useful new "font" tags to give the designer a degree of power over type color, relative size and face and tables enable you to format columns and white space. But the only reliable way to prescribe every aspect of typographic display is to create a graphic image (in GIF format) containing type or to format entire pages and serve them to the web in some format that requires special reader software, as in Adobe Acrobat's Portable Document Format (PDF). The former (for the moment) is faster and more widely accessible than the latter.

Typography and Logos

At first, many newspapers and magazines that went online duplicated their print logos onscreen. Although many still do, the tendency now is to recognize web sites as their own individual media, an outgrowth of the newspaper or magazine from which it derives much of its information, but not a duplication of it (see Figure 6.4).

Philadelphia Inquirer and Daily News

San Jose Mercury News

The Tallahassee Democrat

Figure 6.4

The "nameplates" of the online versions of some Knight-Ridder newspapers. Notice that few nameplates resemble the print products.

The one element of a design where typography plays the most important role in terms of creating familiarity with a publication is the logo. The same is true of online design. You must pay attention to what the typography of the logo says, its point of view, and the image it creates when it first appears (see Figure 6.5). Perhaps the role of type selection here is greater, considering that an average user surfs the web and makes continuous and sequential stops, facing a different logo for each site he visits. After a few minutes of this type of activity, logos (and sites) begin to blend with each other, which is why proper selection of type makes a dramatic difference, not only in creating recognition, but also in distinguishing that last site you visited from the next one.

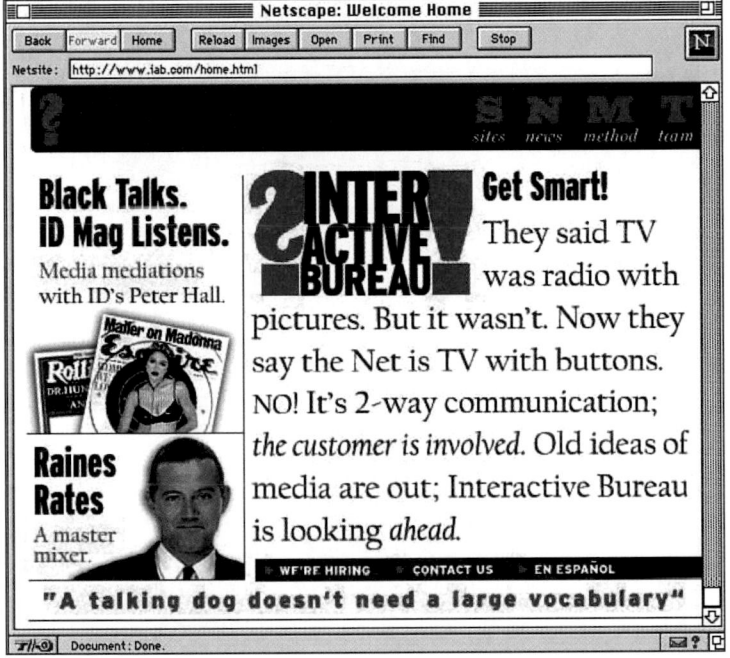

Figure 6.5

Perhaps one of the most type-oriented home pages on the web is that of the Interactive Bureau. It makes sense that one of America's most renowned designers and type connoisseurs, Roger Black, would create such a display of type on his home page. Type becomes art here—easy to read, well spaced, and combining bold sans serifs with stylish serifs.

At Home with Web Design: Roger Black, Interactive Bureau

Roger Black has been a designer for more than 25 years and is best known for his interest and expertise in typography. His design of such publications as Rolling Stone, Newsweek, The New York Times, *and the* San Francisco Examiner, *among many others, reflects the range of his talents. Since 1993 he has devoted considerable time to developing web sites. I asked him about the use of typography on the web and his favorite sites using type well. His comments are included in the following figure captions.*

Figure 6.6

YPN has a hard problem: trying to fit in the entire Internet onto one home page. Interactive Bureau did a redesign last year, but we were not brutal enough editors, and too much got onto the page. Now it is a bit simpler, and downloads more quickly. The daily design work is done by Steve Gullo, an old associate of mine, and his staff at YPN. The interesting thing is the way the type in the GIF files works so nicely with the quiet HTML text.

Figure 6.7

MSN makes the best use of the HTML font call (fontface), which is only appropriate, because it was invented at Microsoft, and the fonts that can be reliably found on a PC are the ones that Microsoft put there. Thus, this site uses more than two typefaces, and still is subtle, dignified, and just slightly cool.

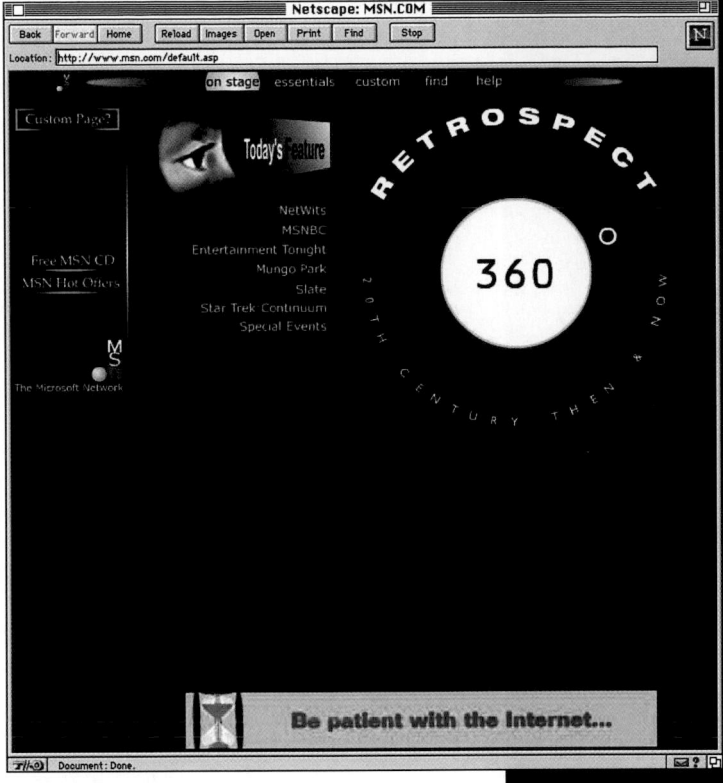

Figure 6.8

The *Chicago Tribune* (http://www.chicago.tribune.com) is my third choice, not *Wired,* or Suck or Word or some more obvious hipster site. That is because when you judge the use of type on a web site (or a in a newspaper) you have to decide how well it is being used for its real purpose. In this case, it is to convey the news. The type is quiet, orderly, and enables the progression of news to take center stage.

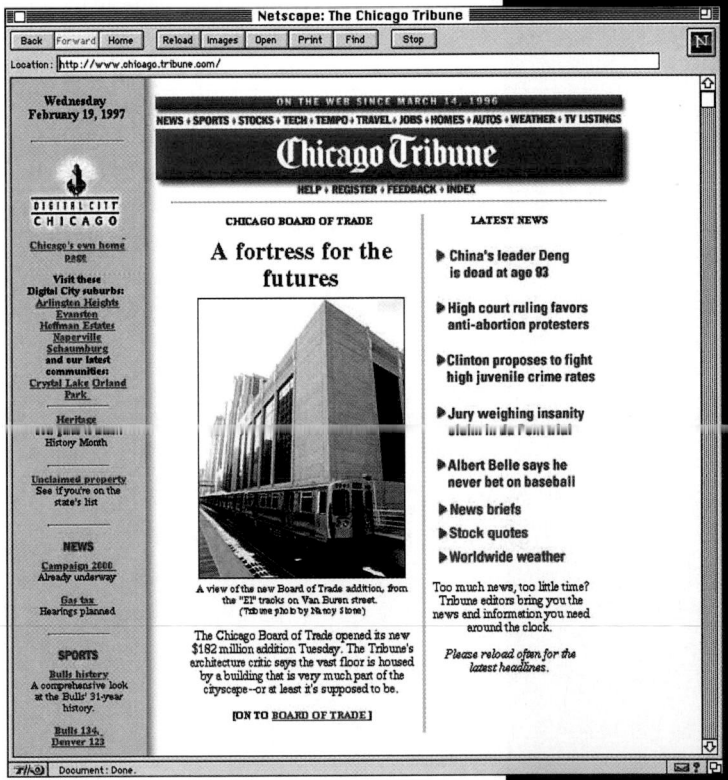

Roger also contributed his web blunders document:

Web Blunders

From the look of things, there are plenty of them out there. For those of you starting a site, we present Five Things Not to Do on the Net.

1. *Don't forget content. People must be compelled to come back to your site. A page full of cute graphics and buttons won't bring anybody back.*

2. *Don't confuse the customer. A site needs to be consistently designed. If you have different pages and different sections, the navigational tools and graphics need to look the same throughout. Make them painfully simple and clear. If someone gets lost, they'll never come back.*

3. *Don't design pages that require a lot of scrolling. Just as 75 percent of people will only read the top half of a folded newspaper, most people will never scroll. People are much more likely to click a button and keep going. This also breaks up the content into bite-size pieces, which is good, because web browsers skim and surf. If you don't give them something quickly, they absorb nothing.*

4. *Don't use a lot of colors. Simply colored pages run faster and look better. Separate your site from all of the color clutter out there! If you get your design graphically right in black and white, you're on the right track. After that, if you want to, add one or two colors. Use red (preferably) or yellow, but don't use them all!*

5. *Don't use big, slow graphics, no matter how impressive you think they are. In our narrow band world, where it takes a lot of seconds to download a meg file, the only acceptable delay for consumer is none at all. Nobody wants to wait a minute for art or seven minutes for video. And if they have to, they'll never come back.*

Serifs, sans serifs, condensed, regular, or hand-xdrawn typefaces: they all seem to play well onscreen. Gone are the problems facing print designers who chose one typeface, only to find that the thin serifs disappeared when the press got through with the job. Typography, and type selection, specifically, become a fun and integral part of the process of designing web pages. Along the way, remember that larger is better than smaller, simpler more elegant than complicated, and legible is more practical than aesthetically pleasing. Also, keep in mind that making type appropriate for the content is one constant to consider when making a selection.

There is also the issue of color or black and white. Both do well, although color type onscreen seems to gain in vigor and in getting our attention. The next chapter looks at the colorization of type, as well as the rest of what appears onscreen.

Chapter 7

Color

Color is the information designer's ultimate tool for conveying feeling, identity, mood, and of course, information. Take a look at the web sites for Ferrari (`http://www.ferrari.it`) and Mercedes Benz (`http://www.mercedes-benz.com`) automobiles and you will find perfect examples of contrast and of color used to convey a feeling that makes a strong statement about the respective products they represent.

Long before we read the first word, or glance at a logo, the colors have managed to convey a variety of messages. Information architects value color for that very reason. More than mere decoration, color is one of the most effective tools to get a message across.

This chapter offers suggestions on choosing colors, from where to obtain valuable technical guidance right at your computer, to those mental choices that every designer must make concerning how to select and utilize a color to convey information. In addition, we try to outline the differences between color use for print and online.

Choosing Colors

Color choices become one of the designer's most vital responsibilities—after making typographic choices. Here are some guidelines to consider:

▶ **Be thoroughly familiar with the content of the site.** Then, suddenly, almost instinctively, a color emerges. So, if the web site is for junior high school students or younger, you might use bright colors—lots of yellow, orange, and metallic hues. If the site is a firm specializing in auto insurance, you might use a stable color, such as blue or gray. One practical and easy test is to use an adjective that describes the essence of the publication. With that one word written down, the thinking process is focused, yet open to possibilities.

▶ **Associate the web site with a color to which the publication, product, or company is linked.** If the nameplate of a newspaper, or the logo of a magazine, includes a heavy orange line or shade, then it would seem natural to incorporate it, somehow, into the web site. You cannot underestimate the power of color association; you must, therefore, capitalize on it.

▶ **Remember that colors are forever linked to environments.** If creating the web site of a Brazilian publication, you might immediately think of bright colors, evoking tropical feelings, and lots of energy. For a Scandinavian web site, you might choose cooler colors, emphasizing pastels, such as lots of blues and whites. In redesigning the web site for *El Tiempo*, of Bogota, Colombia, for example, I made use of gold letters for the logo of *El Tiempo*, evoking the image of pre-Columbian art and jewelry, with its strong gold hues.

▶ **Decide how to use color.** Will you use color as a background emphasis, for typographic accents, or simply to highlight navigational tools (a button, bullet, and so on)?

▶ **Decide how color can be utilized as a vital part of the design.** How many of the colors that appear on the home page, for example, carry through on inside screens? How many simply grab the attention of the users on the home page, but do not make another appearance? In essence, a decision is made as to signature colors versus "spot" colors, which you may use to accentuate a logo, a portion of the site, and nothing else.

▶ **Settle on a color palette.** The palette gives the site a sense of the familiar—an identity, just as it does the same for print publications, and for products that we are used to. A color palette represents part of the visual signature of a publication, site, or product, creating a "color memory." We could not imagine cereal boxes in anything but their bright, sunny, happy colors—because the color palette here has been designed to be bright, to wake up us in the morning and promise us all that comes with the thought of a good day. Web site users, in an unconscious way, will tend to relate the palette—the union of various colors or shades—as part of what reminds them of this web site. The palette (discussed elsewhere in this chapter) gives the site a sense of the familiar—an identity.

Deadly Color Sins

Obviously, each designer is going to have his ultimate list of what not to do with color. All of these lists are subject to be challenged. I have seen many of my "no no's" handled masterfully well by a designer who dared, and triumphed in the process. I still, however, list my absolute sins (and how to avoid them) here:

▶ **Avoid very bright colors.** Whether in print, or on the screen, extremely bright colors, especially yellow, tend to distort the rest of the design. Even if the web site is all about cartoons, try to use a soft version of yellow. Let the sun over your head be the brightest yellow you ever see! Don't attempt to emulate it on the screen.

▶ **Beware of color temperatures.** Nothing can create more unnecessary chaos and confusion on the small canvas of the screen than the mixing of cool colors (blue and green) with hot colors (yellow and red). The Mexican fruit salad may be appetizing when dining in Guadalajara, but on the screen, it dominates, enabling little room for type, illustrations, or other elements to emerge and to communicate anything.

▶ **Be careful when colorizing type.** Avoid colorizing serif letter forms. Color takes better to sans serif typefaces (see Chapter 6, "Typography for the Screen").

▶ **Avoid extremely dark backgrounds with semi-dark type over it.** Whether in print or online, legibility is impaired the moment contrast is lacking. In a sense, nothing substitutes the impact of black type on a white background (or dark type on light backgrounds). It is difficult to imagine a web site developed entirely around black and white, although it is possible and probably would provide for an elegant and sophisticated treatment that would stand apart from all the other sites. It is unlikely, however, that many designers will forego the use of color. Just as in print, however, there are some concerns about how it will reproduce.

Figure 7.1

The Netscape 216-Color Palette.

Designing with Browser-safe Colors

Just as the quality of the paper, the opacity of the ink, and the sophistication of the press determine how color will display in print, the resolution, color capabilities and gamma of the computer screen, the sophistication of the browser software, and the designer's knowledge of how bits translate into dots determine how color will display online.

For the sake of argument, let us assume you have created a stunning GIF graphic using a conservative 256 colors (note that we are talking only about "flat color graphics" here, not photos), thereby matching what passes for an "average" color capability in the wildly various universe of computer monitors. The problem is that only 216 of those colors are shared by the two dominant browsers. If your graphic contains colors other than those 216, your browser will employ dithering to reduce the image's palette and display its best approximation of the colors you specified. If your image employs thousand (or millions!) of colors instead of 256, then the dithering will be even more drastic. We'll leave it to you to imagine the results.

The realist will make sure that her palette relates directly to the actual state of the art on the web by making use of a handy item known as The Netscape

216-Color Palette (see Figure 7.1.); the same 216 colors are shared by Microsoft's Internet Explorer. This indispensable tool is shown here and can be downloaded as a browser CLUT (Color Look-Up Table) from web designer and author Lynda Weinman's site at `http://www.lynda.com/hex.html`. The CLUT can then be loaded directly into Adobe Photoshop for either Mac or Windows, displayed in the "Swatches" palette, and sampled with the Eyedropper tool as you create original GIF graphics. Lynda Weinman's site also discusses the use of color on the web in concise, but useful detail.

Another useful tool is PANTONE's new ColorWeb Internet color matching system, which applies the familiar PANTONE color matching system to web color. The software enables the designer to find the nearest browser-safe, non-dithering match to a desired color for use on the web. For more information, see Hayden's *PANTONE Web Color Resource Kit.*

Figure 7.2

The online version of *Bild's* web site incorporates the same red color that is identifiable in the print version.

Figure 7.3

Tho print vorsion of *Bild*.

Color and Identity

The first function of color in a web site is to convey a sense of identity. Logos will always appear in the same color, and so will certain navigational elements that the user will come to accept as part of the daily routine of operating a web site. Consistency is key.

Identity begins with the color used for the site's logo. In the case of newspapers and magazines that are designing online editions, it helps tremendously to use colors that create resonance between the print edition and its online counterpart.

Many newspapers that, because of tradition, have not used nameplates in color, do, however, create logos in color for their online editions; this is where traditions are being started, not fol-

lowed, and where the medium lends itself to colorization. Newspapers such as *The New York Times* and *The Washington Post*, however, which utilize black nameplates, continue to use black logos in their web sites. Others, such as the German daily *Bild*, emphasize the red for which it is so well known in its printed edition and incorporates it into its home page (see Figures 7.2 and 7.3).

One cannot question the importance of "brand" in products generally. Publications and web sites are no exception. The logo of a well known newspaper or magazine should be used on the web site of the publication. It does not, however, have to be used in a large size, and it does not have to dominate the overall design. The web site is, for all practical purposes, an extension of the publication, but it is not the publication itself. It is a new medium, a new product. As such, you can use a hint of a color to create the resonance mentioned earlier, but you can also add colors, introduce a new color palette, and give users the idea that this is their familiar publication, but stretching itself and conquering new horizons.

The "brand" color can be a line under the logo, even a new logo, a whisper of a presence on the line that underscores navigational words, or the color of the navigational buttons. A presence, yes; an overpowering one, no. In effect, a new color can be introduced for the web site, and it should be able to coexist with the subdued presence of the original brand color.

Color Temperatures

Designers should know about the temperatures of color, which are considered vital to create effective relationships, or contrast, within the space of a screen or a page. Colors are either warm or cool, although red and yellow are definitely hotter than they are warm. If we use the basic definitions of color, red, orange, and yellow are warm, whereas violet, blue, and green are cool. Combinations are possible, so that one could have a green-yellow combination that would be warmer than it is cool. Red-violet could be considered cooler than red-orange, which is a more explosive combination, whether on a screen or a shirt (see Figure 7.4)!

One cannot overemphasize the importance of temperature. Although mixing of cool and warm temperatures sometimes does make for interesting combinations, such mixing must be handled carefully and with great expertise.

Temperature neutrality, if desired, can be achieved through the use of pastel colors, which tend to be less three-dimensional, and blend in the background more effectively.

Neutrality, or the more passive environment provided by pastel shades, is recommended when color is wanted as an accent on the screen, but not as a leading player. A site that wishes to come across as text-oriented, or more serious, may select pastel shades that tend to stay in the background.

Both of the following examples demonstrate what color can do to predispose the user—to inform visually before the words convey any meanings.

One enters the world of Ferrari through the electricity and exuberance that only red can bring to a screen—or, for that matter, to a printed page. The red screen transports us. It conveys passion, danger, sensuality—perhaps fast cars, good times, adventure (see Figure 7.5). The Mercedes Benz web page, in its metallic grays and blues, conveys a more relaxed and elegant environment (see Figure 7.6).

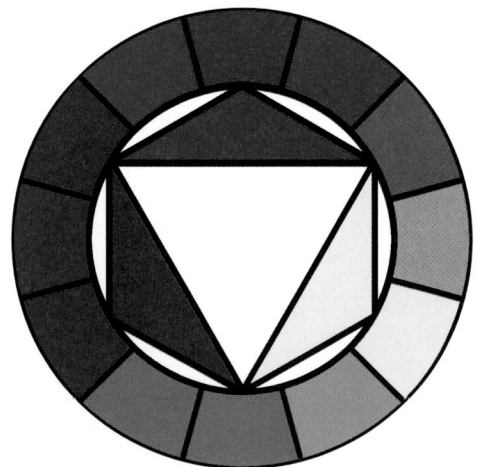

Figure 7.4

One standard color wheel model.

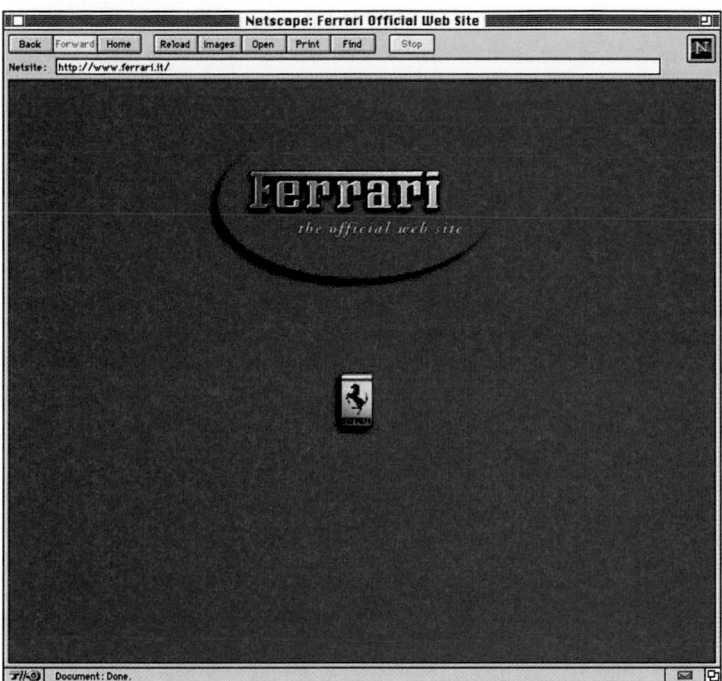

Figure 7.5

This is definitely one of the hottest temperature colors used on a web site. The information designer's intent is to get us excited about this particular sports automobile. The color red does that. One sees himself traveling at fast speeds, on the road to adventure, carefree and happy. All before a word is read, just by using the color red and the yellow Ferrari logo. Two hot colors!

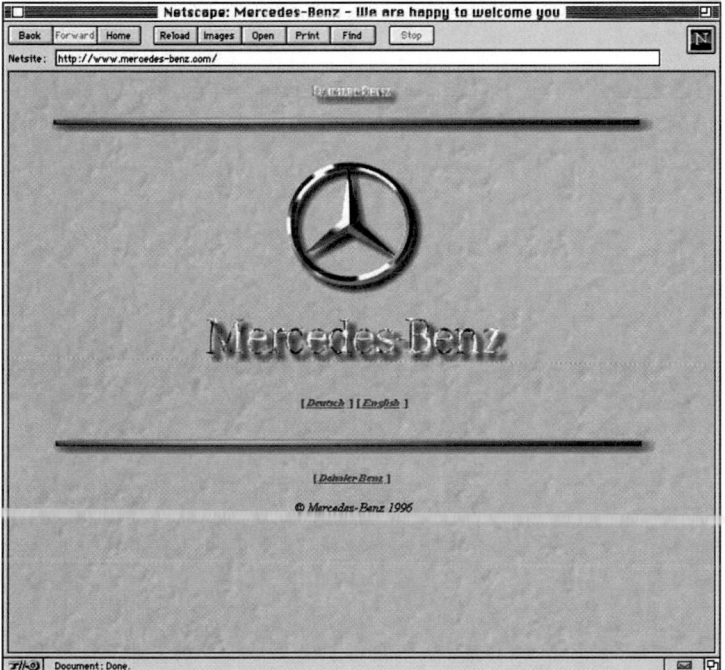

Figure 7.6

On the other side of the color thermometer, Mercedes Benz wants us to relax with its product, and it accomplishes that with cool metallic grays and blues. The mood is less adventurous, but nonetheless, we want to read more, to inquire about this first class product.

Color Hierarchy

Color creates movement wherever it appears. It is the type of movement that comes by color's mere presence. Black and white are taken for granted, a touch of color provides the sort of visual adrenaline that causes us to act, to react, to seek meanings behind words or images. Fashion designers, architects, and artists all know the difference that color can make. Even the presence of black on white paper con-

stitutes a color relationship, as well as a sense of movement and the three dimensional. Because color never appears isolated, it affects the elements surrounding it, be it on a page or on a screen.

Information designers cannot assume that the presence of a strong yellow on the screen will not affect how we attach meaning to whatever surrounds it. Colors always exist in direct relationship to each other and to anything in color surrounding them.

Hierarchy, then, becomes important, whether you are designing on paper or for the screen because it implies relationships between sets of information you are trying to convey. So let us assume that we have a strong presence of a certain color—for example, red— on the screen. That will become the initial point of entry, where the eyes rest for the first 20 seconds on the screen, before taking off in a different direction. It helps not to give this strong lead color competition. Let the secondary colors play in the background, thus helping to establish the sense of hierarchy. Red and yellow, specifically, contribute to impact strongly, perhaps more so than any other colors.

In fact, soft pastel hues, such as mint green, lilac, salmon, light yellow, pink, and light blue, do the opposite. They blend on the screen and do not overpower the design of the site (see Figure 7.7).

Figure 7.7

A site that uses soft pastels effectively is that of Clinique Cosmetics, which blends it all against a white background.

Primary colors have the opposite effect. They tend to become strong on the screen, and, unless they are used with caution, may clash with other elements. Otherwise, strong primary colors can be very attractive to a specific audience and fit perfectly with the web site's theme (see Figure 7.8).

The web designer can relate to and utilize color with greater freedom than the print designer. Just the fact that one does not have to worry as much about color reproduction—the print designer's daily nightmare—is a big step forward. Even the strongest colors (which

I advise to steer away from, even on web sites) can do pretty well on the screen, provided you operate with browser-safe colors. It is easy to see how even the colorful and playful FAO Schwartz web site would have to tone down its colors to print the same concept on a newspaper page. Because one prints on white paper that already has lots of light, the presence of all the yellows and primary bright colors on it would create just too much of a good thing for print. On the screen, well, a more tolerable illumination of shades appear.

Figure 7.8

Famed toy store FAO Schwartz uses a brightly colored palette to appeal to children of all ages who may, upon seeing this home page, almost feel as if they are really entering the world of toys and fun.

Color and Contrast

Web design offers the ideal medium in which to utilize color contrast. Some of the most striking openings for home pages involve the starkness of a black background screen, with few elements, preferably type, swimming on it. Like a star on a very dark night, whatever element is placed against black tends to move forward with vitality (see Figure 7.9).

The Importance of Contrast in Design

Most good design is about contrast, the establishing of visual opposites on the page or the screen: large to small, long to short, thick to thin, bold to light, and color to black and white. Contrast is, however, most important when it comes to how we use color. It is, indeed, where the information designer

can create an instant sense of three-dimensionality that makes the screen look vivid, realistic, and powerful.

Dr. Pegie Stark Adam, of The Poynter Institute for Media Studies, and author of "Color, Contrast, and Dimension in News Design," a Poynter Paper (#6), published in 1995, explains that: "Creating three dimensions in design is an important goal because we want our designs to look vivid, realistic, and powerful. We want the viewer to be engaged, to stop and look. If a design has depth, the viewer is engaged to look "into" the design, to travel through the visual information and clues and to get the maximum amount of stimulus and information from the visual and verbal elements. If a design is flat, with no contrast and therefore no dimension, the reader does not become engaged but simply glosses over the many similar elements because nothing grabs the eye's interest. Nothing stops the viewer. Nothing looks interesting enough to enter and explore. The power of contrast enables us to create dimension. The use of contrasting sizes of small, medium, and large can make one element appear to be in the fore-ground, another element in the mid ground, another in the background. Add various shapes and another contrast is created. Add color and another contrast is created."

I asked color expert Dr. Pegie Stark Adam, my colleague from The Poynter Institute for Media Studies in St. Petersburg, Florida, and an active design consultant, how she viewed the specifics of color contrast for web design. Here are her comments and tips, along with her suggestions of sites that use color contrast well:

Figure 7.9

The official James Bond web site utilizes a black background, making the minimal images stand out more and come to the user right away.

Creating Contrast on Computer Screens

Designing a web site is a perfect environment for creating three dimensions. That's because the medium itself, the computer screen on which you are designing, is a three-dimensional space. Photos, art, type, and colors stay crisp, sharp, true, and realistic. What you see as you are designing is what the viewers see on their end as well. Your design does not go through several generations of print production. Printing often flattens out the dimension that the designer tries to create through contrast of shapes, sizes, and color. Think of the number of times you have created a design on the computer and were disappointed when you saw how it flattened out after it was out of the "machine" and through the production process and printed on a piece of paper.

Color, Contrast, and Dimension

Color is a powerful tool in creating three dimensions in design. By applying a number of color contrasts, the designer can make some elements shout and come forward loud and clear into the viewer's vision. Another color can make elements appear as if they are floating in the background, yet another color can make elements appear to be living in the mid ground. Contrast, then, creates dimension, an important goal to achieve when designing on paper or onscreen because dimension adds interest and provides realistic feel to what you are looking at.

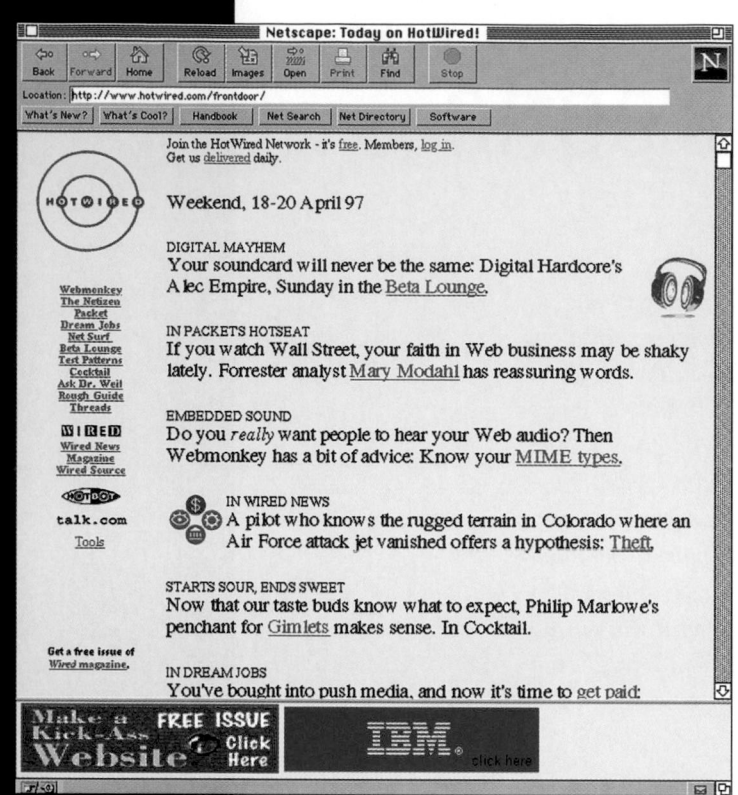

The Color Contrasts

We work with a variety of color contrasts. The most powerful is the contrast of hue (pure color). Strong colors in close proximity create a feeling of movement or vibration in the eye of the viewer. HotWired (http://www.hotwired.com) accomplishes this effect with contrast of hues (see Figure 7.10).

To create a vivid, lively design with a voice that is active, work with pure hues of color next to each other. Be careful, though, when

Figure 7.10

HotWired is a lively and active web site with a clear and definite voice. Its choice of contrast of vivid hue says who it is, and therefore who its readers are. HotWired screens always look as if they are moving because of the extreme contrast of primary hues.

Figure 7.11

http//:www.metadesign.com

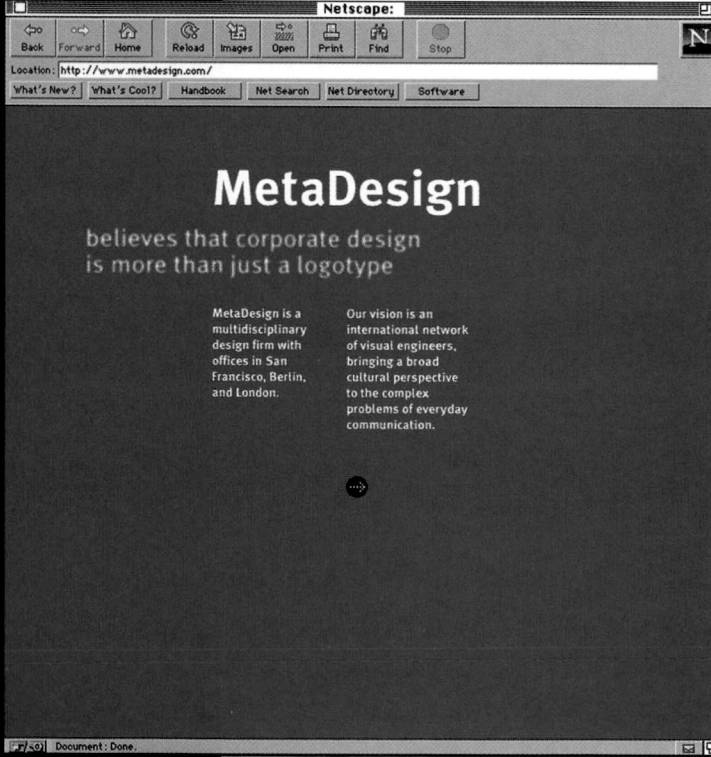

working with type. If you place a pure red word on a pure green background, the word would start vibrating and it would be diffi-cult to read.

Both the MetaDesign and Benetton web sites are good examples of contrast of hues; they illustrate good design that is enhanced by the presence of how color is treated, a sort of invitation for the user to dive in and start navigating the site (see Figures 7.11 and 7.12).

Figure 7.12

http://www.benetton.com

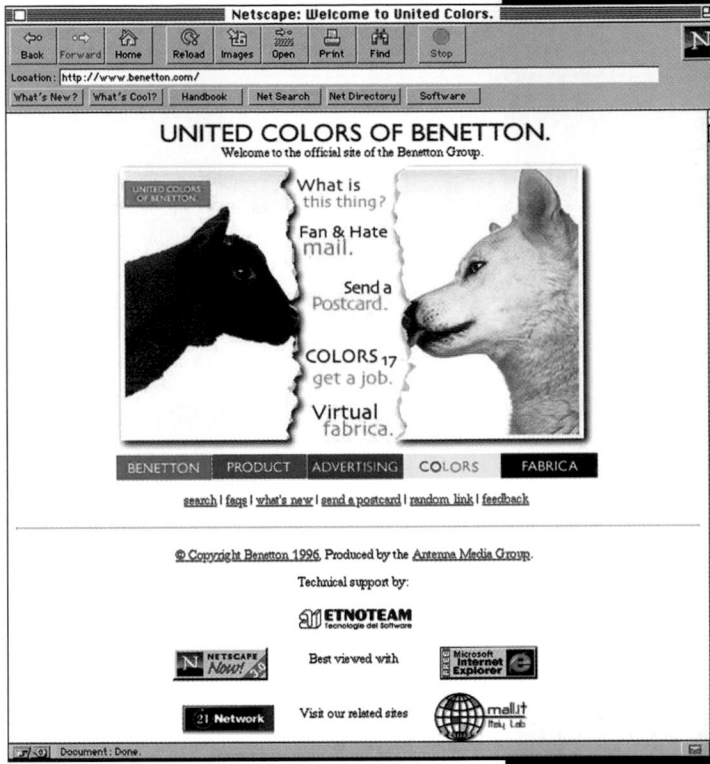

Contrast of Complementary and Contrast of Warm and Cool

Each primary color has a color opposite itself on the color wheel. That color is the primary color's complement. Orange, for example, is the complement of primary blue. Therefore, when you place orange and blue next to each other, a contrast is created. The orange comes forward; the blue goes back. That's because the orange is a warm color and the blue is a cool color. Cool colors recede; warm colors come forward.

The impressionists understood the power of complementary contrast. They anchored warm colors such as orange browns, and deep reds, to the earth. Cool colors, such as blue, green, and light purple, were airborne.

Contrast of Dark and Light, Black and White

Another strong contrast in color is light and dark, the most extreme being black and white. Black and white are exact opposites. So, when they are placed next to each other, the white or black element will appear in front of the other, depending on size, shape, and placement.

As you decrease the percentage of black or darken the white, the less contrast is created. A dimensional object can be formed when a series of percentages of black and white are used in gradation, just as you see in a black and white photograph. The gradation from 100% black through 90, 80, 70, 60, 50, and so on create subtle contrast, thereby creating a realistic image with dimension.

The X-Files web site shows the extreme contrast of black and white. Not only does the site create a multi-dimensional, realistic feel, the mood it sponsors is one of eerie suspense created by the drama of the extreme contrast of black and white (see Figure 7.13).

Any color combination can be made to look more or less dimensional by adjusting the percentage of color, or the darkness or lightness of the color. Remember that a dark color next to a light color will appear more dimensional than a light color next to a light color.

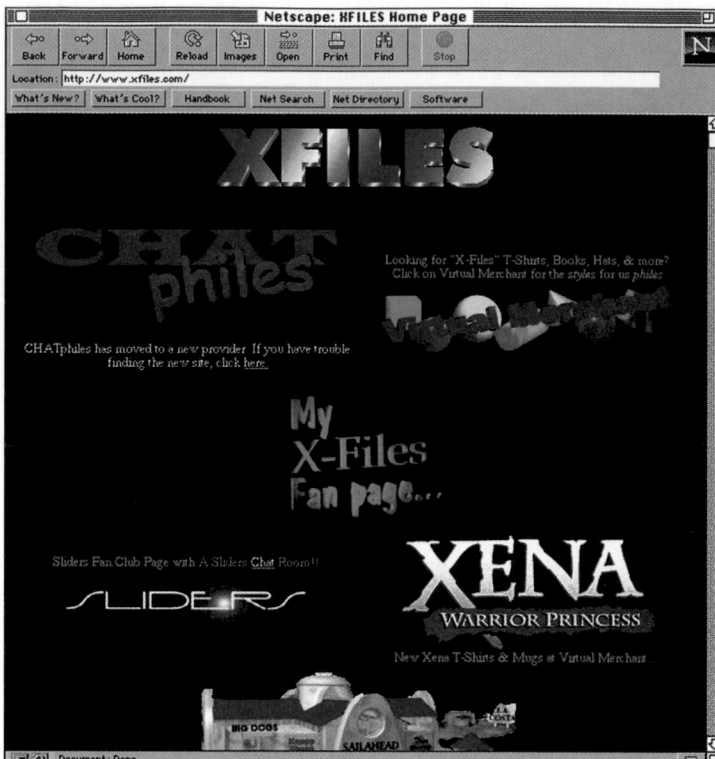

Figure 7.13

http://www.xfiles.com

Contrast of Saturation

The most sophisticated contrast of color is saturation—where one or more colors are either diluted (made lighter by lessening the percentage or by adding white) or dulled (made darker by adding black or the color's complement). One can create a multi-dimensional design with just one color, saturated from a very diluted 5% mix of yellow and red, for example, and gradated through a series of percentages— 10%, 20%, 30%, 40%, and so on, creating a subtle range of color and dimension. Contrast of saturation is difficult to achieve on the printed page because the process of reproduction often does not capture the subtle differences in tone from slight variations of percentages of color. But when designing on the screen, the very subtle variations of percentages are achieved because, once again, there is no mechanical production the color must go through. What you see is what the viewer gets.

Establishing Color Palettes

First come the colors. Long before we react to typography, content, and design, one sees color on the screen. That first 10-second impression conveys tons of information about the product, the publication, or the company. The establishment of color palettes assumes tremendous importance, and should guide the design process accordingly.

The selection of the color palette creates that instant "feel" for the site. So much is said by just the coolness, the warmth, seriousness, playfulness, and so on that a color conveys. Before a word of the site is read, the spirit of it is captured through color. The color palette then drives our first impression of this product, publication, or company, conveying a lasting impression, too. The three main color palettes most commonly used can be classified as classic, medium, and bright. Central to the choice of color palette is the determination of a background color.

Backgrounds

I believe that white still constitutes one of the best colors for screen backgrounds, especially if a lot of type is to be included. Other colors do very well for backgrounds because they tend to become an accessory as opposed to a protagonist in the interplay of elements on the screen (see Figure 7.14).

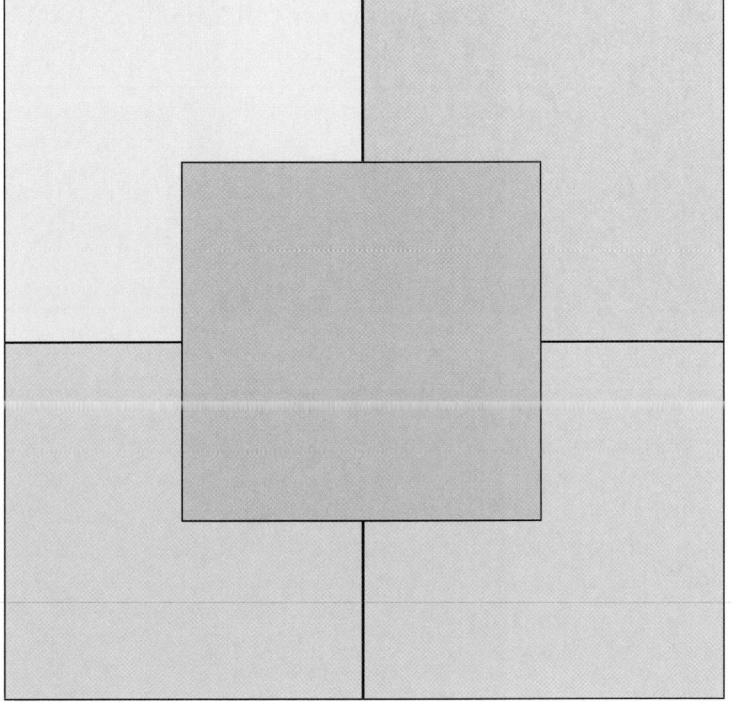

Figure 7.14

A versatile background palette: light yellow, lilac, sand, green, light blue.

The Classic Color Palette

The classic color palette depends on very pale colors to convey feelings that range from subdued to tranquil to sophisticated. When a site appears in classic colors, it is saying that it does not indulge in excesses. This palette reflects the temperatures of winter.

The colors used, especially if dealing with very pale tones, do not move forward on the screen. Take for example a combination of Y10, Y10C10, M10C10 (see Figure 7.15).

Figure 7.15

Pale tones within the classic color palette.

A feeling of serenity, but with stronger tones, can be conveyed as part of a classic palette, based on a combination of dull tones and grayish tones. These are ideal for backgrounds and also for typography, as long as the screen remains white or in a sand color, for the type to stand out. Typical combinations are Y30M10,C30,Y30M10C10, Y30M30C10, and Y10M30C30 (see Figure 7.16).

Figure 7.16

Dull, grayish tones of the classic color palette.

An elegant feeling can be conveyed with soft colors that are also refined and smart, making their presence felt more heavily on the screen. Among some interesting combinations are Y40M30C50, Y30M20C10, Y30M40C70 (see Figure 7.17).

Figure 7.17

Soft, elegant colors of the classic color palette.

The Medium Color Palette

The medium color palette depends on more full-bodied colors that do move forward on the screen, appear happy, combine warm and cold hues, and also convey elegance. When a site appears in a medium range palette, it is saying that it is serious, but having fun anyway. It wants to be seen and enjoyed visually. This palette represents the colors of autumn and early spring.

Three elegant and interesting combinations are Y20M70, M60C70, Y20C50 (see Figure 7.18).

Figure 7.18

Staple colors of the medium palette.

For deeper tones with a bright sparkle within this color palette we can recommend the following combinations: Y100M40C20, Y100M70C20, Y20M100C90 (see Figure 7.19).

Figure 7.19

Deeper tones within the medium color palette.

The brightest within this color palette would combine the happy colors associated with candy wrappers, amusement parks, and toy stores. The colors are pleasantly bright, with almost no dark tones at all, and an overall sense of freshness and sweetness. Ideal for sites that wish to convey a youthful spirit. These are common combinations of the four basic colors: Y80M20, Y80M40, Y80M70, Y40M90, or M90C10, Y50M90 (see Figure 7.20).

Figure 7.20

Bright spots of the medium color palette.

Medium COLOR Palette

The Bright Color Palette

The bright color palette depends on strong colors that seem to burst out of the screen, popping, moving with energy, and representing combinations of the most brilliant colors. When a site appears in a bright range palette, it is saying that it is alive, full of fun and information, sporty, and more spring and summer than autumn and winter.

At its strongest point, this palette includes such combinations as Y100M10, Y100M100, M80C100, Y100C100, or Y100M20, M100, M100C30, and Y70C100 (see Figure 7.21).

Figure 7.21

The bright color palette.

No rule can substitute the information designer's common sense, instinct, and good taste when it comes to selecting color. The web enables us to be more experimental, however, and to push the color envelope beyond some of the traditional rules of the past.

You can benefit from the fact that there are fewer color reproduction problems to worry about, and therefore, you can mix primary colors with pastel hues while creating exciting combinations. More important, however, is to make sure that the choice of color relates completely to the content of the site— that it is appropriate for the mood and point of view of the information conveyed. If, in addition, the visual statement made is attractive and enticing, then chances are color has been effectively utilized.

Having analyzed the four basic components of any design: story structures, architecture, typography, and color, we can now turn our attention to how the whole recipe comes together as we take a set of information and communicate it to an audience on the web. The next chapter takes us into the kitchen where the information designer dons the chef's hat and creates the basic recipe.

bright COLOR palette

Chapter 8

The Basic Recipe

This chapter uses the traditional newspaper model to explain how information can be acquired and transmitted in different formats. There is no evidence that newspapers as we know them will disappear. Perhaps those newspapers that fail to actualize will have difficulty surviving and eventually succumb to factors such as fewer loyal readers, readers with less time, and the paper's incapability to compete in a multimedia environment.

Survival of traditional newspapers will also depend on the editors' ability to present information in a way that is easy to find and fast to absorb. Readers are interested in information, which is not the same as saying they are interested in news. Newspapers and online services have an obligation to both.

"In the future," writes David M. Cole, "rather than having one news desk, newspapers will undoubtedly have three or four of them. One, as usual, will handle the news-print product. The others will figure out how to take the material gathered for the news-print product and extend it to other products: online, CD-ROM, and so on." (★ASNE Bulletin, January 1995, p 11. "Forget paper and focus on reporting the news.")

The Transition from the Print Metaphor

I remember working with the German daily, *Südkurier*, in Konstanz as it prepared its first online edition. My previous work with this newspaper had involved the redesign of its print edition. The very conservative editors had struggled with the changes that a redesign imposes: new typography, a change of writing styles, and, in the case of Südkurier, the introduction of color. The editors were not ready to see color photographs of fires or snowy days, and the first such images on the prototypes made the usually calm Germans quite emotional.

So, when I returned three years later to work with the online team, I brought with me the memories of those encounters. And I did what many designers of online newspapers have done all along, I used the "newspaper metaphor" in the creation of the online version.

It is important to clarify from the start that few newspapers duplicate themselves totally in their online editions, which is why it is incorrect to simply use the name of the newspaper when it goes online. If the newspaper's name is The Gazette, the online edition should call itself The Gazette On-Line, or The Digital Gazette, or some other name.

The online edition is, indeed, more than an edition; it is a new product that ties in with the printed version, but it is not a duplication, if it is done properly.

Let us first review the elements of the newspaper metaphor that create good models to imitate in an online edition.

Sectionalizing

There is no question that newspaper sections enable information to be compartmentalized in a way that makes sense and enables easy access. It does not take much effort for a newspaper reader to find Metro, Sports, Entertainment, or Business sections inside a newspaper.

All publications—and print material—should make an effort to minimize the number of items that appear as navigational tools. A 14-section newspaper must combine some of them (based on common topics and themes) to avoid an imposing column of titles that may intimidate and confuse the user. Likewise, a newsletter going online may limit its navigation to five baskets of information or less, by combining the message from the editor/publisher, letters from readers, and brief notes as one basket. An annual report may combine such items as the history of the company, the outlook for the future, and the names of all board members under one basket, even if these are four or five sections in the printed version.

Indexing

Although newspaper indexes often are not as all-inclusive as readers would want (how often do we reach high levels of frustration when looking for a favorite columnist?), they are as primitive and effective a "navigational" tool as one can find.

All publications going online, regardless of category, must provide good indexing with a sense of hierarchy in mind. An annual report, for example, may choose to begin with highlights of the year as the top navigational item, as opposed to the company's history (which some users might skip, anyway). Newspapers and magazines do well to start with the latest news sections, followed by that which is unique to the site (and does not appear in print). For a magazine web site, the cover story and the second and third best features of the edition are top "buttons" to push, with the horoscope probably at the bottom of the list. These are some of the most vital decisions for an online editor and designer to make—the most difficult and agonizing. After the hierarchy of content has been decided and the topics are narrowed down to bite size, then the visual designing can begin.

Headlines

Well-written headlines are the main entry point to text, regardless of the medium in which they appear. Online editions need good headline writers who can grab your attention as you scroll up and down the screens.

A good headline for a web site has the same elements as the traditional good headline for a newspaper or magazine: enticing words, good action verbs, the best possible summary of what the content is about, and, if possible, a surprise or "hook" that pulls us in.

Graphics

Icons can be extremely useful as navigational tools (see Figure 8.1). More explanatory graphics, however, can help us to understand information. Online edition users welcome graphics that are simple and direct.

When the team who prepared *The Washington Post's* online service, Virtual Ink, described their efforts, they referred to the differences between newspapers and online editions:

"A newspaper…carries information in one direction; an online service operates in two directions, and users of an online newspaper expect involvement and responses from the producers. An online newspaper enables articles to remain available for years; it presents large collections of data that would never appear in the print product; it is read on screens instead of on pages. In many ways, it is not a newspaper at all. At the same time, it contains most of the same articles as today's paper and can be updated around the clock." (*Interpersonal Computing and Technology: An Electronic Journal for the 21st Century—ISSN: 1064-4326, July 1995, Vol. 3, Number 3, pp.64–90 by Melinda McAdams, On-Line newspapers: Virtual Ink, http://www.sentex.net/~mmcadams/invent.html)

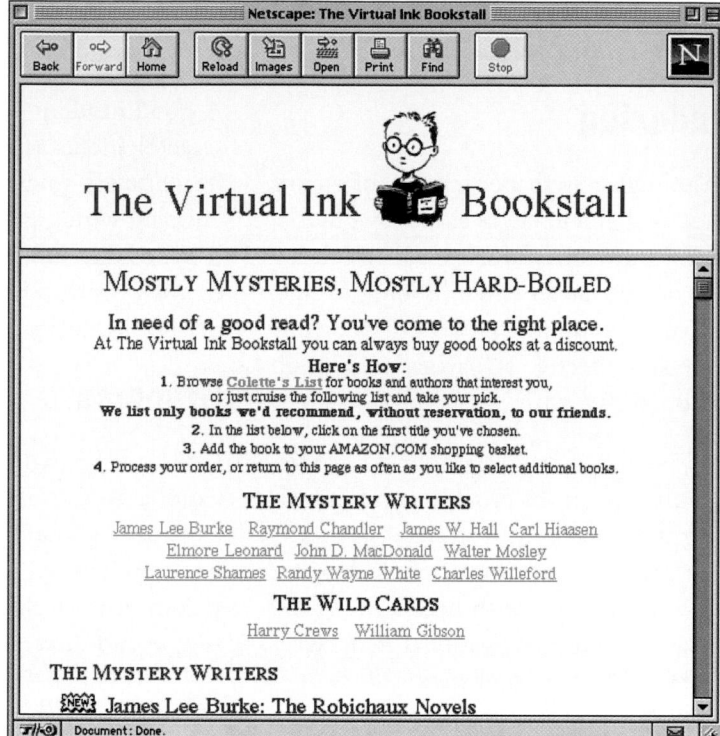

Figure 8.1

Virtual Ink.

Creating Baskets of Information

The first task of organizing a new online edition is to create baskets of information. Look through the printed newspaper, which, in the case of Südkurier, included a main body with news, a local/regional section, sports, and a cultural section. Other supplements appeared at different times during the week. I imitated the logo of the printed version, the blue that characterized the newspaper, the typography, indexing, and content organization (see Figures 8.2 and 8.3). It was an onscreen version of Südkurier. The first reaction from the young staff of the online edition was that it looked too much like the newspaper.

Figure 8.2

This is how the front page of German's *Südkurier* looks, emphasizing the color blue as a signature color that is clearly identifiable to readers.

Figure 8.3

A first prototype for the Südkurier home page used the newspaper metaphor almost identically. The colors, the point of view, and the typographic rhythm all mimicked the printed front page.

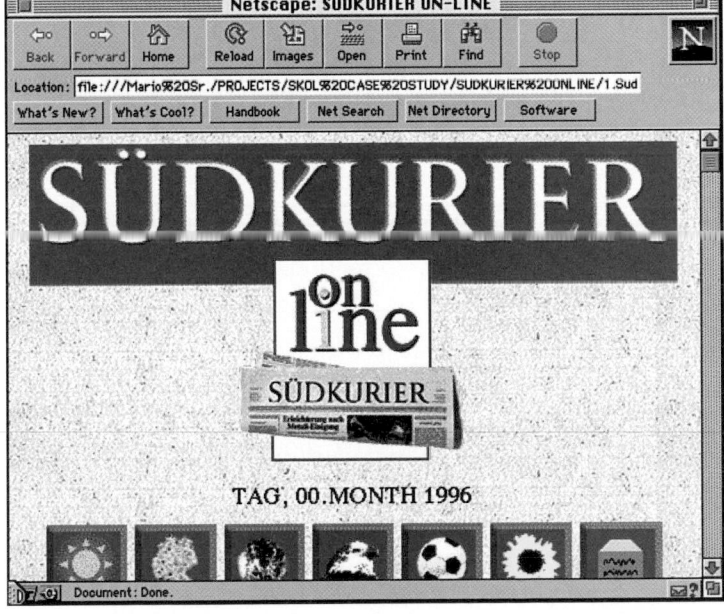

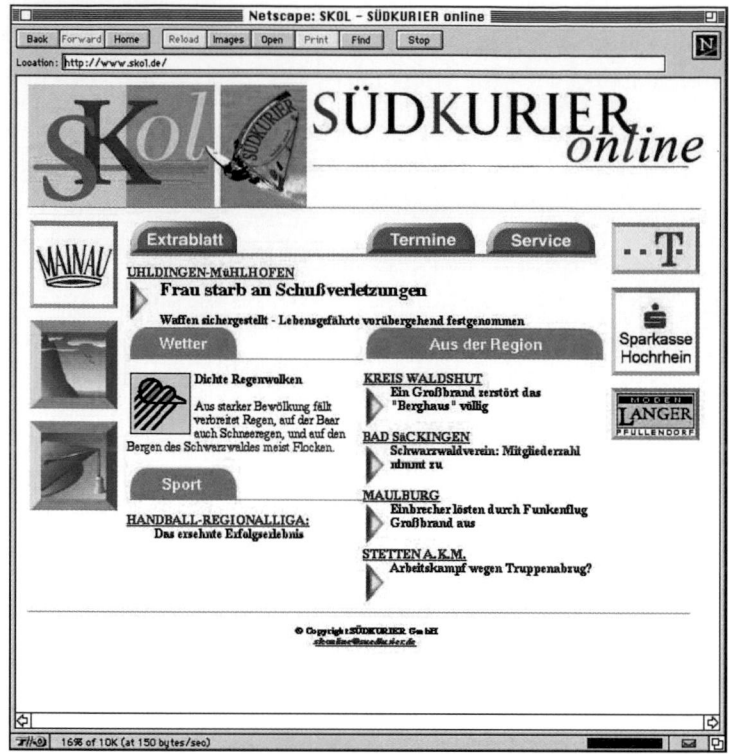

Figure 8.4

The next prototype of Südkurier Online abandons the newspaper metaphor almost completely, with a new logo identity, a different color palette, and a more energized and youthful feel than the paper ever had.

We decided to do some testing with that version while preparing to work on a different one. The online staffers were right. The target audience for whom Südkurier Online was prepared—young university students—did not want their online edition to look like a newspaper (see Figure 8.4).

Online editions are not newspapers. They are to be read, but because they appear onscreen, they must have some of the elements that we associate with television—appealing visuals, movement, energy, color, and a difficult to describe sense of that which is modern.

How does one define "modern"? I don't mean metallic shine on type or animated backgrounds. Instead, "modern" when translated to web site design refers to a systematic retreat from "the newspaper look." Perhaps more than "modern" what I mean here is "open-minded and experimental," welcoming a new medium with new approaches and techniques.

Newspapers, regardless of how colorful they may be, do not represent a modern medium, and perhaps they should not. But online editions are not television. Television is to be seen and to be heard. Online editions are to be read, seen, and sometimes heard. This is an important consideration in moving any printed material to the web.

The new medium requires specific characteristics. Online editions of printed newspapers can benefit, however, from some "visual connection" with their parent publication, while allowing for some unique features as well:

1. A color palette that resembles that used by the printed version of the site can help users identify and relate one medium to the other.

2. The printed edition should include some indexing of the web site, and vice versa. It is desirable to have web site references to content material that may only appear in the print edition.

3. Sometimes the typography of both the web site and printed editions have some common, if not necessarily identical, characteristics.

Name and Identity

An element of the product name must tie back to the printed version of the publication. It is not necessary, however, to duplicate the name or the typeface. Sometimes a new word, such as digital, is added. Or a signature color that is associated with the printed version appears in the online logo. Some online editions scratch the old logos totally, and use new typefaces and names. Each situation should be evaluated separately (see Figures 8.5 and 8.6).

Several existing sites enable you to find out if a selected URL name is already taken by another publication or firm, but the best is hosted by InterNIC ("the landlord of the Internet"). The search engine is called Web Interface to Whois and can be found at: `http://nic.internic.net/cgi-bin/whois`.

The user types in the proposed second-level domain name (times.com) and the search results reveal whether it is available, and if not, who owns the name. This information may come in handy and should probably serve as a first step in the design of a web site. Even the most "original" names a team of designers and editors comes up with may already have a proprietor who had the "brilliant" idea first.

Typeface

The typeface used for headlines and text in the newspaper may be replicated in the online editions, simply because it enables continuity. When moving headlines and text from the printed edition to the online edition, it sometimes helps to use the same fonts, although this is not necessary (see Figures 8.7 and 8.8).

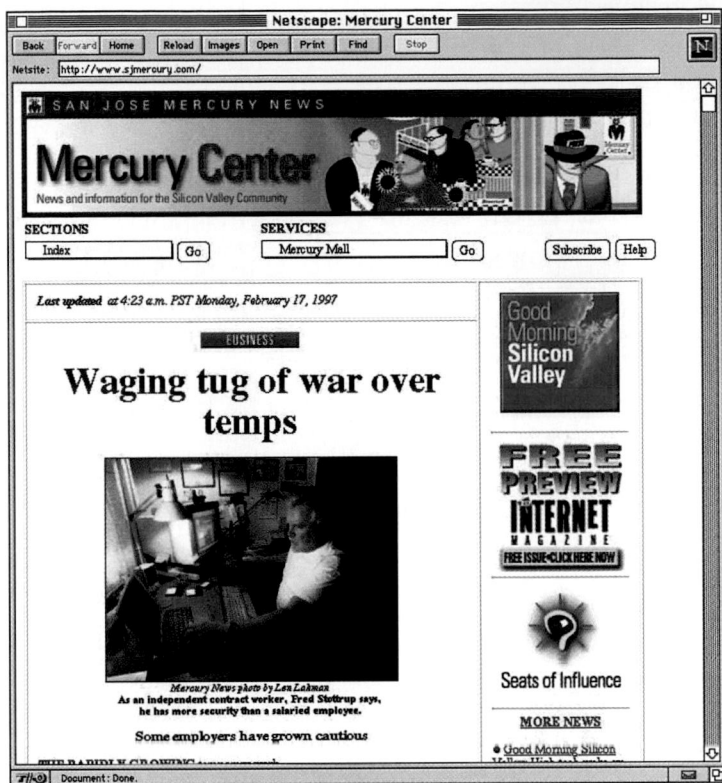

Figure 8.5

One of the easiest news web sites to follow is Mercury Center, from the *San Jose Mercury News*. Simple, uncomplicated, with good navigational devices at the top and right of the screen, the main feature of the day is unmistakably clear to the user, as are ways to seek additional information.

Figure 8.6

These are the main navigational components on the front page of the *San Jose Mercury News* print edition.

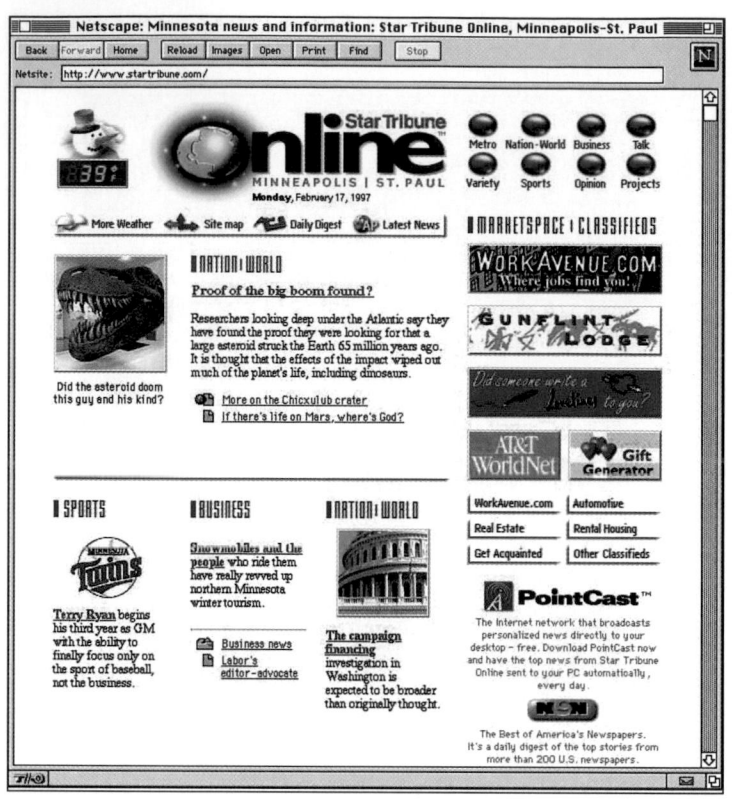

Figure 8.7

StarTribune Online, the web site of the *Minneapolis Tribune,* follows a sort of three-tier horizontal framing, separating news sections of the newspaper from features and advertising. The colors are crisp; the weather information is distinctive and easy to follow; and the buttons to the inside of the site are easy to find (at top right).

Sections

Although it makes sense to create navigational tools centered around the traditional sections of the printed version of the newspaper or publication, that is, sports, business, local, and so on, some online services redefine content organization and assign it different names to facilitate movement (see Figure 8.9). One does not want a crowded home page, which is why more than eight baskets of information may be too much. It is imperative that the online staff determine the most effective way to take the content from the printed newspaper, and then regroup sections accordingly. Culture, entertainment, and the arts, for example, may all be grouped under one heading on the home page instead of three.

STARTribune Online

Telling Stories

If the printed version carries a headline, a summary, and text, it makes sense to have the same story structure when transferring the information to the online edition. The same applies to the treatment of briefs and photo captions (see Figures 8.10 and 8.11).

Figure 8.8

A front page of the *Star Tribune*.

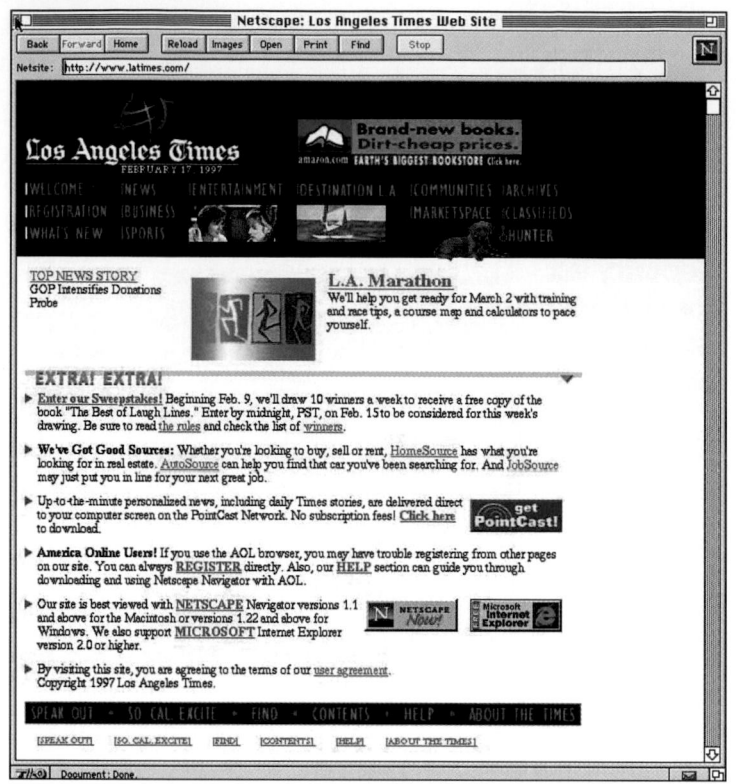

Figure 8.9

The *Los Angeles Times* home page presents headlines and summaries of major stories up front, with a simple and readable index at the top and a small and unobtrusive logo.

Basically, story structures—unlike intact stories—can be taken directly from the print product and incorporated into the web quite effectively. If, for example, a typical story structure for a lead page one story includes a line over the headline, the headline, and a summary paragraph, that entire story structure can be duplicated without major effort on the web edition of the printed publication.

A question often asked in seminars is whether the style of writing for the web should be different from that of other media. Good writing is essential, regardless of the medium, but most writing experts do agree that each medium requires certain expertise to accommodate technical as well as audience differences.

Figure 8.10

A front page of *The News & Observer*.

Figure 8.11

The News & Observer, one of the first newspapers to have its own web site, is also one of the most successful. The lead story normally carries a photograph. Other areas of navigation divide content into regional or subject baskets.

WRITING for Print, BROADCAST, and the WEB

Chip Scanlan, a writing coach and associate at The Poynter Institute for Media Studies, explains these differences:

"In broadcast, you write to video and still images and sound. To accompany, enhance, and amplify what the viewer sees and hears from the screen. Words in broadcast complete the puzzle in the reader's mind.

The writer for print, by contrast, must use language to create in the reader's mind what the television screen provides.

The broadcast writer writes for the screen; the print writer tries to create a screen in the reader's mind that the memory and imagination can fill."

Like the broadcast writer, the writer for the web has additional "electronic texts to work with ("e-texts" include video and still images, animation, sound, as well as words). But just like the print writer, the web writer must use language that is specific, vivid, and accurate. The challenge for the web writer is to use words to provide multiple perspectives—not to repeat information, but to add new layers that deepen the understanding and impact of the story that is being told."

Most importantly, the web writer must inspire the user to scroll for further text, or to click for additional information, just like writers in newspapers and magazines constantly try to make sure readers go beyond a jump to an inside page. The challenge, to hold on to readers, is identical, even if the medium is different.

Layering

One advantage of online editions is that there is no need to worry about the ever-present "newshole" with its space limitations, its advertising/editorial rations (normally 60-40), and the length of stories. That one advantage, however, creates the next challenge. Because online editions do not restrict the content that is included and must enable access to much more information than a newspaper, it is of greater importance to create detailed indexes that make navigation easy and fast.

This takes us to the concept of layers. Home pages that are too ambitious in their presentation of indexing material can overwhelm the user upon entering. Instead, it is best to start with one main entry door that simply places us at the site, using a logo, a symbol or emblem, some familiar color background, and not more than four navigational buttons. One of these elements takes us into the real home page, which can act as the "front page."

Special Features

Next comes the baskets of information that are unique to the online edition, such as a film guide, the chat room, the historic segment, and so on. These are areas that cannot appear in the newspaper because of space limitations; the online edition can make them available for the user to read at his or her leisure. The materials can be updated regularly. It's like carrying a specialized encyclopedia (see Figure 8.12).

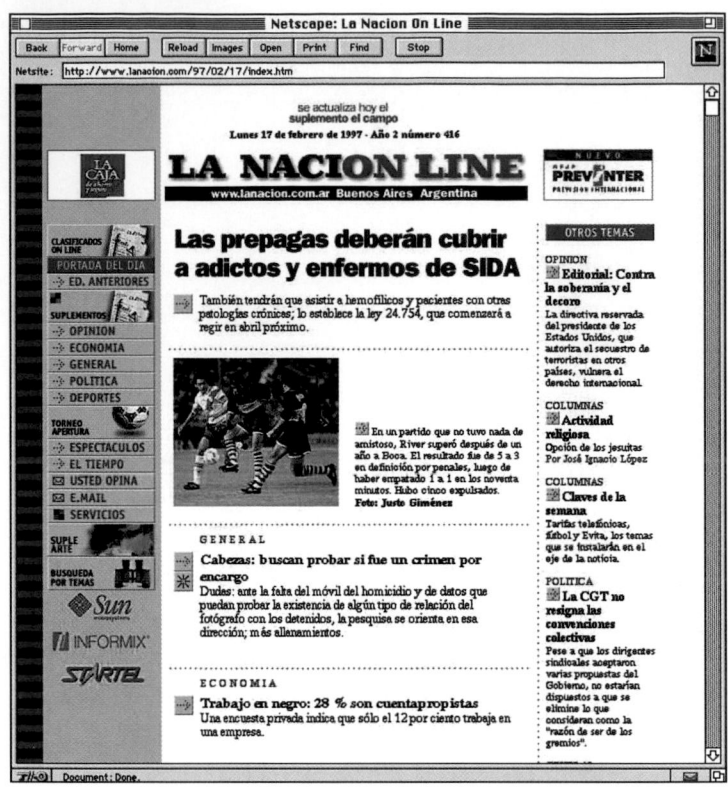

Figure 8.12

La Nacion, of Buenos Aires, Argentina, (www.lanacion.com) uses gray, blue, and black as its signature colors on the home page. A vertical sweep divides the page into three grids, with one navigational column on the left, followed by the wider area for summaries and/or text, and a column for additional topics on the right. Elegant and simple, La Nacion Line stands out as one of the top web sites in South America.

Interaction between Print and Online Publications

Good online editions are going to relate to the printed editions, and vice versa. There must be a daily listing of the online edition in the index of the printed edition, complete with access information, and the online edition, which by virtue of its existence is already a reminder of the printed version, should make reference to the printed version as needed. Some users of an online edition may not be reading the newspaper, and vice versa. The two editions can enhance each other's share of the market.

So much of what is appearing in online publications is experimental and exciting; it is a great possibility that the new media will, indeed, become a source of new readers for the traditional media of print.

The chapter that follows demonstrates what is happening at various newspapers and one television site, where constant updating and redesigning of the products leads to some of the most innovative transitions from print to the web. These sites have found the basic recipe, developed it, and now share it in detail.

Chapter 9

Making the Transition: Case Studies

For some of the online editions profiled here, the change started slowly, following a series of meetings between publishers, editors, and technical people. For others, it was a fast decision-making process instigated by someone in power saying, "We will be online by next month." Others are still working on the prototype, and most confess that their products are in that constant stage of redesign. The idea of the continuous rehearsal, as opposed to the final performance, prevails in the spirit and experimental nature of new media people.

All the cases presented in this chapter involve highly successful sites, and, for the most part, the staffers writing/producing and designing have a background in print. In fact, the model seems to be an editor from the newspaper who expressed an interest in new media and got the job. We are not yet at the stage in new media where staffers come in without previous print or broadcast experience; in some instances, designers have emerged from advertising and public relations backgrounds. The predominant profile, however, is one of a journalist and/or designer from a newspaper or magazine.

As you read through these varied styles of presenting information online, study each for the richness of the experience and how it may contribute to help you with your own transition to web design, or to improving what you already have. Each of the case studies was prepared through interviews, observation, and a careful dissection of the sites on average days. Those sites participating had an opportunity to tell me what made their site unique and to contribute screen pages for sections they considered noteworthy.

The sites shown here portray the work of new media people who have excelled in their experimentation. All agree that they are still in the process of "growing," and the majority are adding content and improving visuals as of the deadline of this book.

Each of the sites profiled excels in one particular area that makes its study interesting:

▶ El Tiempo On-line (`http://www.eltiempo.com`) has the capability to profile community and national events, such as theater festivals.

▶ NandO (`http://www.nando.com`) was one of the pioneer newspaper sites on the web.

▶ Mercury Center (`http://www.mercurycenter.com`) is a great local/regional news site.

▶ StarTribune (`http://www.startribune.com`) shows how photography can be well integrated into online design.

▶ Phoenix Newspapers (`http://www.pni.com`) has one of the best sections for young users.

▶ Arid Lands Newsletter (`http://ag.arizona.edu/OALS/ALN/ALNHome.html`) demonstrates the transition of an informative newsletter.

▶ The Roanoke Times (`http://www.roanoke.com`) presents an extensive community-information network, along with news and features.

▶ CNN Interactive (`http://www.cnn.com`) is an outstanding example of a site that translates broadcast news and content to the web.

The questions asked within the context of each case study do not have easy, neat answers. They are, instead, consistent challenges that arise in various forms every day. Each publication required unique solutions, which varied from day to day.

EL TIEMPO

El Tiempo, Bogota, Columbia (http://www.eltiempo.com)

It was 1993, and two technicians from El Tiempo, Colombia's largest circulation newspaper, published in Bogota for a national audience, got themselves into a tiny room directly opposite the newsroom and started playing with what would become El Tiempo Interactivo, an unambitious project that enabled some interaction between those readers with access to computers and their newspaper.

Using a "bulletin board" approach, the two technicians managed to start placing some stories from different sections of the large newspaper on this electronic bulletin board each day. Mostly, the stories they chose came from politics or local news. El Tiempo Interactivo was a success almost from the start, which prompted executives to move one step further, to start discussing what might be a full fledged online edition of this highly respected newspaper.

Figure 9.1

The front page of El Tiempo's printed edition.

Figure 9.2

Normally, all of the stories on the printed front page translate to the web site opening page.

This was a great success, considering that this was Latin America, and that there were only 2,000 users from the start. Not everyone has a computer. There is an illiteracy rate to contend with among the potential audience, so this really was a good start, and continues to be.

Between December 1994 and December 1995, additional staffers joined the interactive group. A journalist came on board, as well as a designer. Each day, they sort of "put the printed edition of El Tiempo on a table, as in a morgue, and pathologically dissected each section," asking themselves the questions: What belongs online? What does not belong?

They followed the right steps, and asked the right questions during this period of research, trial, and error:

Who uses El Tiempo Online?

El Tiempo used its marketing/data department to conduct surveys and had a daily interactive chat with users as the product was developed.

El Tiempo online registers about 4,000 users a day, many of them Colombians living abroad who access El Tiempo to get much-wanted news about Colombian life and, especially, sports. The rest are university professors, students, and business people (a profile quite similar to that of online users everywhere).

How do we preserve hierarchy from print to web?

To maintain the hierarchy, the online team would take a different section each week, sometimes the local Bogota section, other times Politics, or Sports. How many stories does each department publish per day, per week? What sections appear weekly? Which appear monthly or less often? These became crucial questions in allocating "screen" space and in the eventual development of the home page design.

Must story structures remain consistent from print to online?

The answer was no. El Tiempo includes kickers (overlines) that appear over the headline, then a summary, and then the text. The online edition eliminated the kickers or overlines because they were too obtrusive. More importantly, the story structures of El Tiempo in print are lead stories, secondary stories, columns, briefs, and so on.

"In the beginning," says a journalist involved with the process, "we had to go into the newsroom and beg the journalists to assist us. Nobody really understood much about the Internet, and those who did considered it a competition, a waste of their time. This early stage was pretty much a solo flight for us."

Is everything in the printed edition included online?

No. After the initial architecture of the paper was completed, the staff decided that certain products, such as the Automobile section (highly commercialized) and Home supplements would not join the online edition at the start. And the Sunday edition was too large and complicated for the first online edition. It was introduced a year later. In printed editions there might be 900 plus stories, approximately, of course. As it is, a total of 250 stories find their way into the daily online edition, and even more on Sundays.

One of the highlights of how El Tiempo promotes its online edition is the way it includes a box with information about the web site on the page 2 summary of the newspaper.

What is the best newsroom workflow to transfer text from print to online?

Technically, the El Tiempo engineers created their own system (one offered by a variety of software products) to enable journalists in the newsroom to prepare their text to be transferred to the online staff. The system enabled this version of the text to be sort of "photocopied" to the online staff, who would give the text a name, place it in the hierarchy of how it would appear, and finalize it.

How will we use color?

The initial design of El Tiempo online utilizes bright colors for the logo and icons. At the time of this writing, the site is undergoing its first redesign, one year after it premiered. Some of the changes include:

▶ A new logo, which first appears on what I call a semi-splash page, offering some navigational tools, but also attractive images of Colombian art and/or photos, against a black background. The gold letters in the logo reflect the bright golden hues of pre-Columbian art.

▶ A new direction for the site, which shows that El Tiempo the newspaper continues to be an important presence on the web, but there are many other offerings, such as other publications printed by the same El Tiempo publishing house, as well as extras, such as Theater Festival specials, or the much-publicized and followed Miss Colombia contest.

What are the continuing challenges?

For the online staff, the challenge continues to be to attract more visitors to the site, especially inside Colombia. At a level closer to the staff, the online journalists hope that, with time, and with some systematic approach to training, the newsroom journalists will stop saying: "I work for El Tiempo, the newspaper," and will say, instead, "I work for El Tiempo, the organization," without making distinctions between its print and online editions.

NANDO TIMES

Nando Times, Raleigh, North Carolina (`http://www.nando.com`)

In early 1994, Frank Daniels III, executive editor of *The News and Observer* (Raleigh, North Carolina), began a new venture for the newspaper his family had owned since 1894. A handful of newspapers were experimenting with services distributed electronically to customers with modem-equipped computers. Chief among them were the *San Jose Mercury News* and *Chicago Tribune* on America Online, and the *Fort Worth Star-Telegram* on a local BBS (bulletin board system). Other publications were beginning to talk with AOL, Prodigy, and CompuServe.

Daniels went in a different direction when he established Nando.net, a dial-up BBS that included free accounts for school teachers and students. Nando users could play simple games, venture onto the Internet, read reference materials, and communicate with each other via teleconference and email. Part of the package was a simple, gopher-based, text-only edition of the daily *News and Observer*. Nando.net was intended as an online community, not an online newspaper.

Back then, the World Wide Web was in beta and the Internet was text-only. Mosaic, the "browser" software that would give the obscure Internet a visual, intuitive interface much as the Macintosh had done for computers, did not come into widespread notice until the summer of 1994. By then, The News and Observer was experimenting with multimedia packages and posting a 100,000-word multimedia record of a Nieman Foundation conference on the web, and things were changing fast.

In the fall of 1994, Daniels unveiled the Nando Times, an international news service updated around the clock. There were other news sources on the Internet, but this was the first service, including photos, available free on the web. The wire service stories came through the newsroom's SII system,

Figure 9.3

The News and Observer's print version.

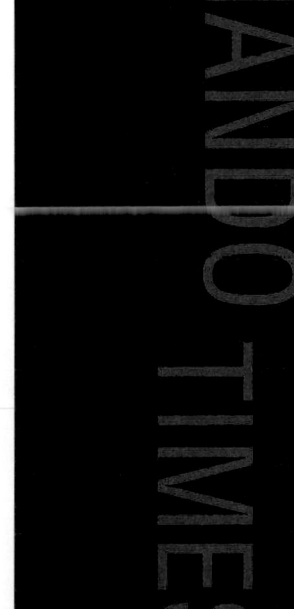

and some programming was done in SII so that a copy editor could select a story and, with just a few keystrokes, add it to the appropriate "page" of Nando Times. The editorial operations of the print newspaper and Nando Times used the same mainframe system and wire services, and some of the same personnel, but the two products were independent of each other. Nando Times still carries national and international news only.

Also in 1994, Nando launched a separate SportServer, with wire and freelance stories on every sport, amateur and professional, major and minor, posted around the clock.

In 1995, the Daniels family sold its newspaper business to McClatchy Newspapers of Sacramento, CA. Nando.net went from online offshoot of The News and Observer to online subsidiary of the McClatchy group. It continued producing Nando Times and SportServer and began developing new services. Nando got out of the low-margin business of providing Internet access for businesses and individuals, cutting the local ties that had started it as an online community.

Now separated from the non-local Nando Times, The News and Observer developed twin web services for its readers and the community it served, North Carolina and the Research Triangle area. In March 1996, working with Nando.net, the newspaper launched a daily web edition, The News & Observer on the web, and GO: The Triangle Guide On-line.

What will be included in the online edition?

The N&O on the web contains only state and local news, sports, business stories and editorials, and letters from the print edition. Rather than put its national and foreign stories online, the service complements the national and foreign news of Nando Times. Raleigh-area users of Nando Times get a locally zoned edition that includes a prominent link to the separate News and Observer front page, much like a national print paper distributed with a local news section insert.

The N&O web edition has stories, some photographs and graphics, and additional resources that supplement stories from the print edition: text of speeches, reports and court rulings, plus links to pertinent web resources for the benefit of readers who wish to explore a topic further. For many readers it functions as an added-value complement to the print edition, and of course it also serves readers not reached by the print edition (see Figure 9.4).

How will we use staff and technology to produce this edition?

It is produced by programs that take edited stories from the newsroom's Quark Publishing System (QPS) each night, strip the QPS formatting and convert each file into a format recognized by a Nando program that takes the stories and combines them into a daily online edition.

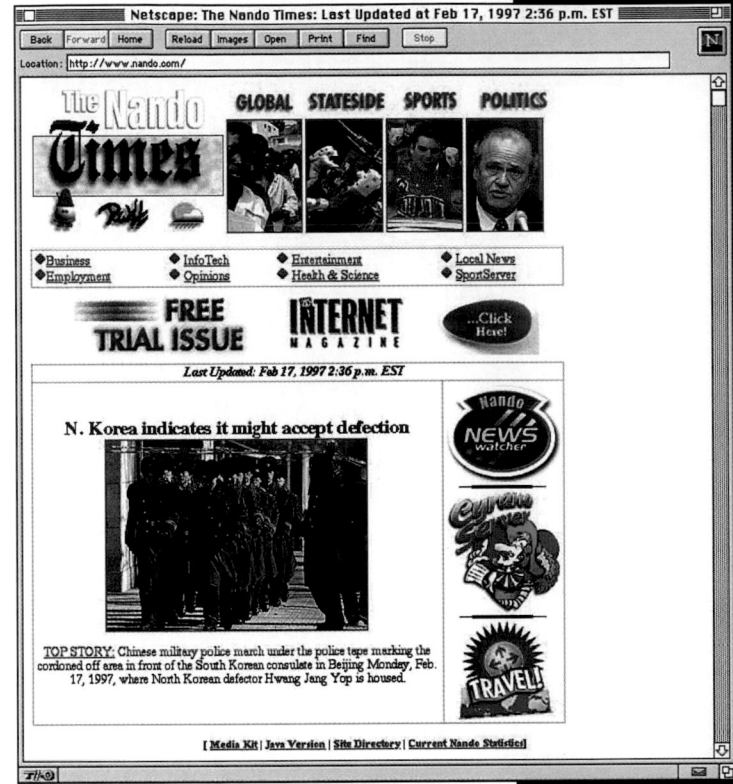

Figure 9.4

The Nando Times web site.

Reporters, editors, and other staffers are using the web to make new contact with their customers. A few dozen employees have personal web pages with links to their clips, and all newsroom employees can be contacted by email.

(This information contributed by Bruce Siceloff, editor of the News and Observer On-Line.)

MERCURY CENTER

Figure 9.5

The print version of the *San Jose Mercury News*.

Mercury Center, San Jose, California
(http://www.mercurycenter.com)

Unlike the thousands of other news web sites now in existence, when Mercury Center was first conceived there were no models. In fact, when the original thinking was underway in 1991 to create an online service, there was no web, let alone web browsers and web sites.

But, writes Mercury Center Managing Editor Bruce Koon, "there was truly visionary thinking at this time that recognized the emergence of new technologies that would impact on the way the public received its news and information. Thanks to the energy of Bob Ingle, who at that time was editor of the *San Jose Mercury News*, a blueprint to the future was first conceived with this mission: to create an experimental electronic service, integrated with the *San Jose Mercury News*, that will offer the public new paths to information, communication, advertising, and entertainment."

This mission intended to extend the life and preserve the franchise of the newspaper. Mercury-Center began its life not on the web but on America Online, launched in May, 1993. It was the world's first complete online newspaper service, offering not only the full text of the newspaper online but also the classified listings. In addition, Mercury Center offered three other services: NewsHound, a customized news service, the News Library, which offered a database of the published articles of the *San Jose Mercury News* and other newspapers, and News Call, an audiotext service.

The AOL site mirrored the structure of the newspaper in that the same subject categories—"information baskets"—were used: Front Page, World, Nation, Local & State, Business, Sports, Living, Entertainment, and Opinion. In addition, there were numerous other content areas that carried breaking news, supplemental news stories, and other information, bulletin boards, and chat areas.

The arrival of Mosaic and the World Wide Web changed the online opportunities tremendously, and Mercury Center was quick to capitalize. By taking the same basic structure created to feed Mercury News content to America Online and translating it to AOL's "Rainman" editing and input format,

Mercury Center's programmers substituted an HTML scripting program to translate Mercury News content to a web server. We were among the first to utilize this "shovelware" application.

Mercury Center on the web was launched in December 1994. The "home page" at that time included a news photograph, a Breaking News digest, and a link to the main menu page that you can still see at `http://www.sjmercury.com/today.htm` (see Figure 9.6). Again, the information basket structure mirrored the newspaper, although some new baskets such as Editor's Picks for web links and special web categories were beginning to emerge.

Throughout 1995, the pace of web development moved quickly, and it became obvious that we no longer needed to mirror the newspaper structure.

Indeed, as browsers became more sophisticated, we discovered we could design on the web. We were among the first sites to experiment with Netscape tables, for example.

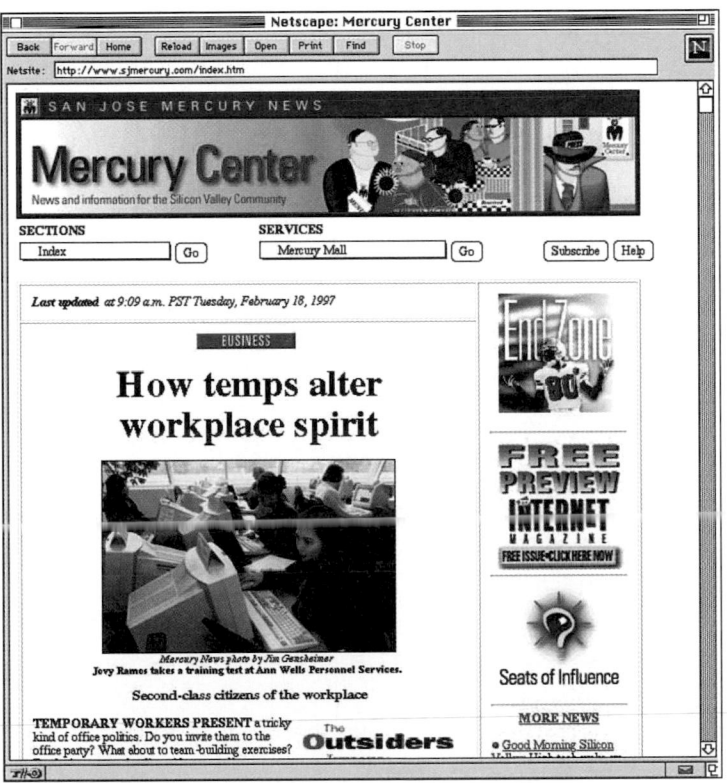

Figure 9.6

Mercury Center web site.

We began a redesign process that led to our current web site. In that design, we set out to accomplish several things:

▶ We wanted dynamic content at the top level. Too many web sites begin with a splash page that has no changing content. As a news site, we felt it important that information exist as quickly as possible. Even if you did not go deeper into the site, you could obtain significant information at this level.

▶ The top level also needed to be the navigation home for the site. Given that real estate was precious, this was a tricky proposition. We wanted to minimize the scroll down the page. At the time, our solution was the pull-down menu, an innovation that we helped popularize.

▶ We wanted our editors to have the ability to display news stories that they chose as the most compelling for our audience and package them as they would a printed newspaper: with photographs, graphics, sidebars, and so on. And rather than give them the printed newspaper's broad range of content, we wanted to narrow our focus to Silicon Valley, which was the natural audience for an online news service at that time. Mercury Center was to become the center of news and information for Silicon Valley. So we needed display space to highlight those stories that reflected this focus. This led to the use of tables to have a "centerpiece" story, an "off-lead" story, and the third cell. Editors were able to assign "weight" to a story by placement on the page.

▶ We wanted a column for advertisement and promotion. This would be an area dedicated to non-editorial features.

This new design was launched in December 1995. What evolved from this new direction was the creation of new, specialized subject areas separate from the newspaper. These can be considered "vertical niches" or "affinity areas" or "information baskets." These sites drew their content not only from the newspaper but from other sources. We began creating new designs to reflect their unique identities. We also began prioritizing the design needs by choosing either original design work or assigning a template.

Today, we are in the midst of our second redesign, one that will modernize the site to reflect the nonlinear structure of the web and the greater content on our site. The *San Jose Mercury News* newspaper, once the core of Mercury Center, remains an important ingredient, however, it is but one information basket. Now there are many others such as Good Morning Silicon Valley, our Sports sites, special news packages (Dark Alliance), and online features (see Figures 9.7 through 9.10).

Figure 9.7

Good Morning Silicon Valley is an additional featured page of the Mercury Center.

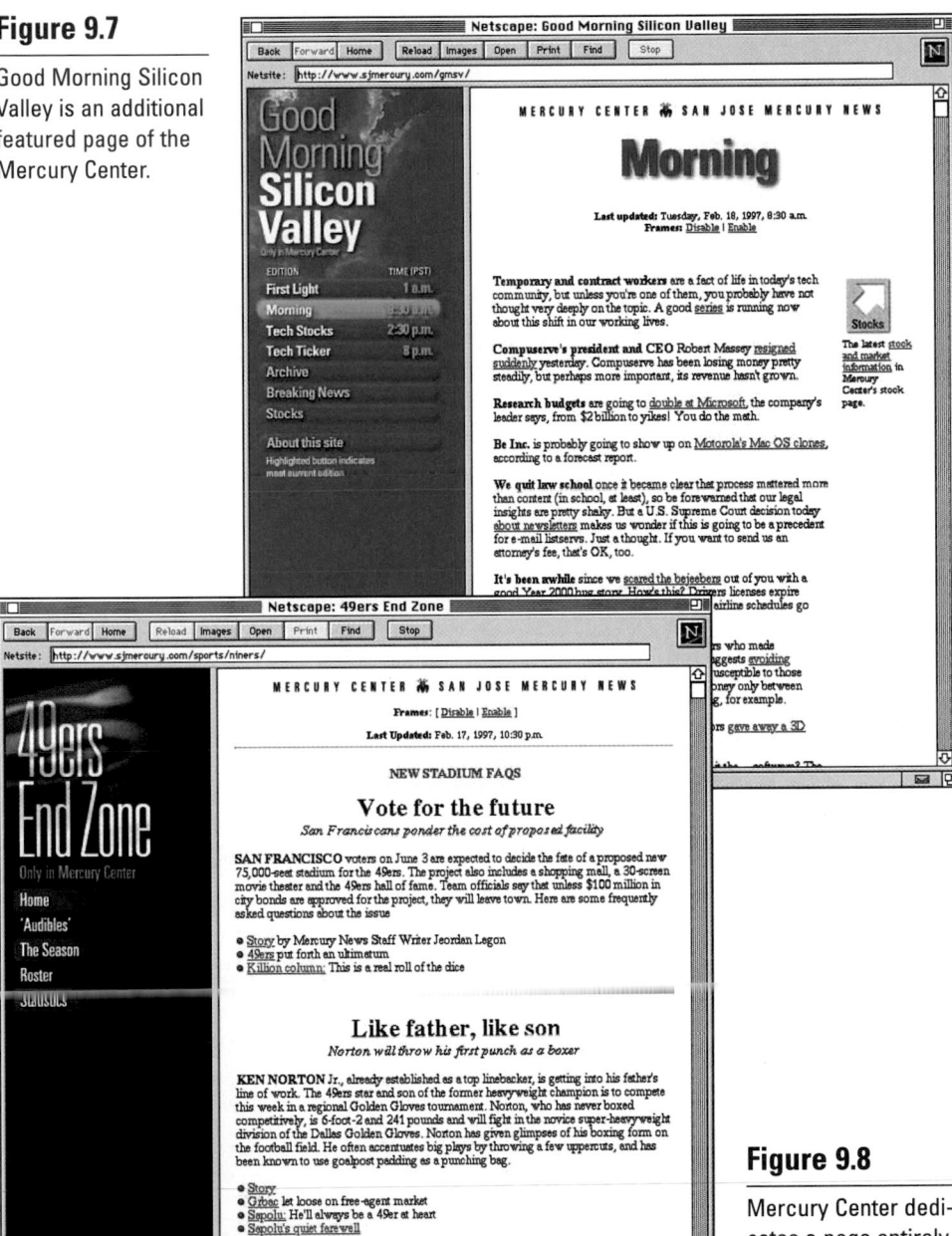

Figure 9.8

Mercury Center dedicates a page entirely to the San Francisco 49ers, the local professional football team.

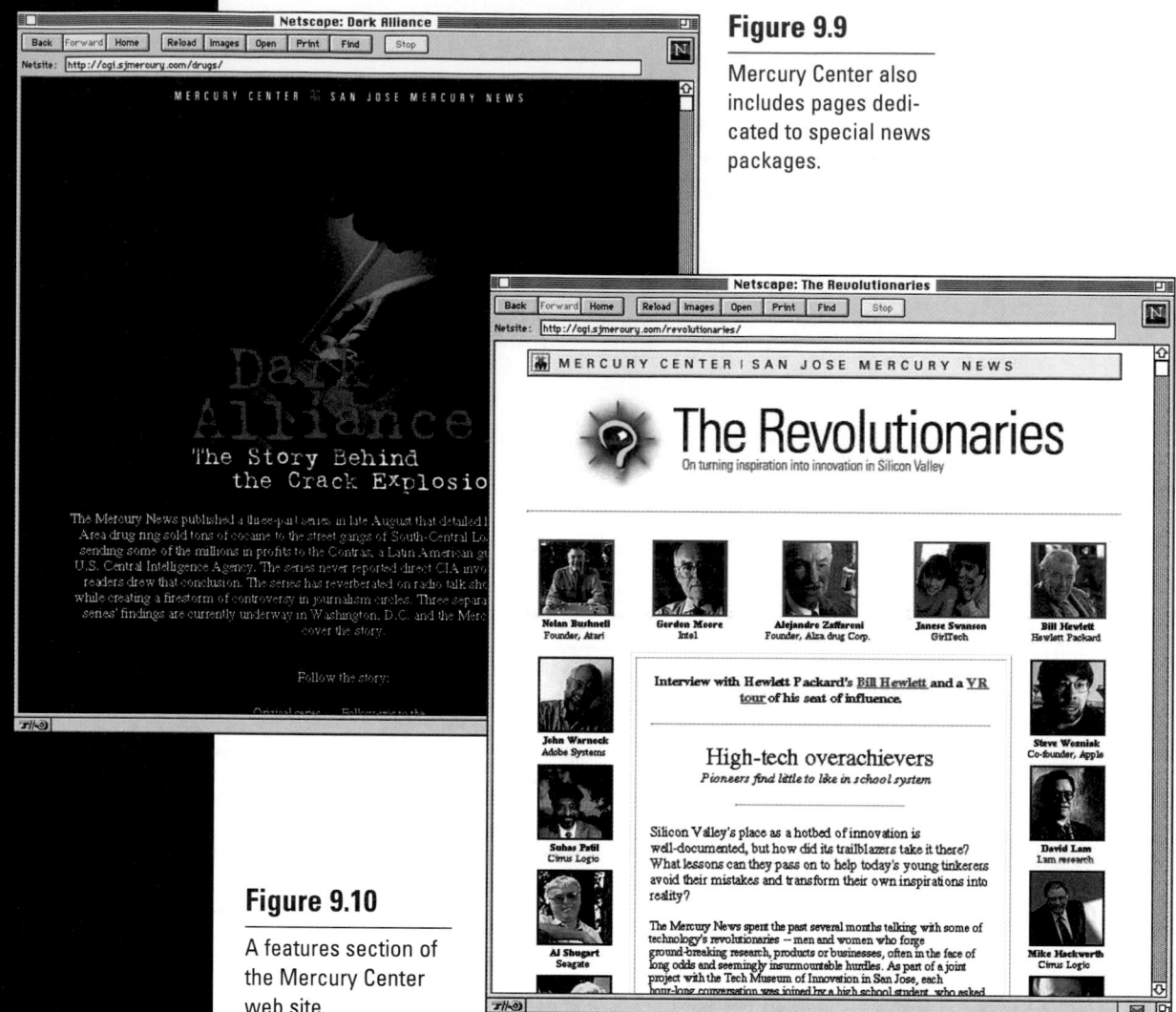

Figure 9.9

Mercury Center also includes pages dedicated to special news packages.

Figure 9.10

A features section of the Mercury Center web site.

What are the differences between the print and online editions?

At the Mercury Center, the online edition is more focused to serve a specialized audience. The Mercury Center's mission is that of serving the Silicon Valley community with news, information, and communication. We define Silicon Valley both as a geographic community—the people who live or work here—and a global "psychographic community"—people whose work or personal interests are strongly influenced by what happens here. Whether you are interested in technology or its effects on society, Mercury Center is the place to get the information you need and discuss it with the people who are making a difference.

Of course, what is of interest to Silicon Valley isn't just technology. Sports and entertainment are major components—and they are growing. But the online edition covers the local angles on these topics that others can't offer, concentrating on local sports teams and the local entertainment scene.

Finally, says Bruce Koon, "we can offer multimedia storytelling that the printed edition can't—audio, video—and interactive forums, databases and archives."

What is the continuing challenge?

Technology represents the greatest challenge, as the changes are taking place constantly, and thus the staff must be flexible enough to adapt quickly while maintaining an existing product. Bruce Koon relates, "Much of our design is on the fly as new innovations present new opportunities or make obsolete yesterday's assumptions. One example of this constant evolution is that the online news audience wants real-time news. We have to create design templates that permit us to report quickly as news breaks and our editors and producers need new skills to be able to offer web packages quickly."

ARID LANDS

Arid Lands Newsletter, University of Arizona (`http://ag.arizona.edu/OALS/ALN/ALNHome.html`)

The transfer from paper to screen of the international research magazine The Arid Lands Newsletter began not long after the web made its largely unremarked debut barely four years ago. In those dark days before Netscape Navigator, few people knew of the web or of the larger Internet. The exceptions were those within the community of scholars, scientists, and government grant makers (largely defense oriented) who needed a fast and reliable way to keep themselves in the information loop that led to project funding.

What were the challenges?

As Senior Editor at The University of Arizona's Office of Arid Lands Studies—a research-oriented outfit at a research-oriented public university, a double whammy that put teeth in the old "publish or perish" imperative—I was wrestling with the problem of a budget that was shrinking while demand for information arising from the office's work in the world's deserts and dry lands was growing. The problem was compounded by the magazine's long tradition of being mailed free of charge to subscribers, who were scattered across every continent but Antarctica. It was then that Michael Haseltine, a colleague in the Arid Lands Information Center, came to my rescue with the news that a promising new publishing medium was beginning to make ripples in the academic pond.

The move from analog to digital was incremental. The process began when I produced an experimental web version of an existing issue, "No. 35: The Deserts In Literature." The result was pretty primitive, featuring straight HTML with the addition of the controversial new "center" tag and a small GIF of the issue's paper cover (see Figure 9.11). The response was disproportionately encouraging. The selected readers I had invited to take a look at the experiment loved it. I immediately repurposed another print issue for the web ("No. 36: Desert Architecture III") and trumpeted the event to anyone who would listen. My colleagues and I also began to make plans to retire the paper version, together with its high production and mailing costs.

With No. 37 ("Conserving Biodiversity") we took a giant leap forward in the form of one small step: I advised the issue's freelance designer that the magazine would be published on the web shortly after its appearance in print. Although my announcement had little impact on design of the paper-and-ink artifact, it helped all of us involved in the project to begin to really think digitally—and ensured that every scrap of the issue was preserved on disk, to speed conversion to HTML and GIFs. The new experiment worked nicely and was as well received as the first. We committed ourselves to moving the magazine to the Internet.

How was the team assembled?

Our next step was to bring Merrill Parsons, who had designed information not only for print and CD-ROM but also for museum displays, on board as Art Director. The new team, with the enthusiastic support and participation of Information Center Director Barbara Hutchinson, published No. 38 ("The Whole Wired World") simultaneously in print and onscreen (see Figure 9.12). The design of both versions changed radically. The print version, the editorial content of which was intended to alert readers to the coming change and to help make them feel more at home on the web, echoed the look of a web publication, complete with "hot links" to information available elsewhere in the global electronic library. The digital version was the first designed especially for the screen. We hadn't yet come fully to terms with the new medium—although we had added an invisible table and a background color tag, the illustration was still adapted from the print cover. But we had made considerable progress in the space of just four issues (a sort of land speed record in the staid academic world).

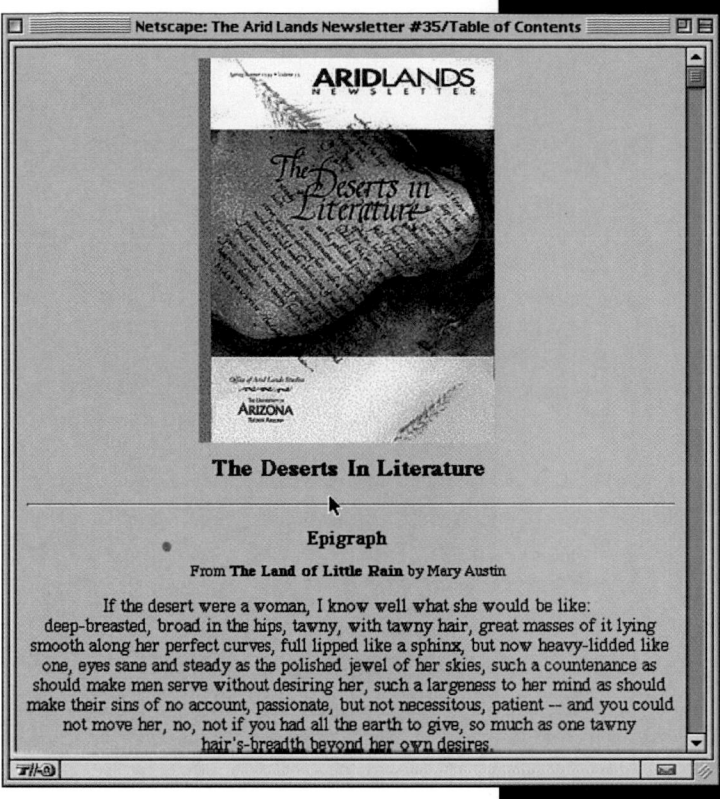

Figure 9.11

Arid Lands Newsletter web site, No. 35.

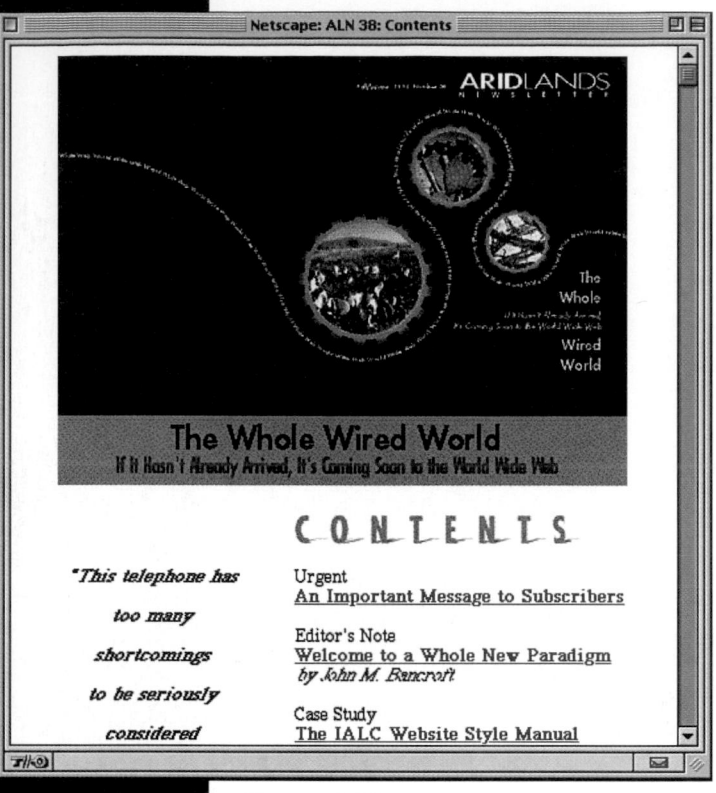

Figure 9.12

The digital version of No. 38 ("The Whole Wired World").

No. 39 ("Borders") was the first issue published exclusively online (see Figure 9.13). The digital Arid Lands Newsletter had arrived—at which point I departed to devote myself entirely to developing for the web as proprietor of my own virtual company, leaving my successor, Katherine Waser, to do the hard work of simultaneously editing a high-profile magazine and staying current with a tsunami of technological change. One of her first coups was to extend the reach of the web version by publishing a text-only edition via an email list server for those former print subscribers with more limited Internet access. And she soon will bring the story full circle by publishing a photocopied abstract of each issue for the small number (we think) of former subscribers with no Internet access at all.

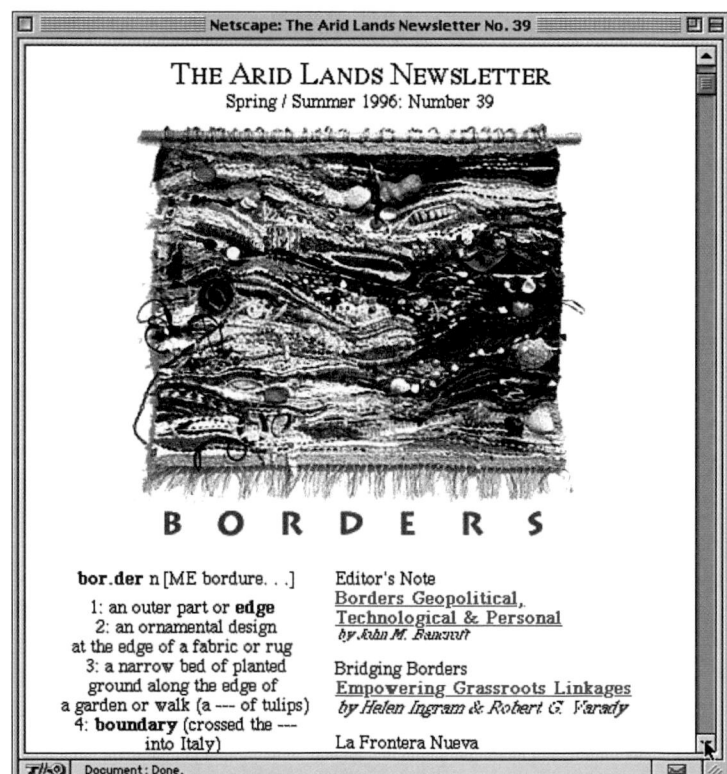

Figure 9.13

The first issue of the Arid Lands Newsletter published exclusively online.

What was the reader feedback?

Reader response has continued to be overwhelmingly positive. They've told us, via the comment forms and "mailtos" in each online issue, that they especially like reducing the volume of paper stored on sagging office bookshelves, the instant links to ancillary information elsewhere on the Internet, and the editor's newfound ability to update articles in real time as new data or sources come to light, without waiting for a new edition to be printed and mailed. (It took the print magazine as long as two months to reach some out-of-the-way international addresses.)

Response within the Office of Arid Lands Studies has been just as enthusiastic. Haseltine and his colleagues in the Information Center are developing an elaborate interlocking web with the ambitious goal of cataloging and linking all electronic resources related to the world's spreading dry lands, as well as repurposing both the wealth of information generated by the Office and that from other sources stored in its tightly focused print collections. Office Director Kennith Foster, who saw the potential in web publishing from the start, has enlisted the Information Center digerati to bring online, too, The International Arid Lands Consortium and The New Uses Council. Students in the university's interdisciplinary Arid Lands Resource Sciences doctoral program, whose research regularly carries them to Latin America, Africa, Asia, and the Middle East, have found in the Office's growing web and associated technology a great way to stay in touch, no matter where they are.

The bottom line? A radical change in publishing philosophy and technique spurred by the hard necessity of cutting costs has ushered in a new age of freely shared information and collaboration on a global scale. I doubt that my former colleagues, having thrown themselves wholeheartedly into the fray, would have it any other way—at least, not now.

Figure 9.14

The *Star Tribune* print edition.

The Star Tribune, Minneapolis, Minnesota (http://www.startribune.com)

In the fall of 1994, the *Star Tribune* began assembling a team to build an online edition of the newspaper. Most of the editors and managers hired for the new venture had solid backgrounds in newspapering. These editors, however, started their planning by largely abandoning the newspaper metaphor. They decided to concentrate, instead, on content that was not in the newspaper. Most importantly, things interactive were top on their planning agenda.

So armed with a group of about ten editors, several developers, some management people, and a designer, http://www.startribune.com was launched, although not before the designer completed what he describes as "some 600 prototypes until we hit upon a composite of the best ideas for the one site we launched."

How was the site initially launched in June 1995?

The *Star Tribune* site emphasizes organization above all by taking the important newspaper categories and combining them with a section called TALK. The planning editors went through tremendous selecting and shifting of content to find common elements of interest. Such individual sections of the printed edition as motoring, books, and travel, for example, could all coexist in one of the most popular and attractive offerings of this site, VARIETY—the lively and easy to follow magazine-oriented section.

Next came the creation of links that enabled users to go beyond the stories as reprinted from the newspaper edition. In a story related to AIDS, for example, the site would offer an icon system to get links and/or contacts providing additional information on other pages or sites, such as the Center for Disease Control. Likewise, stories about state and local government would link up to the offices of the mayor or the governor when available. Taking the user beyond the actual text became one of the Star Tribune online team's top priorities. And they have succeed, as the site receives more than 650,000 hits a day (see Figure 9.15).

Figure 9.15

Star Tribune Online.

How do we structure the editorial system?

At the *Star Tribune*, a liaison editor is stationed in the newsroom, providing the first line of communication with editors of the printed edition, attending all editorial meetings, and networking by letting newsroom people know that the online staff exists. This liaison online editor also queries about things that are coming, including interesting photographic assignments in the making, to see what would translate nicely to the online edition.

As a result, there is good communication between editors in the print and online editions. Editors of the print edition are aware of the online editors, giving them special instructions, such as, "This story is not to go online until such date," or, "We have inserted a specific element for online only."

The Star Tribune uses an Atex system in the newsroom, and all of its material goes into a database. A customized system enables editors to go through a directory to select stories. This is also helpful in creating hierarchy for topics. Although chances are that the positioning of stories online follows

Figure 9.16

Star Tribune Online offers a multi-topic VARIETY section on its site.

pretty closely that of the print edition, it is not necessarily so. Capable online editors look at stories individually and decide whether they will be used at all, then where and how.

How do we approach VARIETY—a special section?

VARIETY, the multi-topic section, and one of the best aspects of this site, was hard to put together as it suffers the most from collapsing a lot of sections that seem quasi-related to entertainment and leisure. This section becomes user-friendly by emphasizing links— such as to a section on books, or cars, while also listing films, concerts, and events of interest (see Figure 9.16).

What was the main information design challenge?

The challenge at the Star Tribune is to convey to users how the different baskets of information are organized and to facilitate navigation to what continues to be a growing site. To the designer, the challenge is where to put things. And, more importantly, how to label things properly so users will know where to look for them.

How do we handle photos?

Photos play a key role in the Star Tribune online site. One of the most successful examples was an AIDS PROJECT, an exclusive investigative report published over six years that the online staff was able to tie together and provide as a coherent unit to their users. The photographer, Brian Peterson, played a key role, talking to the online editors, offering all of his photos, as well as audio cassettes of interviews with his subject. The report involved a photo essay that enabled the photographer to watch the demise of a rural Minnesota family who had been affected by AIDS (see Figure 9.17). Peterson provided the online editors everything he had and processed the photos specifically for the online edition, selecting some that had not appeared in print.

How did the online version of project succeed over the print version? Perhaps by providing the users the ability to see what was a six-year project, with the obvious gaps of time in between, in its entirety. The user could also see the flow of the narrative and the photos, uninterrupted for anyone who wanted to sit and read the entire essay in one seating.

The result? "People sat at the keyboards and cried," explains online designer Jamie Hutt, who reads all of the email that comes to the site. More importantly, he says, this was a good example of how newsrooms can extend themselves, and the result is magic.

As one user put it in her email to the Star Tribune: "I never have been moved by something on the web before…but I cried."

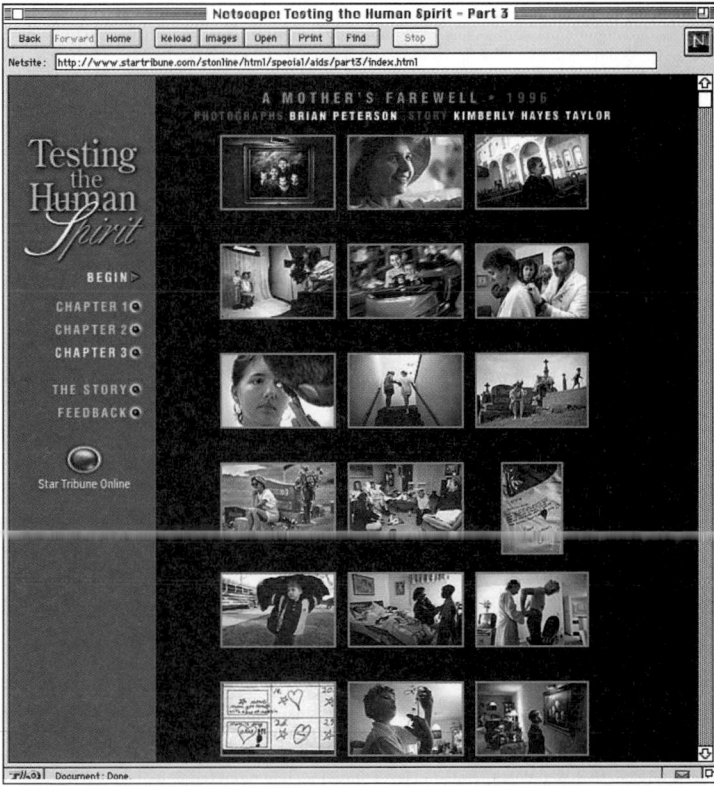

Figure 9.17

A photo essay about a family coping with AIDS is an example of the key role photos play in the Star Tribune Online site.

Figure 9.18

The Arizona Republic print edition.

Phoenix Newspapers, Phoenix, Arizona (`http://www.pni.com`)

When Phoenix Newspapers executive editor John Oppedahl wanted to start preparing the way for the company to explore new ways of information delivery in 1994, he called on Howard Finberg, who had spent his entire 25-year career as a traditional newspaperman—as a reporter, copy editor, graphics editor, assistant managing editor. "It was a very interesting and exciting transition," Finberg says.

"For a long time I had been worried that newspapers were going to lose out if they didn't find new ways to offer information. We don't know if that means special sections, special magazines, information via the fax, via the phone, or information via online. But Phoenix Newspapers wanted to find out. We already had some experiments underway. We had an audio system, which generated about 5 million calls a year; we started working with the delivery of fax information to readers and special groups, and we had a "BBS" or bulletin board computer system for the delivery of information about homes for sale.

"However, we also wanted to explore offering a complete online service to our readers. Yet, I knew there was a difference. And the more I learned about online, the more I realized that there is a big difference.

"In the early days of television, actors would stand in front of the camera and read things, much like radio. In the early days of radio, people would read things from a newspaper. I was afraid that if we used that approach—applied the lessons from one medium onto another—we would fail. Online is a different medium. It is part broadcast; it is part print. More important, however, it is different from its ancestors," explains Finberg.

So Finberg and his team decided that while they could "dump" their newspaper information online, that wouldn't serve customers or the company very well. Instead, says Finberg, they took a hard look at two issues:

▶ What means of delivery should we use? Should we partner with a commercial service?

▶ What kind of information should we deliver?

The answer—at least our answer—to the first question evolved into something Finberg refers to as the "digital newsstand" approach. "We want to provide information to our readers as easily as it is to get the newspaper today. You can get home delivery, you can get it at the grocery store, you can buy it from a coin box on the corner. It is the customer's choice."

That's why the Phoenix Newspapers offer customers two ways to get information from The Arizona Republic (Phoenix Newspapers)—one via America Online and the second via the web.

When it came to organizing information baskets, deciding what to take from the newspaper editions, and what to add as extra baskets, the team in charge of conceptualizing the site for Phoenix Newspapers decided to be innovative, while satisfying the needs of customers. The Arizona Republic's best coverage is that of Arizona and that means everything that makes Arizona interesting—from golf to travel to eating out to local news and politics. "We decided to focus on doing what we do best and developing very deep (that is, complete) niche topic areas," explains Finberg.

"Once we decided 'how' and 'what' to do, we needed to decide 'who.' We have one major advantage over competitors in the online arena—the talent and skills of our journalists. We reached into our newsroom and developed our staff and managers from that group, but we found people with two very important traits. The ability to think outside the 'box'— this wasn't putting out a newspaper, this is a new medium— and a willingness to try new things, to take risks. Once you find those people, you give them the tools, the direction, and get out of their way."

The Phoenix Newspapers web site is not only attractive and easy to use, but it is also quite successful (see Figure 9.19). More importantly, at a time when the commercial side of online services, and especially profit-making among newspaper sites, is a topic of constant discussion, in Phoenix, the group is starting to bring revenue to the company, with the expectation of profit in the very near term, according to Finberg.

PHOENIX
NEWSPAPERS

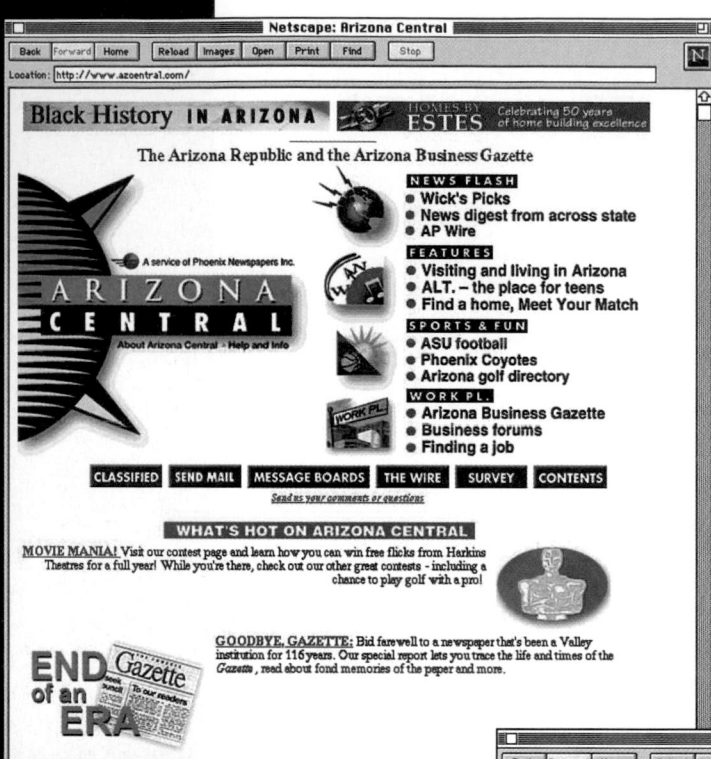

Finberg says that many of his colleagues in newspapers ask him if they (the staff of the newspapers) have changed direction? "Yes," he answers, "but we haven't changed the major destination: deliver accurate and compelling information to our customers."

The Phoenix Newspapers web site treats most information very differently from that which appears in print. The organization of information, especially features, is similar in structure to that of the print products, and columns are labeled as opinion and not news/facts (see Figure 9.20).

Figure 9.19

Arizona Central, the Phoenix Newspapers' web site.

Figure 9.20

Arizona Central's web site organizes feature sections very similarly to the print edition.

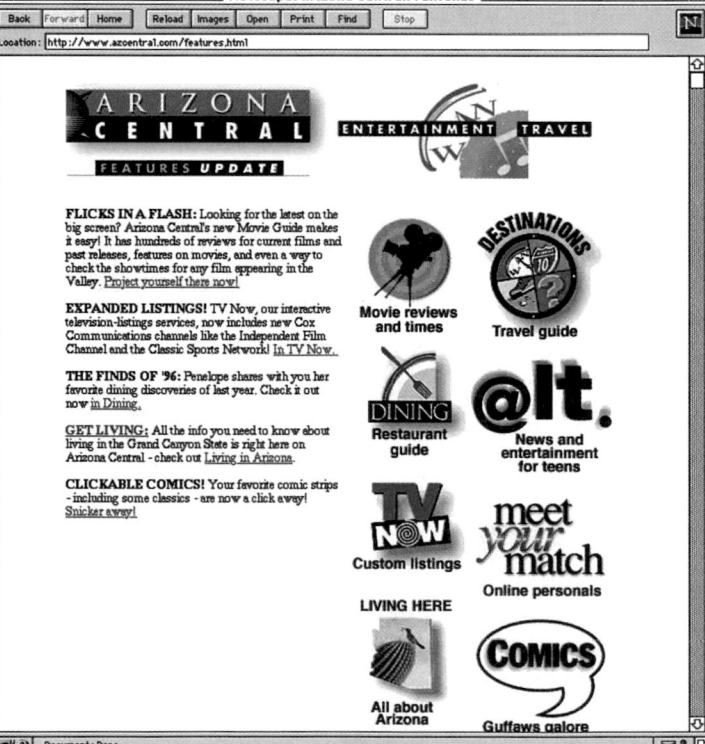

How is the print publication model different from the site?

Everything is different, says Finberg, the pace, the look, the design. You can't bring much from the print world. "We don't have 'above the fold' discussions; we have 'screen/scroll' discussions. We wanted to make sure that the look was always in front of the customer and that there would be little scrolling on the main pages."

And the greatest challenge for a traditional newspaper group to move online?

"The main challenge is understanding this is a new medium. And that it is not a newspaper, even if it is inspired by one," Howard Finberg says.

How will information be routed to the site?

There are two ways for information to come into Arizona Central. One is the "repurposing" method, in which story text is collected from the "filmed" or output directories/baskets of the newspaper's production system. This material is reformatted and organized for presentation on the web and in the site's AOL area. The second method involves the creation of original material. In this case, material is created on both the "front-end" system and via personal computers; it then goes through the online department editors before being sent to the web or AOL.

The editors of this site hope to automate both processes so that more time can be used in the creation and editing of material. The use of this "media server" will greatly speed up the process and handle all file and delivery methods—web, AOL, audio, fax, and broadcast.

What is our user profile?

From research conducted by the marketing department, the company determined that users of the Phoenix Newspapers Online are slightly more male than female, ranging from 35–50 years of age, and generally use the computer at work more than at home.

ROANOKE TIMES

The Roanoke Times, Roanoke, Virginia (http://www.roanoke.com)

The following are not questions, but the main design principles *The Roanoke Times* in Roanoke, Virginia, established at the outset of their online project.

We are not an electronic version of another medium.

Before we established our design principles, two chapters were circulated from "The Fifties" by David Halberstam. One chapter dealt with Milton Berle and the infancy of television. It recounted his roman candle career—rising to fame because he understood the new medium and falling soon after because he didn't grasp the change television underwent as it penetrated the heartland. The other chapter told the story of E.J. Korvettes, the first discount retail chain. The man who built it was the son of a retailer. In order to succeed, he had to willfully ignore everything his father had ever told him.

It was soon after that we decided it didn't make any sense to place the existing newspaper, *The Roanoke Times*, online by itself. Instead, we would build a community-based web site around the newspaper. We would use the extensive data and talent from the newspaper in new ways. Our medium would assume a new voice—we would not be one voice of authority (the newspaper) speaking to many consumers. We would be many voices of interest speaking to many partners within a community. Bill Warren, who was in charge of our site development, deliberately kept these early meetings small and intimate. Each included Jim Ellison, online editor, and David Poteet, owner of New City Media, who we contracted to be our designers.

Our design will have a defining logic that our users will grasp quickly and with which they can remain comfortable.

Because we decided to build a large site around the newspaper, we now had to deal with where to put all the stuff. We began a process of structuring and restructuring the content labeling and location. This continued until "content lock-down," a mutually agreed upon date (five weeks before light-up) with New City Media after which they could confidently finish designing our pages. It was a process of drawing and redrawing grids on paper. As our small circle grew, new voices and new information became available to us. The grids evolved daily until our organizational logic began to unfold. We ended up with a gateway page that displays twelve sub-sites, one of which is the Roanoke Times. Within those sub-sites there are hundreds of choices.

It was at this point that we made our most difficult design decision. It boils down to clicks versus scrolls. We went with the scroll. We decided to have screens with multiple choices, therefore requiring users to drill down, but we get our users where they want to be within three clicks. It is a decision I have alternately regretted and applauded since we made it.

We designed with our users in mind.

We feel our growth will come from users with a mid-range of Internet skills. High-end users don't need us to navigate or organize the web. Low-end users will come online when they are forced to. Because we also sell access, many of our users will see Roanoke.com the first time they go online.

For us, this means that fear and frustration are two design problems. So, we set what we call the "intimidation bar" for our gateway and subsites. The bar determines the level of navigation skills required to use the site. It is set low, for instance, for our community forum and higher for our games site. We'll adjust the bars as we feel the sophistication of our audience changes.

In general, Roanoke.com employs a simple, conventional grid. At this writing, we are trying to establish a type style that will predictably behave on any screen.

Our design will respect our users' time. This means our graphics will be functional.

To reach the broadest audience possible, we designed the site for optimal display on a 640×480 pixel screen and fast trans-mission over a 28.8 bps modem.

ROANOKE TIMES

Users will know when—and where—they are on our web site. They will know what kinds of information they are being presented.

The Roanoke.com logo appears on every page for which we are responsible, thereby reinforcing our brand throughout the publication. Advertising appears in defined spaces.

Art, graphics, and photography will be unique to our web site.

We cannot afford to be generic. If we can download clip-art off a CD-ROM, so can a teenager working at home. We were forced to spend freelance money on local art. The pay-off is a site that looks like southwest Virginia (see Figure 9.21).

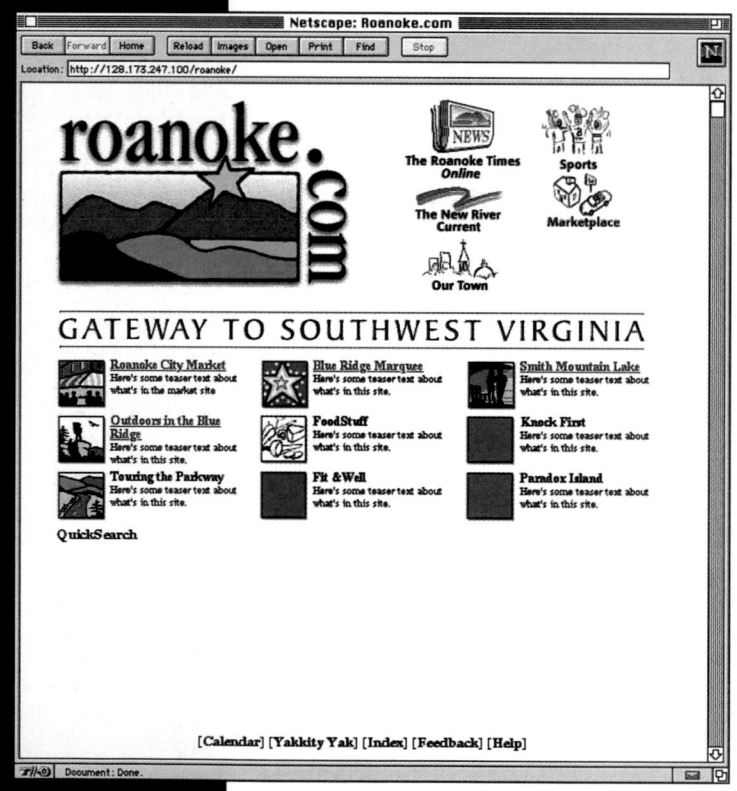

Figure 9.21

Roanoke.com, still under construction at the time of publication.

We will have our own voice.

If we are the host for "many speaking to many," we need help making sense of it all. We hired twelve "site hosts" to do that. The job description is part radio DJ, part print columnist, part master of ceremonies, part librarian.

If I were to characterize the sensibility of the web right now, it would be that you can't see many people there. The institutional voices are, well, institutional. Much of the personal expression is introverted, if not anti-social. I think this is going to change, much like television changed on Berle.

Our site hosts were chosen because they are interesting people who like people. It is a coincidence that many of them have radio experience. As of this writing we are beginning to define just what it is they will produce.

CNN, Atlanta, Georgia (`http://www.cnn.com`)

If going from print to web requires abandoning the newspaper metaphor, then making the transition from a broadcast edition to web is a totally different situation. At CNN, the creation of cnn.com began with the first live edition in the summer of 1995. Unlike the newspaper, where the various sections, from opinion to local to sports, lead to the order of what will appear on the home page, those in charge of the CNN online edition had to wrestle with a tough question:

Do we build the site based on "shows" or develop it around subject areas?

According to Jeff Garrard, executive producer of CNN online, the creators of the site knew from the beginning that they were not doing television, and they were not going to mimic TV as they built the site.

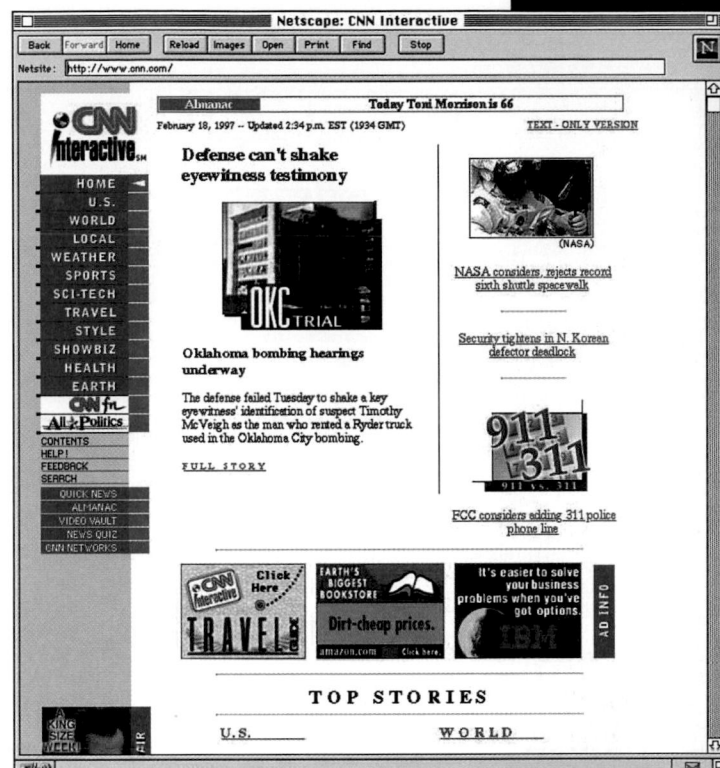

Figure 9.22

The web site for CNN Interactive.

"But we all came from television. Our backgrounds have been as writers, directors, and producers on television shows, so we were predisposed to using images along with the text," Garrard says.

The next most important criteria for the creation team was to make their site as accessible as possible. Speed, they say, was the key, which meant keeping things simple. The team that created the site was composed of editorial, art/design, and technical staffers. Several prototype versions of the site were created before a final one was chosen. That one, which went live, was soon redesigned. In the world of television, redesigning is part of the routine.

"Nothing is edged in granite in television," says Garrard, "so we feel free to experiment with our site, and to change it and to improve it all the time."

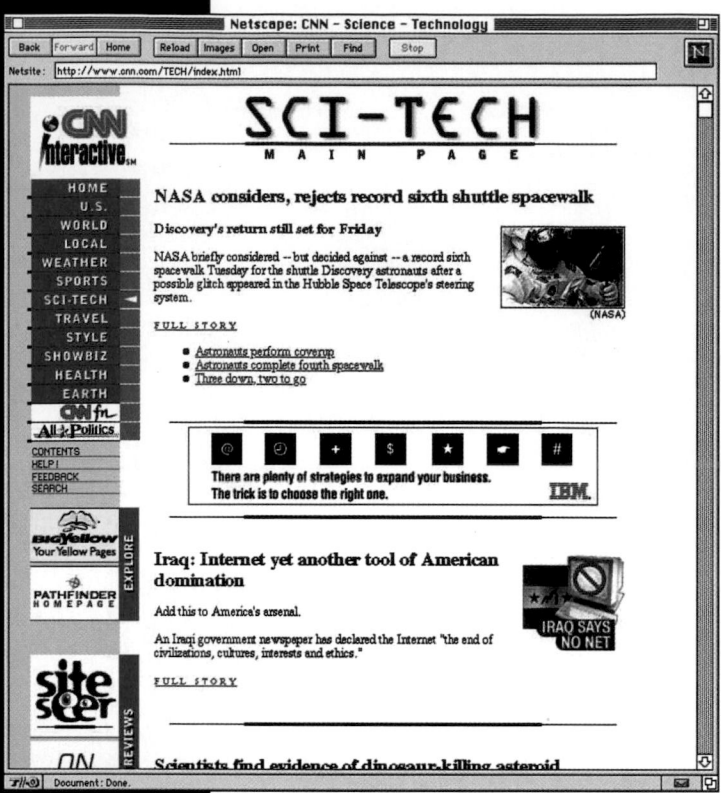

Figure 9.23

CNN Interactive's Science and Technology page.

When cnn.com first appeared, it included subjects that are covered by CNN but not titled according to shows. The creating team decided that the weather would play a key role, as it is constantly updated, but so would news, which is the essence of CNN. The way the system operates, the cnn.com edition benefits from the information available from CNN's 29 bureaus around the world. The news can be updated as it happens, and it is possible for the online edition to include a news item before it appears on the broadcast edition. Scoops, as such, are possible. At the same time, one important basket of information for the online edition is that involving science and technology (see Figure 9.23). This especially applies to stories about the Internet and computer news, which users of the online edition may be particularly interested in.

For the most part, the staff of cnn.com feels that online editions may be closer to print products than to television. They claim, for example, that material to be presented on news broadcasts on television do not require the proper editing and spelling checks that material for the web does. In television the material is read by commentators and reporters, while on the web, it is the users who become the readers.

How do we integrate the copy editor and video?

Copy editors have been hired to watch carefully over all texts, and writers are in demand to prepare text for the online edition. At the same time, at cnn.com these traditional print types combine with television producers who understand that the new medium, although resembling print in so many ways, benefits from and, in a sense, demands the dynamics of television.

Integrating video into the online edition is important to those at cnn.com.

"We think that video will give us options. We will see this as interactive television," says Garrard. "For example, if someone missed our Larry King Show because he was watching something else, he can pick up highlights on our editions the next morning. This enables us to make more of the material, by making it more accessible to more people all the time."

What cnn.com does, knowing the limitations of some users in incorporating video into their sampling of the site, is to provide boxes promoting the availability of video for selected stories, and explaining things such as length (28 seconds), but leaving the decision to the user in any case. To prepare video for online continues to be an involved operation. It may take 30 minutes to make a 30-second clip. Still, at cnn.com, any time good video is available, it is used.

In addition, sound files are used to enhance content. Especially with interview shows, many users like the idea of listening to the actual responses given, and these are available for most stories.

Sound, video, and the latest news updated all the time—these are the characteristics that make cnn.com successful and that invite hundreds of users to email the site daily.

ADDRESSING THE ONLINE PRODUCT

Figure 9.24

The *Göteborgs-Posten*
print edition.

Addressing the Online Product During a Newspaper Redesign

While I was redesigning the Göteborgs–Posten, *one of Sweden's largest daily circulation newspapers, there was no online edition yet. By the time I returned for my first follow-up visit in 1996, the newspaper had published its first electronic edition, with much success.*

The site was designed to emulate the newspaper edition quite closely, and its original design included a wallpapering effect in yellow with the words Göteborgs-Posten repeated several times. In addition, many points of entry appeared on the home page, plus advertising, and even house ads. The users liked it, however, and there was no urgency to change the design.

It was in the second half of 1996 that the newspaper's publisher, Peter Hjorne Jr. asked me to take a look at the design of the G-P online edition. I did and immediately recommended several changes that would not dramatically alter the look of the site, but would enhance it visually:

▶ *Get rid of the wallpaper effect—go with a white background.*

▶ *Develop a system of icons to organize the enormous amount of content and make movement around the screen easier.*

▶ *Redesign the logo to include the letters G-P, as well as a photograph of a lighthouse, a trademark of the newspaper, in which readers constantly send photos of their favorite lighthouses around the Göteborg area.*

Each of these case studies reflects a point of view, a style, and the important fact that each site should accommodate the interests of its users. Notice that all of these cases do have several things in common:

- ▶ The newspaper metaphor dominates the thinking in terms of content, coverage, and organization. This shall change as more information designers begin their careers at web sites and relate less to a print medium in their creation of web sites.

- ▶ Home pages offer a variety of options and navigational techniques, but all emphasize content hierarchy, a strong logotype presence, and a color signature.

- ▶ Typographically, there is little experimentation at this point, although some of the designers have created interesting logos to compensate for what may be almost no variety in the styles of type used for headlines and texts.

- ▶ Emphasis seems to be on how to facilitate access to content— enabling users to get to the information with as few links as possible.

- ▶ Identity is important to each of the sites presented here. Each uses color, type, white space, and illustrations to stand apart visually from other sites.

These constitute "pioneers" in the translating of print matter to the new medium. Five years from today, these trailblazers will look different, less like newspapers or magazines, as they conquer their own identities and establish themselves as what we all would come to identify as web sites.

Chapter 10

A Symphony of Movement

Open the web site for the French version of *Elle* magazine, and a combination of pastel colors, images of beautiful models, and bold, inventive typography all grab the user's attention. Also, one's eyes cannot avoid the constantly pulsating messages above the logo of *Elle* that pull us by our ties, or scarves, or whatever (see Figure 10.1).

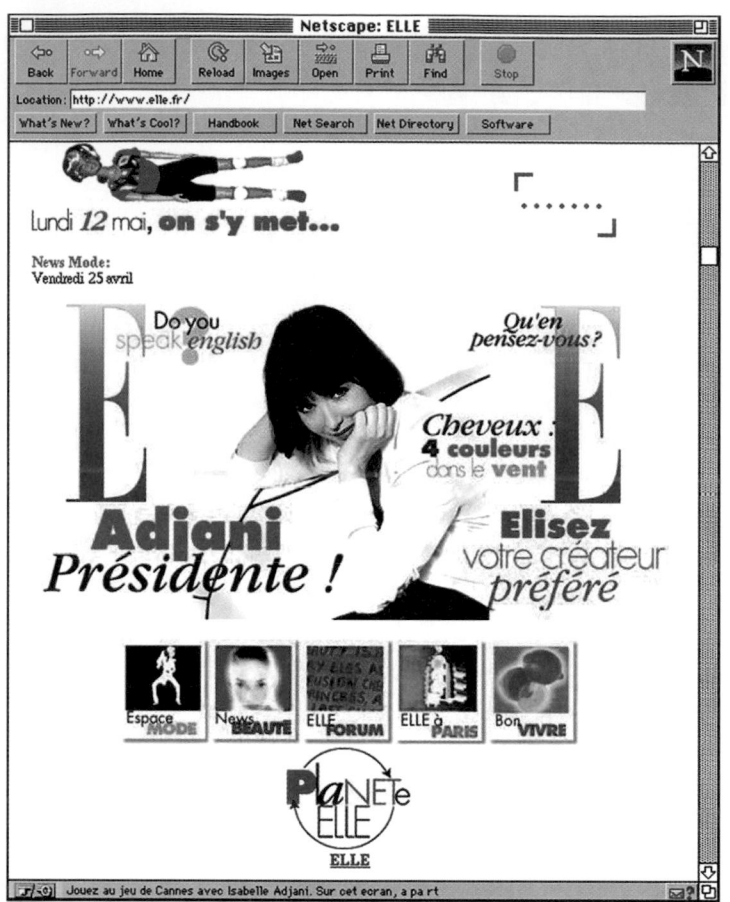

Figure 10.1

Elle magazine's site, `http://www.elle.fr`.

For the *Göteborgs-Posten's* web site G-P, a number of icons lead us to the different information baskets. One word rolls up and down the screen, to alert us to the section Attityd, the young user's own basket (see Figure 10.2.)

In both cases, a symphony of movement has been created. The screen is a combination of layers—some visual, some even more visual—with the effects of animation. And, of course, one enters the site of *El Pais* of Montevideo, Uruguay, as the sounds of the famous tango "La Comparsita" entertain our ears with the tah-rah-tah-tah-tah that tango dancers have stepped to for almost a century (see Figure 10.3).

Figure 10.2

The Göteborgs-Posten's site, `http://www.G-P.se`.

Figure 10.3

El Pais' site, http://www.elpais.com.

station by giving us specific access to how the station works, how those men and women who live in space go about their daily routines while suspended. We emerge from the story with greater understanding.

It is here that one of the most dramatic differences exists between the traditional print product and its online equivalent.

When everything fails in a discussion involving print executives who are contemplating the benefits of going online with their product, there is a surefire way to show how dynamic the new medium of online publications can be: animation.

Seeing such things as arrows moving on the screen indicating the direction of an object, or the silhouette of an Olympic runner as she gets to the finish line, or even the more textbook-oriented rendition of how a part of the body functions, takes the user beyond the mere visual interpretations that we have grown accustomed to through informational graphics in newspapers and magazines. Suddenly our visual awareness combines with a quicker understanding of the material, and our excitement grows. Animation makes the process of receiving information pure fun.

You may read a tremendously informative article about prostate surgery in a men's health magazine, but the online

In all of these examples, animation and sound are the extra layers that appeal to our senses.

In its most basic form, animation may be just a flashing symbol on the screen. Just as three-dimensionality has traditionally added to our visual understanding and enjoyment of illustrations and informational graphics, animation adds a special quality to how the information is conveyed. Animated symbols, graphics, and other elements command our attention, and hold it, as well.

More functional examples of animation are to be found, specifically, in informational graphics. Arrows move to indicate a car chase, or to point how a specific surgical procedure is carried out. In feature web sites, animation could make us see the feet of a dancer tap, or the lips of a singer move, adding to our understanding and enjoyment of the content. Good animations enhance a story about the fixing of a space version takes us beyond, inside, and outside the procedure and the physiology, to let us gain greater understanding.

But can animation be too much of a good thing? Is there a limit to how much animated (or sound) fun one can have on a web site, while still getting the information quickly and effectively? If the new media is a field in its infancy, and thus full of questions for which few scientific answers exist, then the specifics of animation are even more at the early stages of development, and usefulness.

The Role of Animation

Animated graphics are eye-catchers. Many web sites today use animation for advertisements or to highlight elements on a web page that the designers want to make stand out from the rest of the content. Often, moving objects on the page will visually overpower an even larger image. Take, for example, a news home page in which the center of visual impact is a news photo of the day, large enough to constitute the first point of entry. At the bottom of the screen, however, the icon of a fish jumps at us, to advertise a fish market or restaurant. In terms of hierarchy, the photo is much larger than the icon, but the pulsating effect of animation lures the eye. Instantly, we have a problem of visual priorities unique to online design.

Careful Composition

The designer must be very careful to make sure that hierarchy in terms of content is not lost to the "visual noise"

that an unnecessary, or too insistent, animation may cause. Designers who utilize animated elements on their screens must always be aware of how powerful those can be, and that often animated elements will draw attention from the centerpiece or center of visual impact onscreen.

Good animated graphics contribute to and enhance the information within a story, supporting it and enabling the user to gain greater understanding of how a plane crashed, or how fast a track star ran, or the distance from Earth to Mars. Pulsating for the sake of pulsating, the annoying flashing of one word, such as found so often today, indeed falls closer to the category of visual noise.

Like informational graphics in print, animation elements should only be used if they serve a purpose. Simply making something jump up and down onscreen, because it can be done, is not a good reason to do it. In the early days of informational graphics in newspapers, during that famous boom of the super graphics in the 1980s, editors could not wait to show the world that they had an art department, a genius info graphics artist, and the color reproduction to support it. So, starting with the famous *USA Today* weather map and the super graphics of the Challenger shuttle tragedy, to assorted plane crashes, the graphics often became larger and more convoluted than the stories they attempted to tell.

Fortunately, editors and graphic artists soon came to their senses, and the super graphics gave way to more moderate, sensible, and easy-to-follow graphics that did tell what happened without any superficial information.

Animation is such a "treat" for the designer (and, obviously, for the user as well) that we may be tempted to over-animate. If it moves in real life, move it.

If it adds to the story (how a police chase yielded three suspects), then show us the cars, the chase, and the excitement. A little dog wagging its tail for no reason other than it is a dog, and it has a tail, well, let us think twice about that, unless the story is about how the wagging of this dog's tail woke up the household and saved the family from a fire! Sensible animation, such as sensible informational graphics, are a plus—the bonus we offer our audience.

Animated Web Page Features

A wide array of web page features delve into animation for purposes other than visual journalism. Some are related to navigation, whereas others reinforce the branding of the site. See related topics earlier in the book for discussion of those uses.

Animated Informational Graphics

Enter animated informational graphics. Just as visual journalism plays an important part in the newsroom, animation takes the story a step further by giving the user a visual sequence of events in the graphic, aiding the information process and helping the user to understand the story, event, or product. It is added informational value. Suddenly, the world of Disney meets the imaginative thinking of a pioneer of informational graphics such as Nigel Holmes, the much revered guru on the subject, and formerly of *TIME* magazine, who inspired a generation of informational graphic artists, many of whom have made the transition to online design.

Just as Holmes never considered informational graphics as decoration or purely visual entertainment, designers today do not see animated graphics as anything but informational. Says George Rorick, director of the Knight-Ridder Graphics Network (KRT), and a pioneer in animated informational graphics for the web, "I think it's too early to think of animation as entertaining on the web. The technology is not fast enough. The cute stuff or the art that is intended to be entertaining or add excitement quickly becomes annoying."

Animation Dos and Don'ts

Here are some dos and don'ts to remember when considering incorporating animation into web sites:

Animation Dos

▶ *Do understand what animation means. It's not just moving something—it's moving images realistically to create believability and to guide the viewer's attention to important issues.*

▶ *Do think through the entire animation before starting production. The best process to follow is to write or describe the entire animation. The animation, for example, starts with a full screen image of the MD-80 aircraft. Next, the camera zooms in on the tail section. The tail section fills the screen and becomes transparent to reveal the rudder control device, and so on.*

▶ *Do generate a storyboard from the written description.*

▶ *Do assign the script writer to write the voice-over for the animation by using the written description and the storyboard.*

▶ *Do try to master lighting and texture techniques. This adds credibility and believability.*

▶ *Do edit your work to get to the point with clarity and speed. Shorter is better.*

▶ *Do understand how the animation will be used. Will it be a stand-alone, or is it supported with video clips and an announcer?*

Animation Don'ts

▶ *Don't animate without a purpose. Don't just move images to have movement; it confuses the viewer.*

▶ *Don't use special effect techniques to entertain the viewer. Use special effects to give added value to the meaning of the topic, not for decoration.*

▶ *Don't use sound without a purpose. Sound used incorrectly can be distracting and confusing.*

▶ *Don't underestimate the training required to learn the art of animation.*

Animation Tools

There are several developments on the software front making animation an easier technique for the designer as well as making the animations more time- and bandwidth-efficient for the user. (Download times still pose a very large challenge for both designer and viewer, however.) Recommendations here are Mac-centric because the print publishing industry still relies heavily on the Mac operating system, but there are a number of Windows tools in existence as well. Look for animation-related web sites, some of which are linked to sites mentioned in this book, for more information.

GifBuilder

Such tools as GifBuilder (`http://iawww.epfl.ch/Staff/Yves.Piguet/clip2gif-home/GifBuilder.html`) simply helped the evolution of web graphics and design. This freeware program (Mac only, but there are plenty of PC imitations that often charge for their product), which is in version 0.5 at the time of publication, enables users to stack GIFs on top of one another from separate GIF files, a layered Photoshop file, or even from a QuickTime movie. GifBuilder also enables the designer to change the position of the image to essentially reduce the number of pixels in the image, which results in a smaller file size.

Obviously, there are limitations that need to be set to maximize the download time to an animated GIF. Parameters that require attention are the number of cells in the sequence, the height and width size of each image, as well as the number of colors and quality of the output.

Understanding how and where the animation will be used is a major factor to consider. There are several methods for making the file size or the K size smaller. Factors that add to larger size are: larger window sizes, longer animations, the K per second that the animation has been assigned, or added sound. The complexity of the animation, meaning how much in the animation is constantly moving and how fast images move in conjunction with background images, is also a factor. Special effects, such as morphing, transparencies, and RAY tracing, also add file size to the animation.

Know your readers first before you force a large download on them. A more technically savvy user has access to faster modems or T1 lines and can enjoys an informative animated graphic. But a user with slower access may not appreciate a large animated GIF.

3D Rendering Tools

Some very sophisticated modeling and rendering software, such as Electric-Image, Form-Z, After Effects, Shockwave, Infini-D, and Strata 3D, are becoming popular with designers of animation graphics.

When it comes to differences between 2D and 3D animation, it is important to remember that 3D has more impact in multimedia presentations. 2D is for print.

3D means multimedia. Both 2D and 3D can be mixed, but most experts don't think that the user (viewer) expects to see its newspaper on a monitor. He already has a better working model on newsprint.

Also worth noting, print artists increasingly are using 3D rendering applications and even combinations of traditional 2D applications for their work, which is becoming what one may consider a hot topic today. Writes George Rorick: "Using 3D applications as an illustration tool is a great idea. We are training our print artists and illustrators to do that right now. In fact, we have been doing that for quite some time. It's great: You build the model of whatever, apply appropriate surfaces and textures, rotate it to the proper perspective, and render one frame, not an animation. Then save it as a Photoshop file and bring it into Illustrator, add your text, and you have a powerful informational graphic or illustration. It's fast, it's effective, and it's less expensive."

Popular Animations

One of the earliest animated graphics that appeared on a web site with the identity of an informational graphic was done by the *Chicago Tribune* (see `http://www.chicago.tribune.com/news/comet/comet.htm`). An informational graphic done by KRT Graphics was animated to show the sequence of a comet's flight path across the night sky. Another animated graphic in the same package was done to show the comet's path in the solar system. Graphics were originally done by KRT Graphics staff and animated by Knight-Ridder New Media web producer/site interface designer Andrew Devigal.

National Geographic's web site put on a package called "The River Wild" (see `http://www.nationalgeographic.com/modules/selway/`) that took a user through a journey down Idaho's Selway River. During the experience, a user can choose to stop along the way to get more information on, say, how to paddle more efficiently. Through animated graphics, a forward, backward, and turn stroke were demonstrated. This site was designed by Brad Johnson, with graphics by Chuck Carter.

Figure 10.4

KRT Interactive Web where web packages can be obtained.

Recently, KRT Interactive (http://www.krtdirect.com) has made it easier for news content web sites to obtain informational graphics through their services. Among the products that can be accessed from KRT Interactive are recent web packages including animations, graphics, and interaction (see Figure 10.4).

Of course, animation can go beyond providing information to do it in a way that grabs us and keeps us there. If overdone, it can create graphic and visual noise onscreen and delay, rather than accelerate, the information process. Until most users can access animated graphics in less time, it pays to consider how, and if, animation will be utilized.

One area where we are seeing interesting and visually appealing animation is on web feature pages. With topics that lend themselves naturally to animation—from food preparation to exercise and fitness—designers are turning to animation to make their pages move, and the content more vibrant. The next chapter looks at the specific characteristics of designing magazines and features online.

Chapter 11

Designing Magazines and Features Online

If the newspaper metaphor does not always work when applied to the Web, the magazine metaphor seems to have found a comfortable fit onscreen. The reasons for this include the following:

▶ The 8 ½×11 size of a typical magazine page closely resembles the size of a screen.

▶ The best magazine indexes have been, for all practical purposes, "home pages," complete with good navigational tools—for example, large numbers and color headlines that entice the reader to search for the desired material. So the reader can transfer the "index" to the screen and assign linking functions easily.

▶ Magazine and feature designs emphasize color, splashy images, and three-dimensional things that pop on the page. This is, indeed, what comes naturally onscreen.

Many newspaper sites, however, find it hard to flex their muscles in this area. So far, anyway. Because the newspaper metaphor is so consistently used for the development of these sites, features assume a rather secondary position in the hierarchy of things. Even some newspapers that have splendidly designed feature sections do not indulge in the same style design for their equivalent sections onscreen. This, too, will change, and probably fast.

So let's turn our attention, not to newspaper sites, but to some online sites where the magazine cover, the inside page spread, and all its components come alive with energy and color while communicating interesting information. Some of these sites are not based on a print product, but are actually just based on a variety of subjects from paper companies to entertainment centers. All of these sites reflect what good feature design on the web should be.

Visualness

Begin with a visual sorbet of color, type, and texture that immediately communicates to the user that this is not a news site, in other words that he who enters here is doing so to browse through a gigantic Sunday brunch of entertainment material. Click here, and you will read an in-depth interview with a pop star or athlete, punch that yellow arrow and you are cooking with Oprah's chef, and move further to the right, click there, and, presto, Madonna sings a portion of "Don't Cry for Me Argentina," and tells you all about the coaching that led to this coveted role. The talented @Home Web site designer, Ty Ahmad-Taylor, mentions that when he sets out to design the "covers" of his magazine/features he knows that the moods and the expectations of users entering the site are quite different from those who approach a typical news site. It is as if the user is saying, "I am in the ice cream shop now, and I know that I am hungry for ice cream, but I don't know which flavor or how many flavors I want to mix into one cone, or how much to eat. I just know that this is dessert, and I am going to savor it."

Hierarchy

Earlier in this book I discussed the importance of hierarchy—making one element the dominant one on each screen. I referred to type attacks (dominance of a headline or a key word that is larger and more prominent), or a photo attack (the photo as visual lead), or a color attack (the color selected for the background aims at the user first). In the design of features, this has an even greater importance, because not only is the visual dominance necessary for the sense of creating order (for example, a point of entry into the site), but also for establishing that this is a featured site, where you have entered the "ice cream parlor" and are set to have fun, while getting information.

Create a design that is dramatically different from the other sections of the site. Follow the same rules as in Print design; for example, one does not design a Food section the same way one designs the Perspective section—and the same applies to online design. Hierarchy is important, even more so here. One must have lots to look at onscreen, but a single dominant element that commands the reader's attention.

The sketches that follow here are all aimed at providing the "visual gymnastics" necessary for designers to adapt information visually to the screen.

You should decide immediately which onscreen image the users will see first. The second important element is navigation. If the user wants to move out of this screen, how does he access the navigation tool? Hierarchy can be aimed towards a horizontal or vertical slant, or it can cover the entire screen (see Figures 11.1 through 11.3).

Typography

Typography finds its most experimental arena onscreen. Here is an opportunity to emphasize varieties of fonts (many of these done through Photoshop or Illustrator) in order to personalize the site and give typographic impact to the screen. You can play with large and small type, serifs and sans serifs, color and black-and-white (and gray), Romans and italics. Use type to convey meaning, point of view, and instant theme recognition.

Photography

Photography is a key. A photo editor/ designer combination is needed to create the best combinations onscreen. The process of selecting photographs and deciding how to play them—from size to questions of proportion, silhouetting, duo toning—must be handled carefully and with a sense of style and expertise. There is no such a thing as designing a feature section of a web page without photos playing a major role. You'll see this area of web design increasing in popularity in the years to come.

The list of recommendations for photo usage on the web is the same as any other medium: good and meaningful content, quality, and impact through size that translates into making the user want to see, to continue onscreen, and to navigate further as a result. The primary difference between photo use for print and the web, however, is technology-related: resolution.

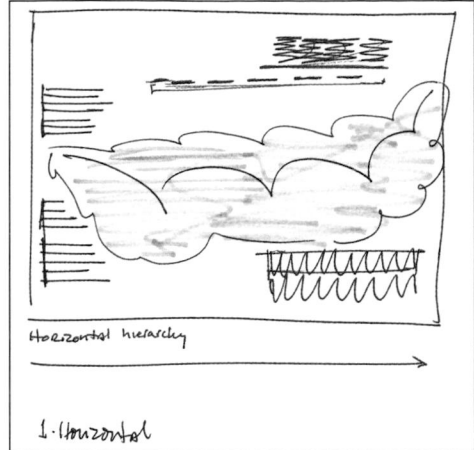

Figure 11.1

Horizontal hierarchy.

Figure 11.2

Vertical hierarchy.

Figure 11.3

Entire screen.

Visual Rules of Thumb

For the information designer, how does this translate into the realities of designing magazines and features? Here are some important aspects of site design to keep in mind.

▶ ***Visuals become extremely important.*** *Lead with a dominant illustration or photo. Do a silhouette, as opposed to a square photo, if the situation warrants it.*

▶ ***Establish a good balance between text and visuals.*** *Remember that although the balance in a news section may be 20% visuals and 80% text, the equation is more likely to be almost 40% visuals with 60% text on a feature/magazine Web site.*

▶ ***Text is important, but*** *one can play with larger type, with wider introductions, in a sense, establishing those traditional differences that made a feature from Vanity Fair look strikingly different from one in the Sunday New York Times. The online feature style, for example, can take us one step beyond those two examples and into the next generation of magazine pages—a combination of information (text), with visual connections (photos and illustrations), and the possibility of animation. Sound and video are also possibilities, which should take more of a center stage position as the technology develops to make transmission quicker and more accessible.*

▶ ***Bring in color*** *as a strategic weapon to wake up the senses.*

▶ ***Give the user the "cover" of the magazine,*** *but with the extras that online design can provide, that is, a touch of animation, a specialized colorized logo or headline, a mixture of typefaces (from elongated sans serifs to the most classic serifs, perhaps all together forming the one sentence that reads: Fishing tips from the pros).*

▶ ***Let your imagination prevail:*** *the cover of a favorite CD, the wrapper of that chocolate bar you crave at mid-afternoon, the texture of the wallpaper on the lead house of Architectural Digest—all those images can inspire you as you dress up the screen, because that is what you do with feature sites: lots of dressing, accessorizing, and experimenting.*

Says Jim Jennings, a photographer as well as an international consultant on photo use for print and web design: "Far too many webmasters seem to forget that the bulk of web users are still dealing with relatively slow modems and put far too much information out in their images. Photographs on the web need only to have a resolution high enough to meet the resolution of screen display, usually 640×480 pixels, 72ppi. Using anything higher only increases file size while *not* improving image quality. The net effect of using higher resolutions is longer download times as the image is redrawn on the screen. This, more often than not, equates to viewer frustration and an early departure from the site. The best rule of thumb I can give is keep the image as small and simple as possible."

The lone exception to this, explains Jennings, involves images with type built into them. Here, it is best to size the image as closely to the dimensions that will be used onscreen to avoid resampling, which has the potential to distort the typography and make it unreadable.

File Formats

Most designers (and photographers, Jennings among them) tend to prefer GIF over JPEG for the web as it has a number of advantages:

▶ Smaller file size with good flat color.

▶ Transparency is easily controlled.

▶ Cuts colors to 256 and thus comparable file size by two-thirds

(creation of images with millions of colors may look really rough when collapsed to 256).

▶ Enables interlacing, which gives the viewer something to look at as the image is downloaded.

Users' Expectations

Users approach feature sections of newspaper sites, and even featured (magazine) sites, differently from how they approach news. It is safe to assert that the user will have different expectations with feature sites, and will be more patient with downloading time for images. You may, for example, decide to forfeit photos when reading *TIME* magazine news portions online, but be more willing to wait for the images of a step-by-step weight lifting tutorial in a fitness magazine. A difference of intention allows for a difference in toleration rates. The information designer must keep this in mind—different sections, different moods, different degrees of toleration.

If one were to stop the user as he navigates his favorite feature site and ask him about preferences and expectations, this is what he would be likely to say:

▶ "I am relaxing as I look at this site that tells me all about how to plant roses. I will put up with a bit of a delay here or there because I want this information, which I plan to use tomorrow as I do my gardening. Pictures are important. I will be patient."

▶ "Let me have whatever text I need to comprehend this story. And, yes, I will read it if it is interesting, well written, and captures my attention. I may even be more patient with this story about someone's journey around the world in a hot air balloon than I would about reading the latest debate over the national budget in Congress."

▶ "Give me good photography. I always like it on my newspapers and magazines, and I am going to appreciate it here, too. Edit those photos well and serve them to me because I have a high interest in photography. I feel that photos can convey the same emotion and power onscreen as they do in print. So don't keep me from seeing good photos."

▶ "I appreciate art and illustration, especially on features, so serve me that delicious caricature of my favorite author or actor. It will make me feel closer to the text I am reading and the subject I am interested in."

▶ "Fill my eyes with vibrant colors, with elegant or funky typography, energize the screen in front of me, and I will click and click and click again. The old turning of the pages is still the same: good content and attractive visuals did the magic before; they still do it, in a different medium."

Let's look at some of the best designed feature sections onscreen. We'll start with the @Home network, which provides an outlook for the best of the Internet (see Figure 11.4). When I describe a home page as a gigantic Sunday brunch, this is definitely one, complete with an interesting menu of interviews, profiles, tips, and self-help content. That so many elements can coexist well on that one home page, and yet hierarchy prevails, is a testimony to the skills of its information designer. Notice that the page includes the glossy cover, including a story of the day clearly identified, and all other elements becoming easy to find, but secondary to it. The functionality of this home page is obvious to the user, with anything in red clickable as a linking element to the inside.

The @Home site is considered by many as the first mass audience for the Internet. Roger Black, the designer who has been involved with @Home since its beginnings, writes that "Anyone with cable (over which @Home is delivered) and a computer is above average in income and education, so the demographics are not mass in the way that, say, network television is. But with 50 million homes passed by @Home's cable partners and affiliates, the potential is an audience much greater than AOL's."

The @Home Network design concept by Roger Black, which includes the creation of its own fonts called At Home Interstate and Miller, provides a variation between serifs and sans serifs.

Although the site has a familiar design from day to day, designers who handle each page screen have the freedom to practice their creativity within the framework of the original concept.

Figure 11.4

http://www.athome.net.

Some designers assemble the art work and type in Photoshop, whereas others do boxes of type and art and dump it into Illustrator or FreeHand. In addition, audio and video add extra components of information to make this online magazine a little print, some radio, and some television.

Colors play a major role in the creation of a feature site, and perhaps this is more evident in the collection of funky colors selected to enhance backgrounds, as well as illustrations in the All Star magazine (see Figure 11.5).

Sports fans can get all the information they want, plus more, in an easy-to-follow, youthfully attractive site that provides some of the most interesting

and creative architectural components of any magazine site, displaying good use of frames to set off material at the bottom of the screen and beyond (see Figure 11.6).

Not necessarily a magazine, but one site that utilizes all the right elements for a possibly wonderful site is that of Samsung products. Its use of icons is particularly of interest to information designers. In addition, photos are well used. Overall, it is a clean, sophisticated magazine look for a site that is intent on selling the image of a product—a company. To complement photos and icons, the design of this site also adds functional use of colors, and, most importantly, of white space (see Figure 11.7).

Figure 11.5

http://www.allstarmag.com.

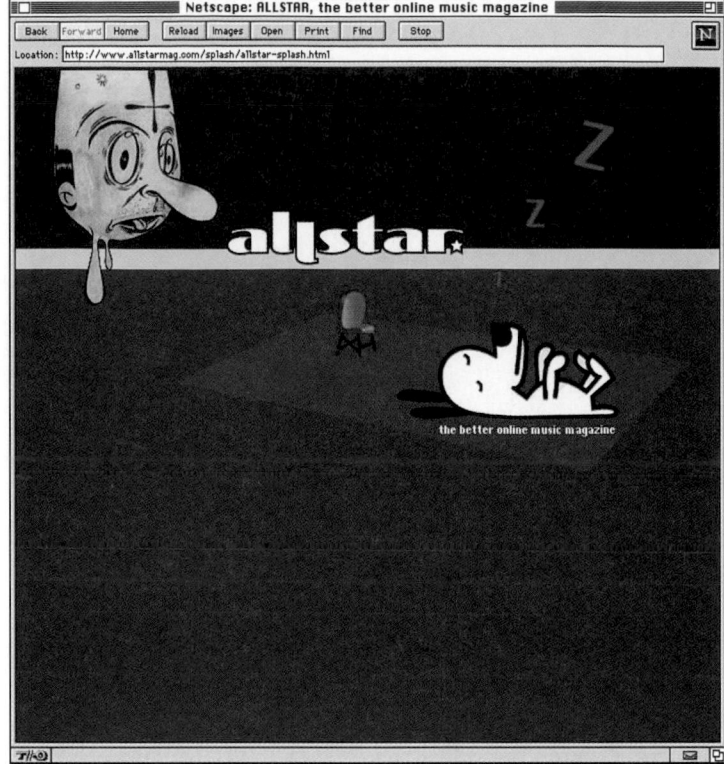

Figure 11.6

http://www.charged.com.

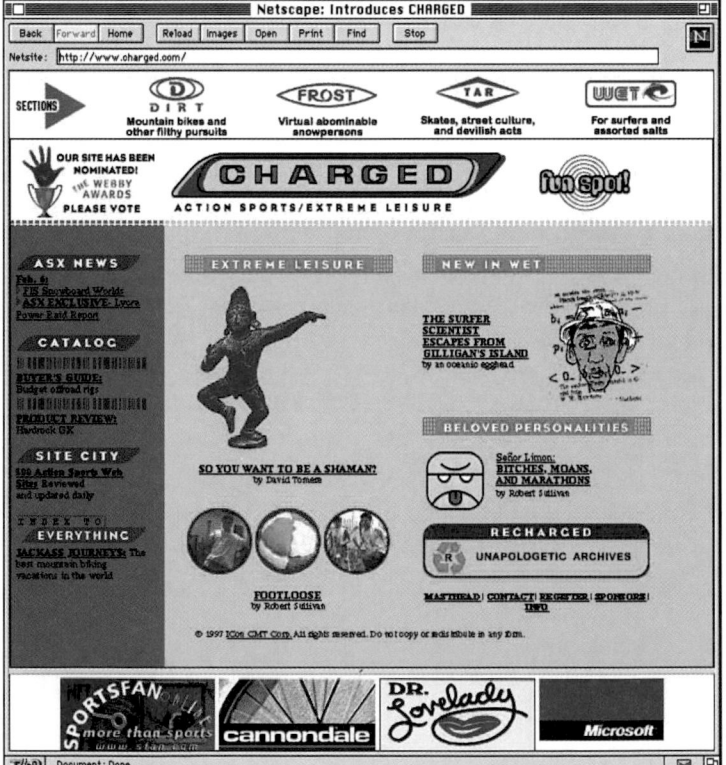

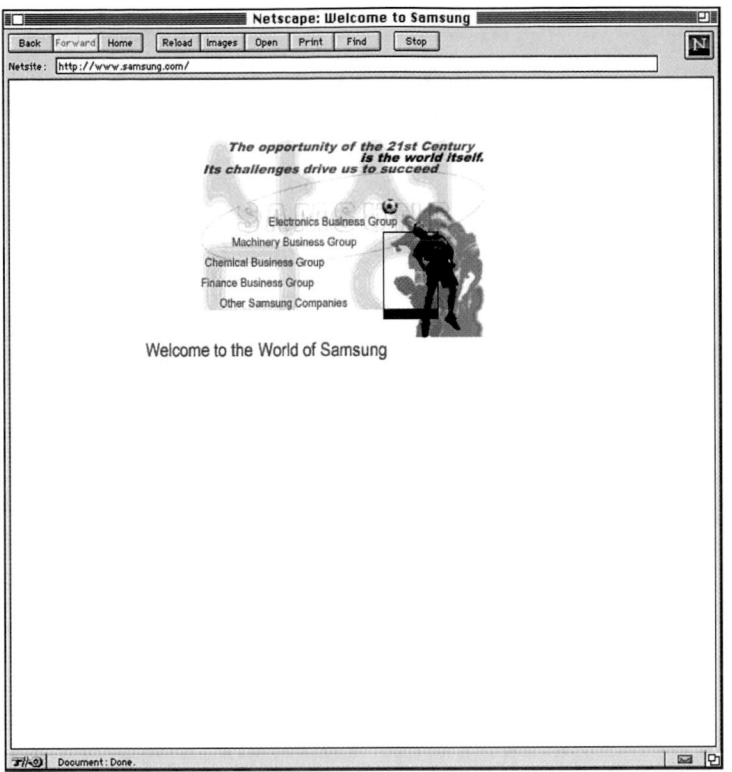

Figure 11.7

`http://www.samsung.com.`

When it comes to the use of a three-dimensional flavor in a feature site, perhaps the best example is to be found at Word, where the architectural background of its designers provides for some of the interesting structures onscreen, as well as easy navigation and lots of rich images that make this one of the most attractive sites on the web today (see Figure 11.8).

This site, targeted at an audience of curious users in a wide range of professions and interests, is a mixture of different subjects, from poems to articles tackling recent issues and culture. It includes interviews with experts on a variety of topics, providing for a highly informational site with the unusual combination of depth for those seeking it and encyclopedic trivia for the more casual reader.

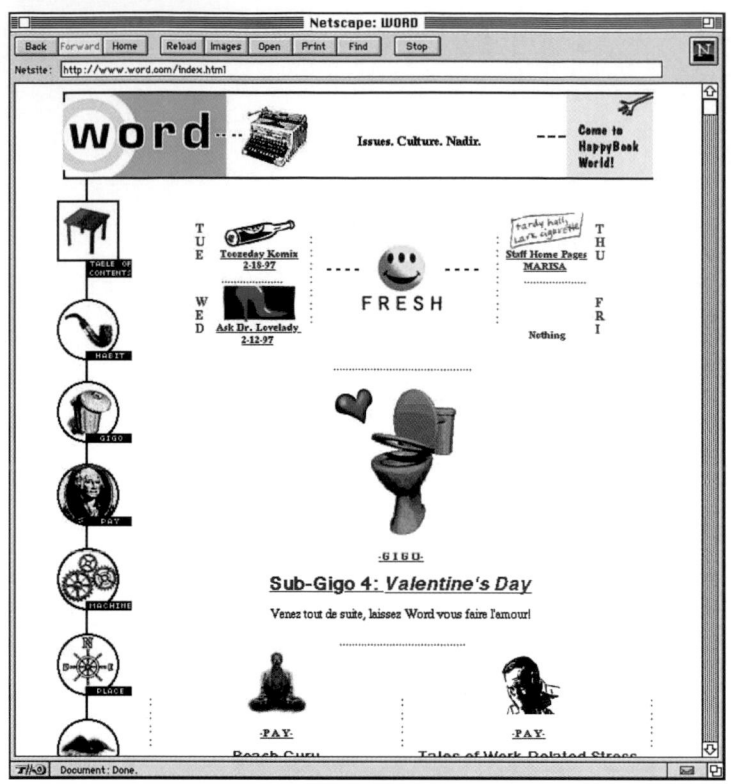

Figure 11.8

http://www.word.com.

Design Considerations and the Screen

If print designers sometimes feel limited by the canvas of a newspaper or magazine page, especially with regard to using large illustrations or type in unusual styles, then the limitations in the size of the computer screen may create much frustration for them. Yet, many of the same principles of proportion, contrast, and overall visual impact still apply.

Features on the web give the designer the ultimate freedom to recreate styles and to draw inspiration from almost any source of light, color, type, and photography/art. It is here that images and text can, as in magazines and newspapers, come to form a perfect union that is visually attractive while communicating a message.

Even the most exciting magazine-style page must be able to meet the next important challenge, that of an effective navigational system, enabling the user to click and move on to the next destination on a web site. The next chapter takes us into the world of buttons, bars, circles, and squares to help us navigate a site.

Chapter 12

Navigation Made Practical

Following the first impression of the overall web site design, the next most important thing is the navigational system. In fact, the traditional index in a newspaper or magazine, although useful, is never as utilitarian as the buttons, arrows, squares, or any other devices created for the user to click and move on to the next destination.

These navigational tools come in all shapes and colors. They may appear to the left of the screen, at the top, across the screen, and sometimes to the right of it. They may be gray or as colorful as M&Ms popping out of a bag. Some tools are big and some are small. In the overall design of a web site, navigational tools are seldom the first concept in the designer's mind; however, ironically, they are usually the first items the user aims for (see Figures 12.1 and 12.2).

Figure 12.1

Ferrari uses a key to designate the English or Italian versions of the site.

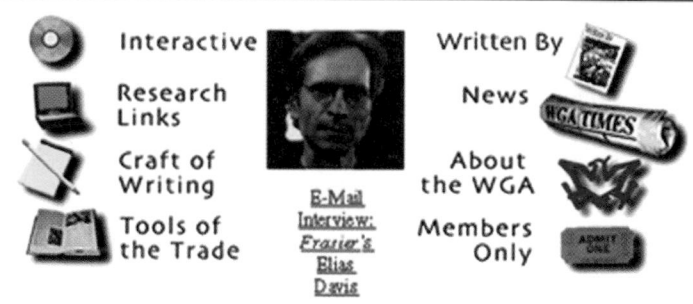

Figure 12.2

The Writer's Guild Of America uses objects used for writing as buttons.

This chapter showcases navigational tools, focusing on which styles work best and showing some designs that go beyond the conventional to add aesthetic value to your web site's design.

One of the greatest advantages of designing for the web is that the various computer companies and software designers have created an entire culture of navigation that is basic to all computer use. Users come to your site already quite adept at manipulating pull-ups, pull-downs, buttons, boxes, and all sorts of click-and-link devices to move from one area to another.

From the development of the Macintosh's pull-down menus to the expanding folders of Microsoft's Windows 95, these computer companies have, in a sense, trained computer users to navigate. Some elements remain constant regardless of the machine you use, and there is a certain "user discipline" that also exists when it comes to navigating web sites. The information can be accessed in a variety of ways, some of which you learn in this chapter. You'll also see some interesting navigational tools that should prove inspirational when you design your next web site.

Clicking the Button

Since the birth of a mouse, users like to click things. They see a button—they click it. And most buttons are implemented simply by a glow and shadow applied to a shape, creating a beveled effect. This simple technique creates a three-dimensional area for the user to expect a reaction if she chooses to click.

Of course, the type of button used will be determined by the personality and content of the site (see Figures 12.3 through 12.5). Just like colors and typography, buttons can also range from conservative to very flashy. The key is understanding the targeted user and selecting buttons that are appropriate for the site.

Tips for Designing Web Site Elements

Figure 12.3

USA Today On-line (`http://www.usatoday.com`) uses the standard rectangular button to help the user navigate through its sections.

Figure 12.4

Boston.com (`http://www.boston.com`) has a sophisticated and modern look of a rounded, beveled button.

Figure 12.5

Yahoo (`http://www.yahoo.com`) uses round and playful navigation tools on the same level as their banner. These are fun to click. The true content of their site, however, lies in the hypertext links below, which overpower their standard navigation features.

Tips for Designing Web Site Elements

For tips and techniques to enhance your web site interface design, check out Andrew Devigal's web site (`http://www.devigal.com/tech/index.html`). Andrew Devigal is a web producer and site interface designer for Knight-Ridder New Media and co-principal of Devigal Design, and he offers basic Adobe Photoshop and Illustrator techniques for use by designers of all levels. For more buttons, backgrounds, and interface design elements, look for Photoshop Web Magic *(Hayden Books).*

Navigation Design

One of the most vital concepts that many Web designers fail to pick up from existing Graphical User Interface design is the consistency of navigation. In almost any application and in any platform, the tools and menus will always be present. While using an application such as Photoshop, for example, the toolbar will show icons to represent individual tools. As a user chooses a tool on the web, the icon does not disappear or move to another part of the screen but rather just changes in appearance (see Figure 12.6).

It may, for example, change its beveled appearance to looking pressed down or even have a change in color. Regardless of the change, the critical point is the fact that the tool does not move or disappear. Placement of these navigational devices may not be as important as their consistency, but most sites have had success in either putting them on the upper or left side of the screen.

Hyperlinks

The idea of underlined words being hyperlinks was among the first great concepts of the early days of the Internet, even before the World Wide Web (see Figure 12.7). This technique and visual cue still serves as a great tool for navigation, especially because it currently is the one way for the user to identify an already-visited page. Some experts and designers assert that the underlined word is still the easiest and most effective way to move us from here to there.

Graphic Type

Many designers use graphic type as their main navigational device. And why shouldn't they? It's far more attractive than regular hyperlink type used by the browser. Graphic type gives better control to the designer. And it's much more attractive than a bevel button of any sort. This technique can be very successful as well; however, the same lesson learned from current GUI can be applied.

The Macintosh pull-down menus in every application (including the Finder) are a great example of graphical type GUI without the physical use of buttons. So why does the Mac GUI work in this case? A menu selection or list expresses to the user that they have options. If, for example, the Finder only had the word "file" on the top of the screen, it would almost seem to be an identifier rather than an option. But as it is, the options are listed with other options, making the list a strong visual navigation tool (see Figures 12.8 and 12.9).

PAGE ONE ↓ NEWS ↓ SPORTS ↓ STOCKS ↓ TECH ↓ TEMPO ↓ TRAVEL
Chicago Tribune
JOBS ↓ HOMES ↓ AUTOS ↓ WEATHER ↓ TV LISTINGS

Figure 12.6

A good example of this technique is the Chicago Tribune (`http://www.chicago.tribune.com`), where the navigational tool, in this case the word "Sports," changes in appearance, maintaining its appearance while letting the user know it has been "clicked."

Figure 12.7

Sudkurier (`http://www.skol. de`) uses words for hyperlinks, facilitating travel from one section to the next. Sometimes key words within text are underlined to indicate that a link to a related story is available.

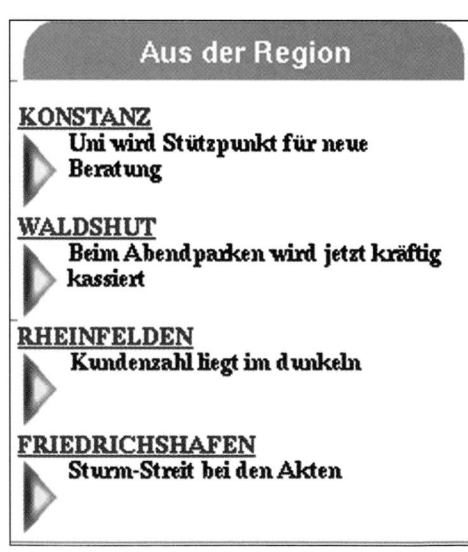

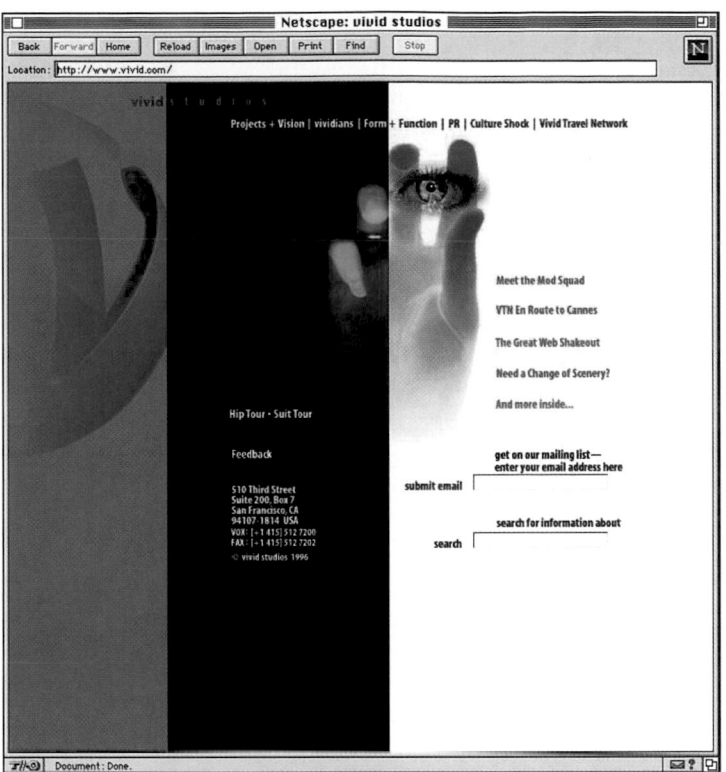

Figure 12.8

Vivid Studios (`http://www.vivid.com/`) creates a consistent navigational device that is clear, simple, and easy to use.

Figure 12.9

Champion Paper (`http://www.championpaper.com`) utilizes attractive sans serif type set in blue for the navigational tools on its home page. The positioning of the words makes the links attractive, yet easy to recognize and uncomplicated to download.

Pop-Up Menus

Navigation using pop-up menus was probably one of the best ideas developed for web site construction. It enables the user to expand his options, while minimizing the real estate occupied onscreen. Although not as attractive as other options presented here, it serves as a great functional tool (see Figure 12.10).

Figure 12.10

Mercury Center (`http://www.sjmercury.com/`) was probably one of the first sites to develop this technique.

Squares, Arrows, and the Rest

Sometimes a designer feels that just one word, or a button, may not be enough, or that there are too many of those on sites everywhere. They come in an array of devices, some more attractive and functional than others. Arrows, half moons, dots, lines, and so on appear on web sites all the time (see Figure 12.11).

Figure 12.11

Clarin (`http://www.clarin.com`), the Argentinean daily, utilizes an interesting tiny symbol of a vertical and horizontal line that come together to tempt us to click. The consistent use of the tool is attractive and functional.

The navigational tool is to the web site what the turning of pages is to the newspaper or magazine. It is the mechanism that moves us forward and onward. It propels us to continue our journey through a site. The navigational tool should be as uncomplicated as the turning of a page and used with the same unconscious effort, requiring almost no attention to the function. But because "screens" don't turn like pages, there is a bit of visual play involved. Color, shape, and functionality make these navigational tools the effective elements they are meant to be.

And, here again, is a dramatic difference between designing for print and for the web. In print, you hope that the content is strong enough that it will compel the user to turn the page to seek more. On the web, after he has been compelled to move on, the user must first find the tool to "turn to the next screen," and then become aware of how to use it (or click on it). These are the buttons, arrows, or other devices of a simple function that ultimately determine how we travel through a site successfully.

This chapter is like the window of the candy store: with colorful buttons and tools that can inspire the information designer when it comes time to design the next bar, circle, or triangle to invite the user to click.

Chapter 13

One More Click

Information designers who design for the web online are, indeed, pioneers as we enter the new millennium. As such, certain responsibilities become important. Fifty years from now media historians will highlight the decade of the 1990s as the period in which information stretched into new positioning—online, the Internet, web sites. They will probably write that the print people looked at the new medium with skepticism, joining only because they had no choice, and because there were "credible" sources telling them it was the thing to do. Historians will probably write that the first news web sites were too much like newspapers, sometimes as complicated as them, and offering little that was new or innovative beyond the platform of the screen as opposed to the page.

Then they will talk about those pioneering online designers and editors, profiling the ones who dared to go beyond newspaper metaphors, to incorporate the first hints of what this new medium was all about. Using the tools they knew best: type, color, architecture, and pure journalism, they brought new life to all of them within the framework of a new platform, revitalizing the way stories were written (and read), experimenting with story structures that seemed suitable for the screen, adapting frames to provide architectural patterns that made it easy to look at the content onscreen, applying color without the doubts of how reproduction would turn out, and using type in an infinitesimal variety of styles all adaptable to the screen and its specific characteristics.

The best pioneers in this new medium will be singled out for their legacy in terms of how they followed their important responsibilities. The following responsibilities come to mind:

Appropriateness

The best informational designers make sure that they create web sites appropriate to the content and organization of their site. Point of view and texture in the design of a site are to be directly linked to what a specific organization is trying to convey to its users. News sites are different from feature and/or advertising sites. The moment the user connects and sees that first image onscreen, an idea is formed in his head. Good informational designers are aware of this and do not simply use the new medium and its vast technological arsenal of toys to indulge in playful motifs. That which moves, or twirls, onscreen may be technically possible and fun to watch, but may not be what the serious news organization wants its first users' impression to be. Colors, simply because they project well onscreen, do not have to be used in abundance, or at all. Typography, too, must set the tone for the content it accompanies.

Design Culture

Web sites, if rolled one after the other and placed fictitiously on a surface, might begin to resemble floats during the Rose Parade: lots of color, lots of fanfare, and after a half hour of floats, a long procession of a visually intoxicating cocktail. Perhaps one or two floats remain in one's subconscious, the ones that had a special meaning, or the ones that stuck pretty close to the one theme that they represented. The same is true for web sites.

When we begin to surf the Net, going from site to site, the visual parade is on. It is at this point that design individuality becomes important. For years, I have maintained to newspaper designers that there are Helvetica towns and Bodoni towns, and one just has to know which is which. In terms of colors, newspapers and web sites from the southwestern United States must incorporate earthtones appropriate to the region, just like Brazilian ones do best with bright colors.

One fantastic source of inspiration for adapting design to its culture is the local galleries and museums, where one can appreciate how local painters use color and design. A link exists between culture and design that is unquestionable. I know that the color palettes of Scandinavian publications tend to be subtle and pastel-like, but so is the "colorization" of the landscape and the way the people dress and decorate. One can take a train ride from Stockholm to Göteborg, Sweden, for example, and never see curtains in any color but white on the windows of small houses, farm houses, or big houses. It is a culture that prides itself in its minimalist furniture, open spaces, white space, and clean landscapes. This must translate to the design of its publications and web sites.

Locations near the oceans, or lakes, or rivers do well with cool colors, just like mountainous terrain invites earthtones. Information designers know this, and simply do not imitate what they have liked in other web sites. They customize, create their own, individualize, and ultimately come out with projects that reflect the culture of the communities in which they exist.

In that huge parade of floats that constitute the Internet, the memorable ones may not be the flashiest ones, but more often the ones that are appropriate for their content and point of view, and true to the culture of their environment.

Creativity

Perhaps no medium offers greater possibilities for creativity than the web. Simply because there is no history, we can write the book, chart the course, create the map, and aim for the highest peaks. The possibilities are immense for developing new writing styles that accommodate the new medium. We have not even begun to scratch the surface of how writing and editing will affect the way people read, or don't read, on the web. In an essay titled, "Thinking Clearly about New Media," Dr. Bill Boyd, of the Poynter Institute for Media Studies, writes: "New media eliminates the excuse of limited journalism because of limited space. Infinite amounts of space are now available for giving added value such as historical background, related articles, and full text of reports of speeches." And he adds that such traditional writing forms as the inverted pyramid, narratives, visual essays and "other story forms not yet invented" have a place in new media.

He also maintains that the new medium may bring about a renaissance of good writing, and, ultimately, great reading. This is perhaps the area with

the most potential for creativity. I can foresee the development of writing styles that will go beyond the New Journalism styles of the late 1960s and early 1970s, to incorporate the ultimate combination of long and short forms of writing. Because the web is an encyclopedic medium, there will be a variety of new styles to present facts, beyond boxes and informational graphics, to articulate factual information in appealing styles. In addition, we shall see the traditional Q&A interview-style enjoy a rebirth, with before and after narrative analysis of the interview, plus all the encyclopedic background of the interviewee. The new medium will enable the quick read, the substantial read, and the encyclopedic read, something that the print media have found it difficult to accomplish.

A new wave of online writing coaches will develop, some of them writers who emerge into their careers without ever having written for print. They will accentuate the nuances of the new medium, from how to make transitions, what words or sentences work best to lead us to a link, when to highlight an encyclopedic element, and so on. This is one book waiting to be written, and an audience waiting to be served.

So it is in writing that I see the greatest possibilities for creativity for pioneers to leave the legacy that historians will talk about. In literature anthologies, we refer to genres and periods. The Romantics, the Realists and the Naturalists always appear next to each other in most such volumes. We know that sometimes the movements were only eight years from one another. What determined a new genre? A group of daring writers who went beyond what the previous group had done. As such, naturalists emerged with their own movement when they dared show more and be more descriptive than the realists.

In the media anthology of the year 2,099, we will have gone from the genre of print journalists, to broadcast journalists, and then to online journalists (the present). But shortly after that we will progress to online information designers, and shortly after that the real New Medium of Information Design, totally disposed of its newspaper metaphor trappings, populated by staffers who never worked in a print medium. In other words, a new animal. Not radio imitating print or early television imitating radio.

And the legacy of today's information designers will have planted the seed, gaining a secured place in that anthology, defining a genre.

The new genre is in its infancy.

This is only the beginning.

Appendix A

New Media Bibliography

Online Articles and Reports

Alexander, Jan and Marsha Tate. "Teaching Critical Evaluation Skills for World Wide Web Resources." http://www.science.widener.edu/~withers/webeval.htm Wolfgram Memorial Library, Widener University, 1996.

December, John. "Units of Analysis for Internet Communication." http://www.usc.edu/dept/annenberg/vol1/issue4/december.html *Journal of Computer-Mediated Communication*, Vol. 1, No. 4.

A special joint issue with the *Journal of Communication*, Winter 1996.

Fulton, Katherine. "A Tour of Our Uncertain Future." http://www.cjr.org/kfulton/journow1.html *Columbia Journalism Review*, Online Version, March/April 1996.

Gunaratne, Shelton A. and Byung S. Lee. "Integration of Internet Resources into Curriculum and Instruction." http://www.moorhead.msus.edu/~gunarat/Internet.html *Journalism and Mass Communication Educator*, Summer 1996, pp. 25-35.

Hume, Ellen. "Tabloids, Talk Radio, and the Future of News: Technology's Impact on Journalism." http://www.annenberg.nwu.edu/pubs/tabloids/ Washington, D.C.: The Annenberg Washington Program in Communications Policy Studies of Northwestern University, 1995.

Lapham, Christine. "The Evolution of the Newspaper of the Future." `http://sunsite.unc.edu/cmc/mag/1995/jul/lapham.html` *Computer-Mediated Communication Magazine*, June 1995.

McAdams, Melinda."Inventing an Online Newspaper." `http://www.sentex.net/~mmcadams/invent.html` First Published by: *Interpersonal Computing and Technology: "An Electronic Journal for the 21st Century."* July 1995, pp. 64-90.

McChesney, Robert W. "The Internet and U.S. Communication Policy-Making in Historical and Critical Perspective." `http://www.usc.edu/dept/annenberg/vol1/issue4/mcchesney.html` *Journal of Computer-Mediated Communication*, Vol. 1, No. 4.

A special joint issue with the *Journal of Communication*, Winter 1996.

McLaughlin, Margaret L. "The Art Site on the World Wide Web." `http://www.usc.edu/dept/annenberg/vol1/issue4/mclaugh.html` *Journal of Computer-Mediated Communication*, Vol. 1, No. 4.

A special joint issue with the *Journal of Communication*, Winter 1996.

Mensing, Donica. "Profit Strategies for Online Newspapers." `http://unr.edu:80/homepage/dmensing/` Reynolds School of Journalism, University of Nevada, Reno, 1996.

Morris, Merrill and Christine Ogan. "The Internet as Mass Medium." `http://www.usc.edu/dept/annenberg/vol1/issue4/morris.html` *Journal of Computer-Mediated Communication*, Vol. 1, No. 4.

A special joint issue with the *Journal of Communication*, Winter 1996.

Newhagen, John and Sheizaf Rafaeli, eds. "Why Communication Researchers Should Study the Internet: A Dialogue." `http://www.usc.edu/dept/annenberg/vol1/issue4/rafaeli.html` *Journal of Computer-Mediated Communication*, Vol. 1, No. 4.

A special joint issue with the *Journal of Communication*, Winter 1996.

Parks, Malcolm R. "Making Friends in Cyberspace." `http://www.usc.edu/dept/annenberg/vol1/issue4/parks.html` *Journal of Computer-Mediated Communication*, Vol. 1, No. 4.

A special joint issue with the *Journal of Communication*, Winter 1996.

RTNDF. "A Seat at the Table: The Role of Journalism in the Digital Era." `http://www.rtndf.org/rtndf/new/brochure.html` The first monograph from the Radio and Television News Directors Foundation's *News in the Next Century* Project, 1996.

Ross, Steven and Don Middleberg. "The Media in Cyberspace Study II." `http://www.mediasource.com/study/index.html` Mediasource, January 1996.

Online Resources and Organizations

The Center for New Media. `http://www.cnm.columbia.edu/` The Center for New Media at the Columbia University Graduate School of Journalism is a working laboratory for developing new ways of presenting information.

The Cole Pages.
`http://colegroup.com` David Cole's online newsletter about new media.

Computer-Mediated Communication Magazine.
`http://www.december.com/cmc/mag/current/toc.html` CMC reports about communication and interaction in online environments.

CyberStrategy Project.
`http://www.fas.org/cp/netstats.htm` A new media project from the Federation of American Scientists, 1996.

The Electronic Frontier Foundation.
`http://www.eff.org/` An organization working to protect privacy, free expression, and access to public resources and information online, as well as to promote responsibility in new media.

Ethics of the Internet: A Conference at UC Berkeley.
`http://www.sims.berkeley.edu/conferences/` This November 1995 conference explored issues of ethics, access, democracy, and the Internet.

Mario Garcia New Media Design International.
`http://www.mariogarcia.com/` A firm devoted to the design of newspapers, magazines, and electronic publishing in its various forms.

Media Lab.
`http://www.media.mit.edu/` MIT's Media Laboratory, founded in 1985, carries on advanced research into a broad range of information technologies.

Poynter Online.
`http://www.poynter.org/` New media resources from the Poynter Institute for Media Studies.

Project 2000.
`http://www2000.ogsm.vanderbilt.edu/` Vanderbilt University's Project 2000 is devoted to the scholarly investigation of computer-mediated environments.

The ProtoPaper Project.
`http://www.grady.uga.edu/ProtoPapers/ProtoPapers.html` A new media project from the Cox Institute for Newspaper Management at the University of Georgia.

Public Interest Journalism: Winner or Loser in the On-Line Era?
`http://www.Nieman.harvard.edu/Nieman/CAgenda.html` Nieman Foundation conference, May 1995.

Stop the Presses: Newspaper New Media News and Analysis.
`http://www.mediainfo.com/ephome/news/newshtm/stop/stop.htm` Steve Outing's *Editor & Publisher* Web Edition column on new media.

Print Articles 1996

Anderson, Heidi. "Cyberspace As Journalism Tool." *Editor & Publisher*, Special Section, February 17, 1996, p. 141. Andrews, Whit. "Surveillance in Cyberspace." *American Journalism Review*, March 1996, p. 13.

Cohen, Jodi B. "Weather On the Internet." *Editor & Publisher*, July 27, 1996, pp. 26-27.

Criner, Kathleen and Jane Wilson. "Big Lesson In Big Web Sites." *Editor & Publisher*, August 31, 1996, pp. 6, 34.

Dreifus, Claudia. "The Cyber-Maxims of Esther Dyson." *The New York Times Magazine*, July 7, 1996, pp. 16-19.

Feola, Christopher J. "Newspapers Gain with Technology." *Quill*, April 1996, pp. 27-29.

Fitzgerald, Mark. "The Effect of the Internet on Print Journalism." *Editor & Publisher*, April 13, 1996, p. 72.

Friedland, Lewis A. and Sheila Webb. "Incorporating Online Publishing in the Curriculum." *Journalism and Mass Communication Educator*, Autumn 1996, pp. 54-65.

Goodman, Fred. "On Fitting In." *Presstime*, April 1996, pp. 31-33.

Harris, John. "On Line with WRAL-TV." *Communicator*, September 1996, pp. 29-34.

Hernandez, Debra Gersh. "A Wave of Protests." *Editor & Publisher*, February 17, 1996, pp. 15, 39.

Hof, Robert D. "Scott McNealy's Rising Sun." *Business Week*, January 22, 1996, pp. 66-73.

Irby, John. "Ridder: Online Products Won't Kill Print Cousins." *The American Editor*, June 1996, p. 33.

Italiano, Laura. "Gimme That On-Line Religion." *Columbia Journalism Review*, January/February 1996, pp. 34-38.

Jacobson, Gianna. "For Journalism Graduates, Opportunities in New Media." *The New York Times*, May 20, 1996, Section D, p. 11.

Johnson, J. T. "Compensation Vs. Copyright—Critical Issue in Cyberspace." *Quill*, March 1996, pp. 18-19.

Mifflin, Lawrie. "Journalist as Broker in Mixed Marriage Next Week of Microsoft and NBC News." *The New York Times*, July 8, 1996, Section D, p. 8.

Mooth, Bryn M. "Home on the Web." *How*, August 1996, pp. 78-83.

Morton, John. "Exploring the Cyberspace Future." *American Journalism Review*, January/February 1996, p. 60.

Niederpruem, Kyle E. "Decisive Ruling Chooses Speech Over Censorship." *Quill*, July/August 1996, p. 52.

Outing, Steve. "Hold On (line) Tight." *Editor & Publisher*, Special Section, February 17, 1996, pp. 41-61.

Pavlik, John V. "New Media Offer Growing Job Prospects." *Nieman Reports*, Summer 1996, pp. 26-28.

Puglisi, Rob. "An Inside Look at MSNBC." *Communicator*, October 1996, pp. 46-47, 49-50, 53.

Ramo, Joshua Cooper. "Winner Take All." *Time*, September 16, 1996, pp. 56-64.

Rebello, Kathy. "Inside Microsoft." *Business Week*, July 15, 1996, pp. 56-67.

Rehe, Rolf. "Typography on the Internet: It's Frontier Time." *Design*, Fall 1996, p. 33.

Regan, Tom. "Cyberspace Job Market." *Nieman Reports*, Spring 1996, p. 37.

Rieman, Richard. "Putting News on the Web." *Communicator*, April 1996, pp. 29-32.

Savell, Larry. "The Internet and the Law." *Editor & Publisher*, September 28, 1996, pp. 22-23, 36.

Schoch, Eric. "Can the Net Be Censored?" *Quill*, March 1996, pp. 30-31.

Singer, Jane B., et al. "Attitudes of Professors and Students About New Media Technology." *Journalism and Mass Communication Educator*, Summer 1996, pp. 36-45.

Soyster, Margaret Blair. "Cyber Law Emerges." *Editor & Publisher*, Special Section, February 17, 1996, pp. 281-301.

Sullivan, Michael J. "Web Site Design: Another Piece in the Communication Puzzle." *How*, August 1996, pp. 90-93.

Tedesco, Richard, Dan Trigoboff and Cynthia Littleton. "Caught in the Web: How Television, Cable and Radio Are Plugging Into the Internet." *Broadcasting and Cable*, Special Report, October 28, 1996, pp. 30-58.

Toner, Mark. "Charting the Course to Digital Cities." *Presstime*, July/August 1996, pp. 60-62.

Wendland, Mike. "Using the Internet: A Crucial Skill for Journalists." *Communicator*, September 1996, pp. 38, 40-44.

Whiteside, Scott. "Web Redefines Who An Editor Is." *The American Editor*, July/August 1996, pp. 4-5.

Print Articles 1995

Agrawal, Rakesh. "Getting the Word Out: Terrorism in Oklahoma." *Quill*, July/August 1995, pp. 32-34.

Albers, Rebecca Ross. "Static on the Cyberbeat." *Presstime*, January 1995, pp. 40-42.

Berkman, Dave. "The Information Superhighway—or Electronic Revolution #4?" *Television Quarterly*, Winter 1995, pp. 77-83.

Borrell, Jerry. "The Emerging Role of Journalists in Multimedia." *Quill*, May 1995, p. 22.

Carter, Margaret G. "Online Advertising." *Presstime*, March 1995, pp. 38-40.

Case, Tony. "Print Person Pontificates: New York Times Managing Editor Gene Roberts..." *Editor & Publisher*, February 11, 1995, pp. 11, 37.

Cochran, Wendell. "Searching For Right Mixture." *Quill*, May 1995, pp. 36-39.

Cole, David M. "The Virtual Library." *Presstime*, September 1995, pp. 47-54.

Egan, Jack and Kenan Pollack. "Cashing in on the Internet." *U.S. News and World Report*, November 13, 1995, pp. 81-83.

Feola, Christopher J. and James Brown. "Gates Hatches MSN: Microsoft Ventures Into Digital News Delivery. *Quill*, September 1995, pp. 34-36.

Fitzgerald, Mark. "Advertising on the Internet." *Editor & Publisher*, March 4, 1995, pp. 30-31.

Gipson. Melinda. "Bill's Online AdVenture." *Presstime*, October 1995, pp. 28-33.

Gordon, Andrew C. "Journalism and the Internet." *Media Studies Journal*, Summer 1995, pp. 173-176.

Grossman, Lawrence K. "The Electronic Republic." *Media Studies Journal*, Summer 1995, pp. 163-168.

Gunther, Marc. "Trying to Bring Journalism With Capital 'J' to Cyberspace." *The New York Times*, August 28, 1995, Section D, p. 7.

Harders, Julie. "Censorship in Cyberspace." *Quill*, October 1995, p. 25.

Hickey, Neil. "Revolution in Cyberia." *Columbia Journalism Review*, July/August 1995, pp. 40-47.

Ingle, Bob. "Newspaper Vs. On-Line Versions: A Discussion of the Old and New Media." *Nieman Reports*, Summer 1995, pp. 17-20.

"Interactive Newspapers '95. Special Pullout Section." *Editor & Publisher*, February 4, 1995, pp. 4TC-26TC.

Isaacs, Stephen D. "The Virtual Water Cooler: Where Journalists Hang Out On-Line." *Columbia Journalism Review*, May/June 1995, pp. 61-64.

Jacobi, Fritz. "Will There Be a Lane For Television on the Information Superhighway?" *Television Quarterly*, Winter 1995, pp. 29-38.

Javers, Ron. "Techs Vs. Lits." *American Journalism Review*, July/August 1995, pp. 16-17.

Johnson, J.T. "Money, Technology Converging to Help Media's Bottom Line." *Quill*, November/December 1995, p. 16.

Lemisch, Jesse. "The First Amendment Is Under Attack in Cyberspace." *The Chronicle of Higher Education*, January 20, 1995, p. A56.

Lightfoot, Linda. "New Electronic Media Present Lots of Legal Questions for Newspapers." *ASNE Bulletin*, February 1995, pp. 12-13.

Linn, Travis. "Station Web Sites." *Communicator*, April 1995, pp. 30-33.

Martire, Greg. "The Information Superhighway: What Newspapers Should Know." *Editor & Publisher*, February 18, 1995, pp. 56, 45.

Maynard, Nancy Hicks. "Managing the Future." *Quill*, September 1995, pp. 24-26.

Millhollon, Michelle. "Citizens in Cyberspace." *Quill*, October 1995, p. 24.

Moeller, Philip. "The Digitized Newsroom." *American Journalism Review*, January/February 1995, pp. 42-47.

Mueller, Jennifer and David Kamerer. "Reader Preference for Electronic Newspapers." *Newspaper Research Journal*, Summer 1995, pp. 2-13.

Paul, Nora. "The Future Past: The Functions of Preserving and Accessing the Past Will Undergo a Revolution of Their Own." *Presstime*, March 1995, pp. S11-S12.

Peck, Christopher. "How Newspapers Can Succeed in New Media." *The American Editor*, July/August 1995, pp. 24-27.

Potter, Walt. "A Guide to Online Avenues." *Presstime*, January 1995, pp. S1-S16.

Poulson, David. "New Web Alliances May Be a Little Dicey." *The American Editor*, December 1995, p. 8.

Ritchin, Fred. "News Photography in Cyberspace." *Nieman Reports*, Summer 1995, pp. 50-51.

Ross, Maddy. "Newspaper's Place in Cyberspace Still Cloudy." *The American Editor*, May/June 1995, pp. 11,13.

Ross, Philip E. and Nikhil Hutheesing. "Along Came the Spiders." *Forbes*, October 23, 1995, pp. 210-216.

Rowe, Chip. "A Journalist's Guide to the Internet." *American Journalism Review*, January/February 1995, pp. 30-34.

Schlender, Brent. "What Bill Gates Really Wants." *Fortune*, January 16, 1995, pp. 35-63.

Sussman, Vic and Kenan Pollack. "Gold Rush in Cyberspace." *U.S. News and World Report*, November 13, 1995, pp. 72-80.

Taylor, Chuck. "Navigating Cyberspace." *Quill*, March 1995, pp. 20-23.

Valovic, Thomas S. "Encounters On-Line." *Media Studies Journal*, Spring 1995, pp. 113-121.

Webb, William. "Public Interest Journalism in the Online Era." *Editor & Publisher*, June 10, 1995, pp. 28-29.

Wooten, Jim. "Editors Take the Plunge Into Unknown Waters." *The American Editor*, May/June 1995, pp. 20, 23.

Print Articles 1994

Benge, George. "Innovation and the Super Highway Belong to the Information Designer." *Design Magazine*, Spring 1994, p. 5.

Birkerts, Sven and Kevin Kelly. "The Electronic Hive: Two Views." *Harper's Magazine*, May 1994, pp. 17-25.

Bogart, Leo. "Newspapers in the New Media World." *Editor & Publisher*, November 5, 1994, p. 48.

Clark, James C. "Who Owns the Information We're Sending Down the Information Highway?" *ASNE Bulletin*, January/February 1994, pp. 14-15.

Cole, David M. "Information Evolution." *Quill*, January/February 1994, pp. 20-22.

Conniff, Michael. "A Short History of the Future." *Editor & Publisher*, August 27, 1994, pp. 3, 39.

Dale, Jack. "Rumors of the Future and the Digital Circus." *Editor & Publisher*, February 12, 1994, pp. 8TC-12TC.

Elliott, Brendan and Thomas Miller. "Newspapers and the New Consumer." *Editor & Publisher*, February 12, 1994, pp. 14TC-16TC, 28TC.

Elmer-Dewitt, Philip. "Battle for the Soul of the Internet." *Time*, July 25, 1994, pp. 50-56.

Fantel, Hans. "New Off-Ramps On Info Highway for Couch Potatoes." *New York Times*, May 15, 1994, Section 2, p. 39.

Feola, Christopher J. "The Nexis Nightmare." *American Journalism Review*, July/August 1994, pp. 39-42.

Fitzgerald, Mark. "Heading for the Information Highway." *Editor & Publisher*, January 1, 1994, pp. 11-14.

Giobee, Dorothy. "Marketing Newspapers in a New Media Age." *Editor & Publisher*, February 12, 1994, pp. 24-25.

Glaberson, William. "In San Jose, Knight-Ridder Tests a Newspaper Frontier." *New York Times*, February 7, 1994, p. D1.

Glass, Andrew J. "The Key to PC Links: Multi-Media Will Always Require Good Data, Analysis." *Quill*, January/February 1994, p. 49.

Gleick, James. "The Information Future: Out of Control (And It's a Good Thing, Too)." *The New York Times Magazine*, May 1, 1994, pp. 54-57.

Hall, David. "How Will the Editor's Job Change?" *Nieman Reports*, Summer 1994, pp. 26-27.

Helle, Steven. "Libel in Cyberspace." *Editor & Publisher*, December 24, 1994, pp. 16, 30.

Isaacs, Stephen D. "The Golden Age, Maybe?" *Columbia Journalism Review*, December 1994, p. 69.

Jennewein, Chris. "Audiotext Gives a Growing Number of Dailies the Chance to Experiment with New Technologies." *ASNE Bulletin*, January/February 1994, pp. 16-17.

Katz, Jon. "Online or Not, Newspapers Suck." *Wired*, September 1994, pp. 50-58.

Koch, Tom. "Computers Vs. Community: A Call for Bridging the Gap Between Two Camps, Two Tools." *Quill*, May 1994, p. 18.

Lail, Jack D. "Newspapers On-Line." *Quill*, January/February 1994, pp. 39-44.

Mandel, Michael J. "The Digital Juggernaut." *Business Week*, Special Issue, June 6, 1994, pp. 22-29.

Markoff, John. "I Wonder What's on the PC Tonight." *The New York Times*, May 8, 1994, Section 3, p. 1.

Moeller, Phillip. "The Age of Convergence." *American Journalism Review*, January/February 1994, pp. 22-28.

Noack, David. "Letters to The Editor Via E-Mail." *Editor & Publisher*, June 25, 1994, pp. 40, 42.

Paul, Nora. "The Electronic Newspaper: Good Reading for the Professional Searcher?" *Searcher: The Magazine for Database Professionals*, July/August 1994, pp. 30-31, 34-35.

Peskin, Dale. "Slaying the Mediasaurus: An Editor Debunks Michael Crichton's View of Media Obsolescence." *Presstime*, June 1994, pp. 51-52.

Potter, Walt. "Free Speech On the Infobahn." *Presstime*, August 1994, pp. 66-68.

Powell III, Adam Clayton, "People of Color Underrepresented on Infohighway." *Electronic Media*, November 7, 1994, pp. 22, 52.

Pryor, Larry. "The Videotex Debacle." *American Journalism Review*, November 1994, pp. 41-42.

Resnick, Rosalind. "Small Newspapers Going On Line." *Editor & Publisher*, February 12, 1994, pp. 34-35.

Seabrook, John. "E-Mail From Bill." *New Yorker*, January 10, 1994, pp. 48-61.

Stewart, Thomas A. "Managing in a Wired Company." *Fortune*, July 11, 1994, pp. 44-56.

Sussman, Vic. "News of the Wired: The Perils and Promise of Electronic Newspapering." *U.S. News & World Report*, May 16, 1994, pp. 60-62.

Tetzeli, Rick. "The Internet and Your Business." *Fortune*, March 7, 1994, pp. 86-96.

Thalhimer, Mark. "High-Tech News or Just Shovelware?" *Media Studies Journal*, Winter 1994, pp. 41-51.

Truitt, Rosalind C. "Rise of the Sysops." *Presstime*, November 1994, pp. 40-46.

Verity, John W. "The Internet: How It Will Change the Way You Do Business." *Business Week*, November 14, 1994, pp. 80-88.

Wolf, Gary. "The (Second Phase of the) Revolution Has Begun." *Wired*, October 1994, pp. 116-121, 150-152.

Wolff, Jennifer. "Opening Up Online." *Columbia Journalism Review*, December 1994, pp. 62-65.

Print Articles 1993

Abernathy, Joe. "Casting the Internet." *Columbia Journalism Review*, January/February 1993, p. 56.

Albers, Rebecca Ross. "Live from the Newsroom: Can Alliances with Television Pay Off for Newspapers?" *Presstime*, June 1993, pp. 48-51.

Alridge, Ron. "Will Journalism be Road Kill on the Superhighway?" *Electronic Media*, December 20-27, 1993, p. 29.

Balboni, Philip S. "Memo To: All Journalists Re: The New Information Industry." *Columbia Journalism Review*, July/August 1993, pp. 49-50.

Bender, Walter. "Riding the Digital Highway." *Presstime*, May 1993, pp. 54-55.

Conniff, Michael. "The Dinosaur Is Starting to Dance." *Editor & Publisher*, March 6, 1993, pp. 4TC-6TC.

Crichton, Michael. "The Mediasaurus: Today's Mass Media is Tomorrow's Fossil Fuel." *Wired*, October 1993, pp. 56-59.

Davis, Nancy M. "The Joys of Toys: Electronic Gadgets and Services are Management Musts for a Few Adventurous Newspaper People." *Presstime*, September 1993, pp. 24-26.

Easterly, David. "The Brave New World of Media." *Editor & Publisher*, August 14, 1993, pp. 4-35, 44.

Elmer-Dewitt, Philip. "Take a Trip Into the Future on the Electronic Super-highway." *Time*, April 12, 1993, pp. 50-58.

Garneau, George. "The New Media Landscape." *Editor & Publisher*, May 8, 1993, pp. 14-15.

Glaberson, William. "Creating Electronic Editions, Newspapers Try New Roles." *New York Times*, August 16, 1993, p. A1.

Gordon, David. "Information Haves..." *Presstime*, December 1993, pp. 56-57.

Hernandez, Debra Gersh. "Free-lancers and the Information Highway." *Editor & Publisher*, December 11, 1993, p. 39.

Leccese, Mark. "Electronic Corner Tavern Connects You to Journalists, Sources Around the World." *Quill*, January/February 1993, pp. 12-13.

McKenna, Kate. "The Future is Now: Newspapers are Overcoming their Fears of Technology and Launching a Wide Array of Electronic Products." *American Journalism Review*, October 1993, pp. 17-22.

Morton, John. "Papers Will Survive Newest Technology." *American Journalism Review*, June 1993, p. 48.

Oppenheimer, Todd. "Newsweek's Voyage Through Cyberspace." *Columbia Journalism Review*, November/December 1993, pp. 34-37.

Potter, Walt. "Changed Marketplace, Changed Attitudes: Newspapers and the Bells Have Changed their Tone as They Seek Common Ground." *Presstime*, September 1993, pp. 27-30.

Sims, Calvin. "The Uncertain Promises of Interactivity." *New York Times*, December 19, 1993, p. 6.

Tewlow, Jules. "Newspapers and Media Convergence." *Editor & Publisher*, June 12, 1993, pp. 86, 96.

Tierney, John. "Will They Sit By the Set or Ride a Data Highway." *New York Times*, June, 20, 1993, pp. 1, 12.

Wright, Robert. "Voice of America: Overhearing the Internet." *The New Republic*, September 13, 1993, pp. 20-27.

Books 1994-1996

American Society of Newspaper Editors. *Come the Millennium: Interviews on the Shape of Our Future.* Kansas City: Andrews and McMeel, 1994.

Basch, Reva. *Secrets of the Super Net Searchers.* Wilton, CT: Pemberton Press, 1996.

Bates, Mary Ellen. *The Online Deskbook.* Wilton, CT: Pemberton Press, 1996.

Carter, Mary E. *Electronic Highway Robbery: An Artist's Guide to Copyrights in the Digital Era.* Peachpit: Addison-Wesley, 1996.

Dizard, Jr. Wilson. *Old Media/New Media: Mass Communication in the Information Age.* New York: Longman Publishing, 1994.

Evans, James. *Law on the Net.* Berkeley: Nolo Press, 1996.

Featherstone, Mike and Roger Burrows, eds. *Cyberspace / Cyberbodies / Cyberpunk: Cultures of Technological Embodiment.* Thousand Oaks, CA: Sage Publications, 1996.

Fidler, Roger. *Mediamorphosis: Understanding New Media.* Thousand Oaks, CA: Pine Forge Press, (Available 1997).

Garrison, Bruce. *Computer-Assisted Reporting.* Mahwah, NJ: Lawrence Erlbaum Associates, 1995.

Garry, Patrick M. *Scrambling for Protection: The New Media and the First Amendment.* Pittsburgh: University of Pittsburgh Press, 1994.

Gates, Bill. *The Road Ahead.* New York: Penguin Books, 1995.

Gilster, Paul. *Finding It on the Internet.* New York: John Wiley & Sons, 1996.

Grossman, Lawrence K. *The Electronic Republic: Reshaping Democracy in the Information Age.* New York: Viking, 1995.

Hafner, Katie and Matthew Lyon. *Where Wizards Stay Up Late: The Origins of the Internet.* New York: Simon & Schuster, 1996.

Hahn, Harley. *The Internet Complete Reference.* Berkeley: Osborne McGraw-Hill, 1996.

Hamel, Gary. *Competing for the Future.* Boston: Harvard Business School Press, 1994.

Harris, Linda M. ed. *Health and the New Media.* Mahwah, NJ: Lawrence Erlbaum Associates, 1995.

Helfand, Jessica. *Six Essays on Design and New Media.* New York: William Drenttel, 1995.

Jones, Steven G. *CyberSociety: Computer-Mediated Communication and Community.* Thousand Oaks, CA: Sage Publications, 1995.

Kahin, Brian and James Keller, eds. *Public Access to the Internet.* Cambridge, MA: MIT Press, 1995.

Koch, Tom. *The Message is the Medium.* Westport, CT: Praeger, 1996.

Lane, Carole A. *Naked in Cyberspace: How to Find Personal Information Online.* Wilton, CT: Pemberton Press, 1996.

Levine, Jayne, ed. *The Federal Internet Source.* Washington, DC: National Journal, 1995.

Levy, Steven. *Insanely Great: The Life and Times of Macintosh, the Computer That Changed Everything.* New York: Viking, 1994.

Marsh, Harry. *Creating Tomorrow's Mass Media.* Orlando: Harcourt Brace and Company, 1995.

Maxwell, Bruce. *Washington Online: How to Access the Federal Government on the Internet.* Washington: Congressional Quarterly Books, 1995.

Negroponte, Nicholas. *Being Digital.* New York: Alfred A. Knopf, 1995.

O'Leary, Mick. *The Online 100.* Wilton, CT: Pemberton Press Books, 1995.

Pavlik, John V. *New Media Technology: Cultural and Commercial Perspectives.* Boston: Allyn and Bacon, 1996.

Reddick, Randy and Elliot King. *The Online Journalist: Using the Internet and Other Electronic Resources.* Fort Worth, TX: Harcourt Brace, 1995.

Reeves, Byron and Clifford Nass. *The Media Equation: How People Treat Computers, Television, and New Media Like Real People and Places.* New York: Cambridge University Press, 1996.

Resnick, Rosalind and Dave Taylor. *The Internet Business Guide.* Indianapolis, IN: Sams.net Publishing, 1995.

Schuler, Douglas. *New Community Networks: Wired for Change.* Reading, MA: Addison-Wesley, 1996.

Schwartz, Edward. *NetActivism: How Citizens Use the Internet.* Sebastopol, CA: O'Reilly and Associates, 1996.

Shields, Rob. *Cultures of Internet: Toward a Social Theory of Cyberspaces and Virtual Realities.* Thousand Oaks, CA: Sage Publications, 1995.

Smith, Richard J. *Navigating the Internet.* Indianapolis, IN: Sams Publishing, 1995.

Straubhaar, Joseph and Robert LaRose. *Communications Media in the Information Society.* Belmont, CA: Wadsworth, 1996.

Tilton, Eric, et al. *Web Weaving: Designing and Managing an Effective Web Site.* Reading, MA: Addison-Wesley, 1996.

Tittel, Ed, Susan Price, and James Michael Stewart. *Web Graphics Sourcebook.* New York: John Wiley & Sons, 1996.

Turkle, Sherry. *Life on the Screen: Identity in the Age of the Internet.* New York: Simon & Schuster, 1995.

Turlington, Shannon R. *Walking the World Wide Web: Your Personal Guide to Great Internet Resource.* Chapel Hill: Ventana Press, 1995.

Van Hoff, Arthur, et al. *Hooked on Java.* Reading, MA: Addison-Wesley, 1996.

Ward, Jean and Kathleen A. Hansen. *Search Strategies in Mass Communication.* New York: Longman Publishing Group, 1996.

Wendland, Mike. *News in the Next Century. Wired Journalist: Newsroom Guide to the Internet.* Washington, DC: Radio and Television News Directors Foundation, 1996.

Williams, Frederick and John V. Pavlik, eds. *The People's Right to Know: Media, Democracy, and the Information Highway.* New Jersey: Lawrence Erlbaum Associates, 1994.

Willis, Jim. *The Age of Multimedia and Turbonews.* Westport, CT: Praeger, 1994.

Wilson, Stephen. *World Wide Web Design Guide.* Indianapolis, IN: Hayden Books, 1995.

Books 1988-1993

Abramson, Jeffrey B., Christopher F. Arterton and Gary R. Orren. *The Electronic Commonwealth: the Impact of New Media Technologies on Democratic Politics.* New York: Basic Books, 1988.

Compaine, Benjamin M., ed. *Issues In New Information Technology.* Norwood, NJ: Ablex Publishing, 1988.

Cotton, Bob and Richard Oliver. *Understanding Hypermedia: From Multimedia to Virtual Reality.* London: Phaidon Press, 1992.

Dizard, Wilson P. *The Coming Information Age: An Overview of Technology, Economics, and Politics.* New York: Longman, 1989.

Donnelly, William J. *The Confetti Generation: How the New Communications Technology is Fragmenting America.* New York: Holt, 1986.

Gerstein, Marc S. *The Technology Connection: Strategy and Change in the Information Age.* Reading, MA: Addison-Wesley, 1987.

Heim, Michael. *The Metaphysics of Virtual Reality.* New York: Oxford University Press, 1993.

Hiltz, Roxanne Starr. *The Network Nation: Human Communication via Computer.* Cambridge, MA: The MIT Press, 1993.

Koch, Tom. *Journalism for the 21st Century.* Westport: CT: Greenwood Press, 1991.

Malamud, Carl. *Exploring the Internet: A Technical Travelogue.* Englewood Cliffs, NJ: Prentice-Hall, 1993.

Neuman, W. Russell. *The Future of the Mass Audience.* New York: Cambridge University Press, 1991.

Paulik, John V. and Everette E. Dennis, eds. *Demystifying Media Technology: Readings from the Freedom Forum Center.* Mountain View, CA: Mayfield, 1993.

Pimentel, Ken and Kevin Teixeira. *Virtual Reality.* New York: McGraw-Hill, 1993.

Rheingold, Howard. *The Virtual Community: HomeSteading on the Electronic Frontier.* Reading, MA: Addison-Wesley, 1993.

Salvaggio, Jerry L. *The Information Society: Economic, Social, and Structural Issues.* Hillsdale, NJ: Lawrence Erlbaum, 1989.

Schrage, Michael. *Shared Minds.* New York: Random House, 1990.

Weitzen, H. Skip. *Infopreneurs: Turning Data Into Dollars.* New York: John Wiley & Sons, 1988.

Wilson, Kevin G. *Technologies of Control: The New Interactive Media for the Home.* Madison, WI: University of Wisconsin Press, 1988.

Wriston, Walter B. *The Twilight of Sovereignty: How the Information Revolution is Transforming Our World.* New York: Scribner, 1992.

Appendix B

Site Catalog

Compiled by Jessica Helfand

A beautiful typographic animation done by my former intern, Peter Cho, now finishing up his degree at MIT:

`http://highlander.media.mit.edu/Users/pcho/portfolio/A.html`

For a funny, goofy look at borderless frames and some fairly quick-loading display type (it helps that the screen size is minuscule, designed for the teeniest laptop):

`http://www.jinx.com/index2.html`

Jonathan Hoefler's Type Foundry site, simple but quite beautiful:

`http://www.typography.com`

The Review, a publication written, edited, and designed by students at the Interactive Telecommunications Program at New York University:

`http://www.itp.tsoa.nyu.edu/~review/current/contents/contents.html`

In particular, Elizabeth Roxby's piece:

`http://www.itp.tsoa.nyu.edu/~review/current/focus/Roxby1.intro.html`

... and Jessica Safran's interview with Joseph Squier, with links to his site:

`http://www.itp.tsoa.nyu.edu/~review/current/profile2/jsintro.html`

Finally, while most magazines on the web are badly repurposed, there is one I love:

`http://www.rollingstone.com/Home.asp`

Appendix

Appendix C

HTML Reference Chart

Included here is the HTML code:

▶ Main elements

▶ Type

▶ Layout

▶ Images

▶ Lists

▶ Forms

▶ Tables

▶ Frames and frame attributes

▶ Multimedia

▶ Style sheets

▶ Paragraph style properties

Main Tags

Element	Description
<HTML></HTML>	Start/End tags of the HTML document
<HEAD></HEAD>	Identifies the document head
<META	Meta-info about document (must be in head)
<META HTTP=EQUIV="name">	Binds element to HTTP response header
<META HTTP=EQUIV="Refresh" _CONTENT=n>	Refresh page every n seconds
<META HTTP=EQUIV="Refresh" _CONTENT=n; URL>	Refesh page in n seconds by jumping to URL
<TITLE></TITLE>	Denotes title of HTML page (must be in head)
<BODY></BODY>	Specifies body of document
<BODY BACKGROUND="URL">	Background texture
<BODY BGCOLOR=="#RRGGBB" _or "colorname" ></BODY>	Background color
<BODY TEXT="#RRGGBB" _or "colorname"> </BODY>	Text Color
<BODY LINK="#RRGGBB" _or "colorname" ></BODY>	Link Color
<BODY VLINK="#RRGGBB" _or "colorname" ></BODY>	Visited Link Color
<BODY ALINK="#RRGGBBå _or "colorname" ></BODY>	Active Link Color

Type Related	Description
<Hn></Hn>	Heading (n=1-6 with 1 as the largest heading)
<Hn ALIGN=LEFT|CENTER| _RIGHT|NOWRAP|CLEAR></Hn>	Align heading 3.0

Type Related	Description
<CODE></CODE>	Text in monospace computer code
<TT></TT>	Teletype font
<FONT SIZE=n></FONT>	Font Size (n ranges from 1-7; default is 3)
<FONT COLOR=="#RRGGBB" _or "colorname"></FONT>	Font Color
<FONT FACE="fontname"> _</FONT>	Specify Font (ususally common system fonts)
<BASEFONT SIZE="n">	Changes the base font value (where default basefont is 3) n=1-7
<B></B>	Bold
<I></I>	Italic
<U></U>	Underline text
<S></S>	Strikeout text
	Subscript text
	Superscript text

Layout	Description
<BLOCKQUOTE></BLOCKQUOTE>	Block indent
 	Line break
<BR CLEAR=LEFT|RIGHT|ALL>	Clearing line break
<CENTER></CENTER>	Center
<DIV>	Division of a document
<HR>	Horizontal rule
<HR ALIGN=LEFT|RIGHT| _CENTER>	Aligns horizontal rule
<HR SIZE=n>	Thickness of horizontal rule (n=number in pixels)

continues

Layout	Description
<HR WIDTH=n>	Width of horizontal rule (n=number in pixels)
<HR WIDTH=n%>	Width of horizontal rule defined by percentage of page
<HR NOSHADE>	Solid black horizontal rule
<NOBR>	Prevents line break
<P>	Paragraph return
<P ALIGN=LEFT|CENTER|RIGHT>	Align paragraph
<PRE></PRE>	Preformatted (displayed with browser default font, usually Courier)

Links	Description
<A HREF="url"></a>	Hypertext link
<A HREF="url" TARGET=_"window">	Link opens a new browser window
<A HREF="url" TARGET=_"framename">	Link loads in a frame specified by frame name
<A HREF="url" TARGET=_"_self">	For Frames: link loads in frame where the link was clicked
<A HREF="url" TARGET=_"_parent">	For Frames: link loads in the immediate FRAMESET parent of document
<A HREF="url" TARGET=_"_top">	For Frames: link loads in the full body of the window

Images	Description
<IMG SRC="URL">	Display image
<IMG SRC="URL" ALIGN=TOP|_BOTTOM|MIDDLE>	Align image relative to text baseline
<IMG SRC="URL" ALIGN=_LEFT|RIGHT>	Align image relative to page
<IMG SRC="URL" ALT=_"alttext">	Alternative/Descriptive Text displayed when images are turned off

Images	Description
<IMG SRC="URL" ISMAP>	Image is an image map
<IMG SRC="URL" USEMAP>	Image is a client-side image map
<IMG SRC="URL" WIDTH="n" _HEIGHT="n">	Image dimensions (in pixels)
<IMG SRC="URL" BORDER=n>	Image border (in pixels)
<IMG SRC="URL" HSPACE=n _VSPACE=n>	Specifies horizontal or vertical spacing (in pixels)
<IMG LOWSRC="URL" SRC= _"URL">	Specifies low-resolution load of image

Lists	Description
<DL></DL>	Definition title
<DD>	Definition
<DT>	Definition term
<LI>	List item (bullet when used with <UL>, numbered list with <OL>)
<OL></OL>	Ordered list
<OL COMPACT></OL>	Compact ordered list
<OL TYPE=A|a|I|i|1>	Format of list items (caps, small, numerical, roman, or default)
<LI TYPE=A|a|I|i|1>	Controls format of list item
<UL></UL>	Unordered list
<UL COMPACT></UL>	Compact version of unordered list
<UL TYPE=DISC|CIRCLE| _SQUARE>	Specifies bullet style

continues

Forms	Description
<FORM ACTION="URL" _METHOD=GET|POST></FORM>	Define form
<INPUT TYPE="TEXT| _PASSWORD|CHECKBOX|RADIO| _SUBMIT|RESET">	Input field for HTML form
<INPUT NAME="fieldname">	Field name forms
<INPUT CHECKED>	Checked checkboxes or radio boxes forms
<INPUT SIZE=n>	Field size (in characters)
<INPUT MAXLENGTH=n>	Maximum length (in characters)
<OPTION>	Option (items that can be selected forms)
<SELECT></SELECT>	Selection list forms
<SELECT NAME="listname"> _</SELECT>	Name of list forms
<SELECT SIZE=n></SELECT>	n=number of options
<TEXTAREA ROWS=n COLS=n> _</TEXTAREA>	Input box size
<TEXTAREA NAME="boxname"> _</TEXTAREA>	Name of box forms

Tables	Description
<TABLE></TABLE>	Defines table
<TABLE BORDER></TABLE>	Table border (on or off)
<TABLE BORDER=n></TABLE>	Table border (width of table border)
<TABLE CELLSPACING=n>	Spacing between cells
<TABLE CELLPADDING=n>	Thickness of cell borders
<TABLE WIDTH=n>	Desired width (in pixels)
<TABLE WIDTH=%>	Width percent (percentage of page)
<TD></TD>	Table cell (must appear within table rows)

`<TD ALIGN=LEFT|RIGHT|CENTER _VALIGN=TOP|MIDDLE|BOTTOM>`	Alignment
`<TD NOWRAP>`	No linebreaks
`<TD COLSPAN=n>`	Columns to span
`<TD ROWSPAN=n>`	Rows to span
`<TD WIDTH=n>`	Desired width (in pixels)
`<TD WIDTH=n%>`	Width percent (percentage of table)
`<TH></TH>`	Table header
`<TH ALIGN=LEFT|RIGHT|CENTER _VALIGN=TOP|MIDDLE|BOTTOM>`	Alignment
`<TH NOWRAP>`	No linebreaks
`<TH COLSPAN=n>`	Columns to span
`<TH ROWSPAN=n>`	Rows to span
`<TH WIDTH=n>`	Desired width (in pixels)
`<TH WIDTH=n%>`	Width percent (percentage of table)
`<TR></TR>`	Table row
`<TR ALIGN=LEFT|RIGHT|CENTER _VALIGN=TOP|MIDDLE|BOTTOM>`	Alignment
`<CAPTION ALIGN=TOP|BOTTOM> _</CAPTION>`	Specifies table caption

Frames	Description
`<FRAMESET></FRAMESET>`	Hosts the frame elements (must be placed in the header)
`<FRAMESET COLS=n>`	Column widths
`<FRAMESET ROWS=n>`	Row height
`<FRAMESET SPACING=1|0>`	Frame Spacing adds additional space between frames
`<FRAME SRC="URL">`	Single frame
`<IFRAME SRC="URL">`	Floating frame

continues

Frame Attributes	Description
<FRAME ALIGN=left|center|_right>	Frame alignment
<FRAME FRAMEBORDER=1|0>	Frame border (1 is default, 0 is no border)
<FRAME NAME="name">	Frame name
<FRAME NORESIZE>	Prevents resizing of frame
<FRAME SCROLLING=yes|no>	Scrolling frame
<FRAME MARGINHEIGHT="n">	Frame height (in pixels)
<FRAME MARGINWIDTH="n">	Frame width (in pixels)

Multimedia	Description
<EMBED SRC="url" WIDTH=n _HEIGHT=n>	Indicates an embedded object (used for Shockwave

Style Sheets	Description
<STYLE TYPE="text/css"> _</STYLE>	Start and closing tags for the style element (must live in the head of the document)

Paragraph Style Properties	Description
P{ color: color name }	Text color of paragraph
P{ background: color }	Background color of paragraph
P{ padding: length, %, _auto }	Controls spacing between text and border of paragraph; can specify up to four values in order of padding for top, right, bottom, left
P{ font-size: size in _points or pixels }	Font size of text in paragraph (must have pt or px suffix)

Style Properties	Description
P{ font-family: font name }	Specifies font
P{ letter-spacing: }	Controls spacing of letters

P{ text-align: left| _right|center|justify }	Alignment of paragraph
P{ text-indent:length _or % }	Controls indent of first line of paragraph
P{ border-color: color }	Specifies color of border
P{ border-width: thin| _medium|thick }	Specifies width of paragraph border

Link Style Properties	**Description**
A:link {color: color name}	Link color
A:link {font-size: size in _points or pixels}	Size of font (must have pt or px suffix)
A: link {font-family: _font name}	Specifies font

Appendix D

Colors by Name and HEX Value

Table D.1 contains a list of all the color names recognized by Netscape Navigator 2.0 and also includes their corresponding HEX Triplet values. To see all these colors correctly, you must have a 256-color or better video card and the appropriate video drivers installed. Also, depending on the operating system and computer platform you are running, some colors may not appear exactly as you expect them to.

Table D.1   Color Values and HEX Triplet Equivalents

Color Name	HEX Triplet
ALICEBLUE	#A0CE00
ANTIQUEWHITE	#FAEBD7
AQUA	#00FFFF
AQUAMARINE	#7FFFD4
AZURE	#F0FFFF
BEIGE	#F5F5DC
BISQUE	#FFE4C4
BLACK	#000000
BLANCHEDALMOND	#FFEBCD
BLUE	#0000FF
BLUEVIOLET	#8A2BE2
BROWN	#A52A2A
BURLYWOOD	#DEB887
CADETBLUE	#5F9EA0
CHARTREUSE	#7FFF00
CHOCOLATE	#D2691E
CORAL	#FF7F50
CORNFLOWERBLUE	#6495ED
CORNSILK	#FFF8DC
CRIMSON	#DC143C
CYAN	#00FFFF
DARKBLUE	#00008B
DARKCYAN	#008B8B
DARKGOLDENROD	#B8860B

Color Name	HEX Triplet
DARKGRAY	#A9A9A9
DARKGREEN	#006400
DARKKHAKI	#BDB76B
DARKMAGENTA	#8B008B
DARKOLIVEGREEN	#556B2F
DARKORANGE	#FF8C00
DARKORCHID	#9932CC
DARKRED	#8B0000
DARKSALMON	#E9967A
DARKSEAGREEN	#8FBC8F
DARKSLATEBLUE	#483D8B
DARKSLATEGRAY	#2F4F4F
DARKTURQUOISE	#00CED1
DARKVIOLET	#9400D3
DEEPPINK	#FF1493
DEEPSKYBLUE	#00BFFF
DIMGRAY	#696969
DODGERBLUE	#1E90FF
FIREBRICK	#B22222
FLORALWHITE	#FFFAF0
FORESTGREEN	#228B22
FUCHSIA	#FF00FF
GAINSBORO	#DCDCDC
GHOSTWHITE	#F8F8FF
GOLD	#FFD700

Color Name	HEX Triplet
GOLDENROD	#DAA520
GRAY	#808080
GREEN	#008000
GREENYELLOW	#ADFF2F
HONEYDEW	#F0FFF0
HOTPINK	#FF69B4
INDIANRED	#CD5C5C
INDIGO	#4B0082
IVORY	#FFFFF0
KHAKI	#F0E68C
LAVENDER	#E6E6FA
LAVENDERBLUSH	#FFF0F5
LEMONCHIFFON	#FFFACD
LIGHTBLUE	#ADD8E6
LIGHTCORAL	#F08080
LIGHTCYAN	#E0FFFF
LIGHTGOLDENRODYELLOW	#FAFAD2
LIGHTGREEN	#90EE90
LIGHTGREY	#D3D3D3
LIGHTPINK	#FFB6C1
LIGHTSALMON	#FFA07A
LIGHTSEAGREEN	#20B2AA
LIGHTSKYBLUE	#87CEFA
LIGHTSLATEGRAY	#778899
LIGHTSTEELBLUE	#B0C4DE

Color Name	HEX Triplet
LIGHTYELLOW	#FFFFE0
LIME	#00FF00
LIMEGREEN	#32CD32
LINEN	#FAF0E6
MAGENTA	#FF00FF
MAROON	#800000
MEDIUMAQUAMARINE	#66CDAA
MEDIUMBLUE	#0000CD
MEDIUMORCHID	#BA55D3
MEDIUMPURPLE	#9370DB
MEDIUMSEAGREEN	#3CB371
MEDIUMSLATEBLUE	#7B68EE
MEDIUMSPRINGGREEN	#00FA9A
MEDIUMTURQUOISE	#48D1CC
MEDIUMVIOLETRED	#C71585
MIDNIGHTBLUE	#191970
MINTCREAM	#F5FFFA
MISTYROSE	#FFE4E1
NAVAJOWHITE	#FFDEAD
NAVY	#000080
OLDLACE	#FDF5E6
OLIVE	#808000
OLIVEDRAB	#6B8E23
ORANGE	#FFA500
ORANGERED	#FF4500

Color Name	HEX Triplet
ORCHID	#DA70D6
PALEGOLDENROD	#EEE8AA
PALEGREEN	#98FB98
PALETURQUOISE	#AFEEEE
PALEVIOLETRED	#DB7093
PAPAYAWHIP	#FFEFD5
PEACHPUFF	#FFDAB9
PERU	#CD853F
PINK	#FFC0CB
PLUM	#DDA0DD
POWDERBLUE	#B0E0E6
PURPLE	#800080
RED	#FF0000
ROSYBROWN	#BC8F8F
ROYALBLUE	#4169E1
SADDLEBROWN	#8B4513
SALMON	#FA8072
SANDYBROWN	#F4A460
SEAGREEN	#2E8B57
SEASHELL	#FFF5EE
SIENNA	#A0522D
SILVER	#C0C0C0
SKYBLUE	#87CEEB
SLATEBLUE	#6A5ACD
SLATEGRAY	#708090

Color Name	HEX Triplet
SNOW	#FFFAFA
SPRINGGREEN	#00FF7F
STEELBLUE	#4682B4
TAN	#D2B48C
TEAL	#008080
THISTLE	#D8BFD8
TOMATO	#FF6347
TURQUOISE	#40E0D0
VIOLET	#EE82EE
WHEAT	#F5DEB3
WHITE	#FFFFFF
WHITESMOKE	#F5F5F5
YELLOW	#FFFF00
YELLOWGREEN	#9ACD32

Index

C

T

U-V

W

X-Y-Z

REGISTRATION CARD

Redesigning Print for the Web

Hayden Books

Name _____ Title _____

Company_____Type of business _____

Address _____

City/State/ZIP _____

Have you used these types of books before? ☐ yes ☐ no

If yes, which ones? _____
_____

How many computer books do you purchase each year? ☐ 1–5 ☐ 6 or more

How did you learn about this book?_____

☐ recommended by a friend   ☐ received ad in mail
☐ recommended by store personnel   ☐ read book review
☐ saw in catalog   ☐ saw on bookshelf

Where did you purchase this book? _____

Which applications do you currently use? _____

Which computer magazines do you subscribe to? _____

What trade shows do you attend? _____

Please number the top three factors which most influenced your decision for this book purchase.

☐ cover   ☐ price
☐ approach to content   ☐ author's reputation
☐ logo   ☐ publisher's reputation
☐ layout/design   ☐ other _____

Would you like to be placed on our preferred mailing list? ☐ yes ☐ no e-mail address _____

☐ **I would like to see my name in print!** You may use my name and quote me in future Hayden products and promotions. My daytime phone number is: _____

Comments _____
_____
_____

Hayden Books   Attn: Product Marketing ◆ 201 West 103rd Street ◆ Indianapolis, Indiana 46290 USA

Fax to 317-581-3576   Visit out Web Page http://WWW.MCP.com/hayden/

Fold Here

- -

BUSINESS REPLY MAIL
FIRST-CLASS MAIL PERMIT NO. 9918 INDIANAPOLIS IN

POSTAGE WILL BE PAID BY THE ADDRESSEE

HAYDEN BOOKS
Attn: Product Marketing
201 W 103RD ST
INDIANAPOLIS IN 46290-9058